DANCING DIPLOMATS

HANK & DOT
KELLY

Illustrations by Gustave Baumann

To

THE AMIABLE PEOPLE OF IQUITOS

this book is fondly dedicated

Foreword

*T*HE DEATH of Henry W. Kelly, in his last venture at shooting the rapids of the Río Grande, deprived many of us of a delightful companion and priceless friend. It also deprived a much larger community of a promising young writer.

As an undergraduate at Harvard he had made certain historical studies, later published by the University of New Mexico, which were of unusual finish, historical value, and literary quality for undergraduate work. On his return from his tour of duty as Vice Consul in Peru, an arduous service which he had undertaken out of pure patriotism, he set about writing the narrative of his unusual experiences there which now appears as DANCING DIPLOMATS.

This was his first venture into purely literary writing; the original draft possessed many of the faults inseparable from such ventures. Nonetheless, it was quite apparent even in the early draft that this was the work of a coming writer. I had the pleasure of criticizing the work and egging on the worker.

He had planned, as his wife indicates in the Prologue, to turn from the narrative of a specific experience to a subject which he knew *entrañable*, New Mexico. He knew this state as a native son, as a cattleman and sheepman, as a merchant, a scholar, and as a liberal, curious-minded, keen young fellow who spoke fluent Spanish. His writing would have added formidably to the literary product of a state which, at present, is only too much known for the products of immigrant writers. It is truly lamentable that he was silenced just as he was beginning to master his craft.

DANCING DIPLOMATS is a warm story, full of keen observation. One recognizes the real writer, as well as the devoted husband, in Hank Kelly's free use of the excellent material provided by his delightful relationship with his wife as well as by the important part she played in his dealings with the people of Iquitos. There is no room for doubt of his general liking and appreciation of the people among whom he had lived.

His book is before you. I leave you to it, confident that in it you will find good writing, much to enjoy, and more than a glimpse of a singularly delightful and most complete man.

OLIVER LA FARGE

Contents

Prologue

*H*ANK ALWAYS read a prologue or a foreword before he read
the book. Said he liked the brief view behind scenes before the
play began. I, Dot, having spent my callow years in China, find
the Chinese approach more logical and always read prologues
afterwards, if not backwards. Prologues are written last anyway,
so maybe my Chinese viewpoint has something, at that.

In September, 1942, Hank and I converged on Washington
from our respective homes. I came by boat—two months' voyage through three seas on the exchange ship *Gripsholm*. Only
half of my family was out of the holocaust of war in China, my
brother and I. My mother and sister were to be internees for
many months to come. I had had the hot breath of war on my
face for a year from the inner sanctum of the American Consulates in Canton and Shanghai. Hank came fresh, but troubled
too, from his home and family in sunny New Mexico. Turned
down by the draft because of poor eyesight, he was determined
to "do" something and had obtained an appointment as Vice
Consul in the Foreign Service.

I like to think that we brushed shoulders in Washington as
we clipped down the checkered halls of the old Department of
State Building and as we pored over reports on Peru. I had been
transferred from my post with the American Consulate General
in Shanghai to the Embassy in Lima. Hank, who loved all things
Spanish, having majored in both the language and history of
Spain and the Spanish-speaking peoples of the South Americas,
had also been assigned to Peru as Vice Consul, in sole charge of
the Consulate in the jungle village of Iquitos, on the banks of
the Amazon River.

Destiny winked an eye in sly good humor and we almost met

one day at the Naval Dispensary, where civilian and military personnel alike, about to depart overseas, poured in a steady stream for their shots—smallpox, yellow fever, typhus, tetanus, cholera, typhoid. Where the husky, six-foot marine in front of me fainted dead away when a certain pharmacist mate, with a sadistic gleam in his eye, approached with a needle in each hand; and the puny clerk behind me took both jabs at once with a sick little grin. The Navy was certainly long on serums! Hank, the smarty, had made his own master control chart, whereas I had had double helpings of everything before my attendant agreed to believe my wail that I had been vaccinated four times in three months, viz., before getting on the boat in Shanghai, by an over-zealous health officer; before getting off the boat in New York, because I couldn't produce a new scar; and now twice by the Navy's conscientious pharmacist mate, because he had lost my chart.

And so we winged our separate ways to Lima, the beautiful City of Kings, where we met quite formally, as you will see. The time was ripe, the place was perfect, and we were married. Our jungle honeymoon began—and that is our story.

There was romance everywhere in Iquitos—even in the almost primitive struggle of it. We grew close in the struggle and shared the romance. Hank was always an intimate part of the immediate world around him. He did not merely stand off and observe. He was an ardent and enthusiastic seeker of truth. And so we made our job and our pleasure one. We explored together the passionate story of rubber, the miracle of barbasco root, and the "chew" in Mr. Wrigley's chewing gum. We were awed together at the spectacle of gigantic mahogany log booms, a small family of jungle Indians with all their household chattels nonchalantly perched on top, floating downstream on the muddy breast of the great Amazon River on their way to the Iquitos mill—and thence to a PT boat perhaps?

Being tucked away in a dripping Amazon forest behind the towering Andes, where uncertain roads made air travel the only feasible route to our guiding mentors at the Embassy in Lima, is something I want to remember long after Chalet Tacu Tacu, in which we spent many troubled but happy hours, may have disappeared into mildewed oblivion. Why did we go there? is another question still to be answered in that sum total of activity that defends a way of life we believe in. It will demand many more young and venturesome diplomats to fill non-spectacular positions in the out-of-the-way corners of the world.

Hank's venturesome spirit and enthusiasm was certainly not dulled when we returned from the glamour of foreign fields to the relative quiet of his beloved home town, Santa Fe. There was the romantic and adventurous story, still untold, of the beginnings and growth of his own family firm, pioneers in the West when our country was still young. And there was another Río— the Río Grande. Perhaps he saw something in the waters of the Río Grande that reminded him of the far away Amazon on which he learned to feel at home. He had negotiated river rapids numberless times, but with the last attempt the Río Grande claimed him.

For a long time after this loss of a devoted husband, the daily notes of our several years of activity in the diplomatic service, that we had gone over together, failed to have any meaning or importance. Then, gradually, they took on a new value for our two children, who, as they grow up, can share with me ever bright remembrances of their father.

Out of these notes, I leave Hank to tell you the story.

Santa Fe, New Mexico   DOROTHY KELLY
August, 1950

*C*HALET TACU TACU, the suburban residence of Señor y Señora Kelly, was located on Avenida Coronel Portilla—a street of red clay known to its intimates as Punchana Road—about a mile downstream from the Plaza de Armas, of Iquitos. The setting was more rustic than suburban. Tacu Tacu and the city were connected only by an intermittent line of palm-thatched houses. Behind the houses on one side of the road was the jungle, spotted with occasional cleared plots of pasture or farm land. Behind the houses on the other side of the road was a steep embankment dropping off some fifty feet into the Amazon River. A quarter of a mile beyond Tacu Tacu, the road entered Punchana Plaza,

The Pearl of the Amazon

a spacious square of bare earth, empty, except for a run-down chapel, and flanked on three sides by more palm-thatched houses, two small retail stores, and the battlemented brick and stucco barracks of the Guardia Civil. In dry weather the municipal buses extended their service as far as Punchana Plaza.

Chalet Tacu Tacu faced the river, while across the road on the river's bank lay the Punchana Naval Base, still under construction in 1943, the headquarters of Peru's Amazon flotilla of gunboats.

The Vice Consular chalet was wedged snugly between two other chalets, the three forming an isolated trio in a line of primitive, mud-floored, *irapai*-thatched houses. It is one of the sacred mores of the Loretan metropolis that every country home must be called a *chalet*—the Spanish term *quinta* for country home is never used. To give your chalet individuality, a name is added. Custom demands that the name chosen must appear in bright-colored letters on a board tablet nailed to the veranda, for the edification of all passers-by.

Viewed from the road, our neighbor to the right displayed a sign reading Chalet Crandall; our neighbor to the left advertised Chalet María Antonieta, after Louis the Sixteenth's country-loving queen.

Chalet Crandall was an unlovely, albeit imposing, frame structure of two floors perched six feet off the ground on a forest of concrete pilings. Its unpainted board walls were weathered a moldy gray by a thousand tropical storms. The galvanized iron roof had long lost its shiny gleam and was now streaked with rust. To complete the sad picture of this decadent tropical palace, each of the concrete pilings was girded with a strip of burlap sacking, soaked in creosote to prevent ants from invading the house. The creosote had run in streams from the gory bandages towards the ground.

Crandall is hardly a Latin-sounding name, and the inmates of the Chalet Crandall were not descendants of Loretan pioneers. The Peruvian Government had engaged the Crandall Engineering Company, of Boston, to build the Iquitos dry dock. The Crandall engineers rented the large, airy chalet conveniently located only a stone's throw from the site of the dry dock. At first the work progressed rapidly. The embankment was cut back and huge pilings of the rot-resistant *huacapú* tree were driven into the mud bottom. But Madama Amazonas, no respecter of schedules, threw her formidable weight against the project as the line of pilings extended beyond the protected embayment into the seven-mile-an-hour current. Stout Ben Deveau, the diver, found the current too swift and treacherous except during the short period when the river was low. The Amazon added to the Crandall miseries as it crept toward its crest by sweeping tons of silt into the embayment and about the pilings. The feeble scoopings of the primitive dredge were only a frustrating reminder that man was fighting a losing battle against the majestic power of the Amazon. A powerful dredge was ordered from the States, but wartime priorities, Nazi U-boats, and the remoteness of Iquitos combined to produce month after month of disheartening silence regarding its whereabouts.

So our Boston neighbors sat on the veranda of Chalet Crandall, scratched their chigger bites, and learned the patience of the Amazon.

Compared to Chalet Crandall, our neighbor on the other side—Chalet María Antonieta—was a doll's house, sitting on pilings hardly a foot high. It was the week-end home of Dr. Luis Felipe Morey, a justice of the Superior Court of the Department of Loreto. Doctor Morey, his young second wife, a flock of small children, and a retinue of Indian serving maids would alight on Saturdays from a taxi, laden with hamper baskets of food for the week-end visit.

The Latins have a gift for bestowing apt nicknames on their associates. The one the community had given Dr. Luis Felipe Morey was a masterpiece. He was called (behind his back, of course) *La Carachupa,* the Loretanism for armadillo. The nickname was a neat physical description of the good justice. He was short-legged, barrel-shaped, and his head rested on his shoulders without an intervening neck. But most of all Dr. Morey was a carachupa in his waddling gait.

So much for Chalets Crandall and María Antonieta, flanking Chalet Tacu Tacu, into which Dot, the bride, moved one August day with all her worldly possessions. Chalet Tacu Tacu had, if nothing more, as much character as its name painted in red on a board nailed to the front porch. Somehow you couldn't take Tacu Tacu seriously. You felt that it was more like the packing-box club house you had built as a kid than a real-life home where you would eat, sleep, hang your clothes, and entertain your friends day after day. Dottie was very sweet as I followed her from room to room. She said nothing until the tour of inspection was over. She kissed me. "It's darling," she said. "It has wonderful possibilities. But are you sure it won't blow away in a storm?" We laughed, and I knew that Dot would convert my packing-box club house into the residence of Señor VEEsay CONsool Norteamericano y Señora.

Dot, of course, was "Shanghai Dot," whom I met for the second time in the dining room of the Pensión Morris in Lima on the evening of the first day of my two month's stay there while receiving my final training.

Dynamic Hope Morris, the auburn-haired American widow who ran the pensión, presided over the large table of unmarried Embassy staff members. Between spoonfuls of papaya cocktail, I marveled at the unabashed flow of Spanish that Hope directed in the most Texan of accents at the two white-coated waiters. She could meet any emergency in Spanish. Her secret was to keep talking and to bridge the potential hiatuses with an Anglicism or a descriptive play of her hands.

The main dish arrived on a huge platter. Hope, for the benefit of the newcomers, announced that it was eggs *a la Huancaina,* a specialty of the house. We were very much impressed. At that moment, a tall, brown-haired girl breezed into the room and took the empty chair at the far end of the table. She had been shopping after work, she explained. I gaped. "It couldn't be!" I told myself. But it was. None other than the hypodermic rebel of the Naval Dispensary in Washington.

I remembered her well as the girl with nice legs who was several places ahead of me in line for the Navy's numerous shots. She submitted to the first three needles with resignation. However, with the approach of the fourth she blew her top.

"Why don't you people ever believe anybody!" she cried in desperation. "I've already had double helpings of everything." She paused for breath and continued, "They pumped me full of all this stuff *three* times just before I left Shanghai on the *Gripsholm,* and now you give me more!"

This was my first introduction to "Shanghai" Dot.

"Mr. Kelly," said Hope, "this is Miss Smith. She's with the Embassy, too."

After dinner I maneuvered a conversation with Miss Smith. I told her that her single-handed revolt against the embattled pharmacist mates had won my deep admiration. "And you work in the Embassy, too," I said.

"Yes, I've been here almost a month," she replied.

"But I don't remember seeing you when I toured the premises today with Mr. Boyce."

"Did Dickie Bird fail to show you the file room, the nerve center of the whole shebang!" she exclaimed with a laugh. "I'll speak to him tomorrow about it. I'll bet you if Patty Cake had shown you around he wouldn't have overlooked my bailiwick."

"Who's Patty Cake?" I blurted, somewhat dazed by this gush of intimacies.

"You mean that Dickie Bird didn't introduce you to Patty Cake! That's a shame because he's a dear and, besides, he's Chargé while his nibs is away."

"You don't by any chance mean Mr. Patterson?" I ventured.

"Yes, I met him. But, how long does one have to know the boys before one may feel free to dispense with the formal address? I always thought these career lads were sticklers for protocol."

"Oh, we never use those names to their faces," Miss Smith hastened to assure me. "We file room gals only use them among ourselves. After all, we have to do something to relieve the pressure in that sweat shop."

About a week after my arrival in Lima, Pensión Morris lost its star boarder as far as I was concerned. Dot Smith, along with Virginia McAuliffe, another Embassy-ite, and Dot Jester, of the Pan American Sanitary Bureau, moved to an attractive little house in the select residential district of San Isidro.

It seems that a legion of smug little angels with yellow wings, who frequented one of Hope's two "chicagos" precipitated the girls' move to a new home. Hope's hostelry was a mansion of colonial vintage whose Old World charm was most ruggedly apparent in its plumbing. The day I arrived, the house boy startled me by pointing out the bathroom nearest my room. "*Señor, éste es el chicago.*" The Windy City's fame had indeed risen to exalted heights, for the term "chicago," as I afterwards learned, has generally replaced the antiquated W. C. in many localities of coastal Peru. Sure enough, the blue enameled letters in the toilet bowl spelled *Chicago.*

The plumbing was not only meagre but senile. The toilets had no zest, the water trickled with agonizing slowness into the tub, and, after a few run-ins with the temperamental geyser, you were glad to sponge off in cold water. All the while, creakings in the hall outside told you that your fellow *pensionistas* were becoming restless. The walls, from the floor to the height of five feet, were lined with tile, each square containing a prim blue-gowned *angelito* with yellow wings and the most exasperatingly beamish expression on his face. You would swear that their prim smiles changed to puckish leers when the water stopped running and left you stranded, your face covered with soap.

"It's those fiendish angels," concluded Dot. "I can't stand them another day."

The old saw about absence and the fonder heart has its grain of truth, for hardly had Dot moved to San Isidro when she and I began our piecemeal exploration of the City of Kings. Lima, in the more than four hundred years since Pizarro traced out the original streets, had grown to a bustling, modern metropolis of a half million inhabitants. We used every available moment to explore the city.

My first problem in our exploratory program was to reconcile Dot to the more democratic units of Lima's public transportation system. Although Peru has her own oil fields, and taxis were both reasonable and plentiful, exclusive use of them was beyond my Vice Consular pocketbook. But Dot balked at my suggestion of streetcars and buses. Born in Richmond, Virginia, she moved, while still very young, to Canada and then to China, where her father was a tobacconist with an American company. Reared since childhood in the favored lap of Shanghai's extra-territoriality, she patiently explained to me that "one simply doesn't take omnibuses and trams. One rides in an automobile or a rickshaw."

We compromised. The omnibuses were ruled out. So we rode the streetcars by day to Herradura Beach, to the Acho bull ring, down to the port of Callao. In the evenings we explored Lima's Chinatown, San Francisco's senior by two centuries. A chop suey joint is called a *chifa* in Peru. If you think it's hard to talk to a Chinese person in English, you ought to try it in Spanish. Dot had impressed me by saying she could speak Chinese, but she was no help in getting us something to eat. I became suspicious. Her alibi, though, was good. "I speak the Mandarin dialect," she claimed. "These chifa people are all Cantonese." I combed Chifa Row for a Mandarin restauranteur to no avail.

The Grill Room of the Gran Bolívar offered dinner dancing and two excellent orchestras that alternated, one playing *el swing* and the other the traditional *criollo* waltzes, rumbas, tangos, and sambas. Shanghai Dot might have been rusty on her Cantonese, but her samba was perfection. ,

One morning between Christmas and New Year's, I was called into the office of the administrative officer. He raised his head from a pile of correspondence, with the harassed look that administrative officers are entitled to assume. "Kelly," he said, "I believe that you have about completed your indoctrination at the Embassy. Although the going may be a little tough until you become experienced, you are very fortunate to have your own post. A single officer at a small post is not confined to some special task as he is in a large establishment. Iquitos is under the direct supervision of the Embassy, and you will route all correspondence with the Department through the Embassy for approval and forwarding. Once you reach Iquitos, Mr. Gembs, who has been temporarily assigned there since last May, will remain with you for about a month to acquaint you with the details of the work. Be ready to leave in ten days."

This abrupt resurgence of a no longer remote Iquitos, with its Malecón Palace Hotel offering "rooms only" at one dollar a day, came as a shock. The fiesta in Lima was over.

Strange to say, there was much ignorance in Lima regarding Iquitos and the Department of Loreto. To the average, well-informed Limeño, whether Peruvian or foreigner, the *montaña* (the flat, forested region of Peru east of the Andes, drained by a network of rivers flowing into the Amazon and amounting to over one-half of the national territory) is an unknown quantity. It is a vast, empty, mysterious region from which fantastic stories of perils and high adventure seep through the Andean barrier to furnish arresting conversation at cocktail parties.

The most disconcerting of my informants on the montaña were the self-styled jungle experts who haunted the Bolívar lounge at tea time. The tales of these hardy adventurers were a little upsetting until I discovered that they had never strayed from the environs of the metropolis, and never intended to. "Ah!" they would say, surveying me as if I were a very unfortunate creature, "so you're going to live in Iquitos. What a shame." Then would come yards of warnings and counsel. Did I know that the streets of Iquitos were crawling with snakes? Did I have a mosquito netting and plenty of quinine? Was I taking along a year's supply of tinned food? This was essential because Iquitos was famine ridden. So, I was unmarried! I wouldn't be for long, for the Amazons of Iquitos were extremely voracious.

I rushed about Lima's compact shopping district collecting amenities to tide me over in my exile. When I stopped for breath, my wallet was clean, and I owned a radio with phonograph attachment, an album of Mexican folk songs, a guitar, an anthology of world poetry, and subscriptions to *Time, Life,* and *The New Yorker*. Shielded thus from mental rot during the long jungle nights, I insured my creature comforts by raiding the Embassy's supply room and making off with two electric fans.

My time was running out. The New Year's dance at the Country Club would be the final fling. Between shopping and packing, I hadn't seen Dot for several days, but I assumed that the track was clear. I drifted down to the file room about closing time. "The Club is fine," she replied, "and that's where I'm going. Ken asked me quite a while ago."

"Who's Ken? Don't tell me you've taken up with one of those FBI gumshoes on the seventh floor."

"Don't be difficult. Ken is a chap I knew before you even reached Lima. He's from 'the hill.' He's with Cerro de Pasco, at Oroya."

"A damn miner!" I snorted.

I went to the Country Club with Dot's roommate, Dot Jester. We celebrated with grim vengeance. Her original date, also with the Cerro de Pasco Mining Company, couldn't get off "the hill" at the last moment. I had only one dance with Dot—very beautiful in a black lace gown. She accused me of trying to monopolize her and ruin "Ken dear's" evening.

A little digging among Dot's feminine intimates during the next couple of days made it clear that my stake in the Dorothy Turner Smith homestead was pretty wobbly. Highest sources reported that the miner had proposed and that matters were in a state of flux.

The situation demanded action—and pronto! There was no time for more pros and cons.

I got hold of Dot at the noon hour; walked her all over downtown Lima. Our feet gave out in front of the University of San Marcos, and that's where I burned my bridges. "With me it's all er nuthin'," I said.

The next two days were hell. Hope Morris served broiled lobster from Chimbote, up the coast, but I couldn't touch it! *Ay, corazón!*

Still no verdict from Dot. Again I waylaid her at closing time and tried a new approach. We didn't walk. We rode—seven miles to Callao harbor, on the interurban express. Then we walked some more until we couldn't walk any farther because we were standing on the end of the pier at La Punta. It was a wild, stormy night. The breakers dashed against the pilings, shaking the pier. Across a bleak, white-capped sea loomed the hulk of San Lorenzo Island, dark except for the lights of the naval base.

"Looks like Hong Kong from Kowloon," Dot said. "But much more beautiful."

The indigestion passed. I knew then that I could eat Hope's lobster.

2

*D*OT AND I had agreed not to announce our engagement—not until I got settled in Iquitos and figured out a way to release Dot from the Embassy.

I had been instructed to fly to Iquitos. The famous Pichis Trail had been abandoned several years before with the advent of air service between the coast and the montaña. The *tambos* or trailside inns had been left to rot in the jungle, the mules sold, and the trail overgrown.

However, even the air route to Iquitos contrived to be complicated. There was no beeline service over Andes and jungle to Iquitos, which would have been a trifling matter of six hun-

The Bachelors' Table

dred miles. Topography made this route not feasible. The Faucett Aviation Company would take me by land plane about five hundred miles northward along the coast to Chiclayo and from there eastward over the Andes another three hundred miles to the jungle town of Yurimaguas, on the Huallaga River. At Yurimaguas, I was to connect with a hydroplane of the Línea Aérea National (LAN). Another 250 miles by LAN and the little jaunt would be over.

I arrived at Faucett's Santa Cruz airport with only five minutes to spare. There was no time for famous last words. As I climbed into the single-motored plane—painted orange all over—Dot thrust four tennis balls into my coat pocket. "There are none in Peru," she shouted above the roar of the engine. "I bought these in Washington, two at a time." George Widney, the Ambassador's *simpático* personal secretary, said nothing; with a nasty leer, he handed me a pocket edition book. It was De Kruif's *Microbe Hunters*.

The plane taxied down the field. Through the window I saw my bare-legged Dot in her red turban, stomping and switching like a nervous filly to keep the sand flies from eating her up.

The three-hour flight to Chiclayo was restfully uneventful. The Peruvian pilot was the epitome of nochalance. For the first hour, he combed the pages of *El Comercio*, Lima's leading daily, glancing up now and then to see that the prevailing southwesterly wasn't blowing us too close to the Andes. Then he turned to the crossword puzzle, and finally drew out his serious reading for the day, *El Mundo es Ancho y Ajeno* (its more euphonious English translation: *Broad and Alien is the World*) by Peru's popular novelist, Ciro Alegría.

15

At last we sat down at Chiclayo, with the flight over the hill scheduled for the next morning, when the seven Iquitos-bound passengers boarded another Faucett plane. It was single-winged with one triple-bladed propeller and painted orange for ready detection in the background of jungle green in the event of a crash landing.

We took off at 8:15 and headed north-northeast into the towering Andes. I breathed a sigh of relief when our pilot showed none of the earmarks of a bookworm. Soon we were over the lesser ridges of the cordillera, whose slopes were at first as barren as the coastal shelf. As we travelled eastwards, they became covered with shrubs and heavy timber. In an hour we were over the raging Marañón River, a tributary of the Amazon, its turbulent waters racing northwards in a deep, V-shaped gorge.

A few minutes later we winged so low over a grassy divide that we startled some pack mules off the rutted trail. A Peruvian lieutenant, who had been pointing out the landmarks, yelled over the roar of the engine, "That's Pishcuhuañunan Pass—the high point of the trip." The pilot later told us that we had been flying at 11,500 feet when we crossed the pass, a low gap in the Andes. The sky was almost cloudless and we were told how fortunate the passage had been. "Frequently," the pilot said, "the weather sets in early over the *sierra,* and I have to climb to 20,000 feet to get above it. It's hard on the passengers at that elevation with no oxygen tubes. And there are many times," he added, "when we can't find a hole through the stuff and can't get above it, either. Then we return to Chiclayo to try again the following morning."

Soon we were over Moyobamba, a mountain city, the capital of the Department of San Martín. From Moyobamba eastward, the lush, Andean slopes dwindled rapidly into the immense, flat, tropical rain-forest of the Upper Amazon basin.

At ten o'clock we landed on the soft turf field at Yurimaguas, the second city of the Department of Loreto. The Department of Loreto! I repeated the words with a warm proprietary feeling. At last I was within the sacred borders of *my* department: the hugest and most thinly populated hunk of land in the sovereign Republic of Peru!

My musings were swept away by a blast of oven-like air as I stepped onto the field. A mob of barefooted gamins seethed about the plane, engaged in spirited combat for possession of the passengers' luggage. Our motley safari wound through the red clay streets of Yurimaguas, past flimsy houses roofed with palm-thatch, rusty galvanized iron sheets, and red tile. I had eight pieces of luggage and was soon in a lather trying to keep a running tally on my eight porters. A half-mile walk brought us to the agency of the Línea Aérea Nacional.

Again we were in luck. Less fortunate travelers have been forced by unfavorable weather to endure the hotel-less charms of Yurimaguas for many days while awaiting the arrival of the LAN planes. We waited only an hour and a half under Señor Puga's portal, overlooking the broad Huallaga River, when our plane arrived. The twin-engined Grumman Widgeon came down on the water with beautiful smoothness, making a neat, shiny incision in the muddy breast of the river, and tied up alongside a balsa-log raft moored to the embankment. The pilot and co-pilot, members of the Peruvian Air Corps, were dressed in khaki.

The Faucett plane had scaled a land on end, a vertical night-mare of chasm and ridge that extended to eternity. LAN now moved above a new kind of eternity—one ironed out flat. The Upper Amazon basin is something that you have to see and think about many times under many circumstances before you even dare to voice a feeble expression. I do so with a great feeling of inadequacy. The most overwhelming emotion that sweeps over you is the unspeakable vastness that surrounds your tiny plane. The grasslands of Texas; the wheat fields of the Dakotas; the lakes and forests of the Canadian shield—all these in consolidation will approximate the vastness of Amazonia. Like the ocean, the horizon curls under in all directions without a rumple in the emerald carpet. Like the ocean sky, the clouds march on in flat-bottomed array beyond the range of vision. Through that limitless carpet run the shiny threads of many rivers. The pattern of flow is universal and identical—twisting, looping curves as if the rivers have nowhere to go and plenty of room to wander in. Myriads of lakes—oxbow lakes, lakes shaped like cashew nuts, round lakes, and lakes of irregular contour—litter the rain-forest carpet. Countless scars show through the covering of jungle, marking the former channels of rivers. The erosion of eons of geological time has worn the boundless valley down to base level so that there remains not a single speck of land which at one time has not been the bed of a roving river.

After two hours of this awesome monotony, the Peruvian lieutenant pointed ahead through the window. "Iquitos!" he said. We craned and peered. By now we were flying over the Amazon River proper.

The Grumman settled into the broad anchorage in front of the city. The contact with the water was made without a jolt, but it sounded as if the hull of the ship were being hauled over a gravel bed.

We taxied across the anchorage and entered the narrow Itaya River. Dugout canoes slipped out of the way of the advancing plane, paddlers maneuvering so that our wake did not strike their canoes broadside. In the shallow water, Indian women washed clothes. The palm-thatched houses lining the bank were built on balsa-log rafts or high off the ground on pilings.

About a half mile up the river, we came to the Itaya Air Base, headquarters of the Peruvian Fourth Aviation Squadron. The co-pilot cranked down the wheels and, with engines revved up and much creaking, the plane climbed the brick ramp to the hangar.

Vice Consul Anthony Gembs, authentically tropical in white linen and lion tamer's hat, met me. He looked disgustingly fit for a veteran of eight months' service in Iquitos, not a symptom of malnutrition.

As we drove out of the reservation area, I was impressed by the brick road which led up a slight rise to the bench on which the city lay. However the brick ended with the sentry station. From there on we bounced along over rutted dirt streets. We rode through the entire length of Iquitos. The cane and palm-thatched houses of the suburbs gave way to more pretentious buildings of brick and stucco and colored tile. The main street, *Jirón Lima,* was not paved from curb to curb. Instead, there were two pairs of brick runways affording a narrow hard surface "railroad" for the wheels of the automobile. Our chauffeur, however, was worried about his threadbare tires, for he carefully straddled the ragged brick runways.

"*Al Hotel Malecón Palace,*" Gembs directed the driver. The words startled me. Ages ago I had read something in the encyclopedia . . . "It's really very convenient," Gembs said, as if he had read my thoughts. "The Vice Consulate is on the second floor, and our rooms are on the third."

The taxi pulled up in front of the hotel. The encyclopedia had been right about those "ambitious buildings." The Gran Hotel Malecón Palace embodied the ambitions of the garish Iquitos of yesterday: the Iquitos of the fabulous era of black gold, when ocean-going steamers formed queues awaiting their turn to take aboard the pungent balls of wild rubber that caused the names of Iquitos and Manaos to ring through the world as synonyms for wealth, inflation, adventure, and intrigue.

There was something melancholy about that elegant pile. It symbolized the last flush of crazy activity before the Amazonian bubble burst. The Malecón Palace was completed in 1912, on the threshold of the dramatic collapse of the price of wild rubber, that brought stagnation to Iquitos. There it stood, dominating the waterfront, the skyscraper of the Upper Amazon, its three floors topped by a penthouse. The building stood on a street corner, its two wings forming a right angle. The entire façade from street level to the roof was of multicolored Portuguese glazed tile, bearing geometric designs. The rooms on the upper floors opened on to miniature silvered balconies through arched French windows. Where the two wings joined in a V at the street corner were three grand balconies, one above the other. From the wrought-iron balcony of the second floor projected a flagpole, at the base of which was fastened a circular shield bearing the legend: *Consulado de China.*

"We'll drop cards first on your colleague, the Chinese Consul," said Gembs as we unloaded our suitcases. "It is not only his consular prestige that makes Don Victor Israel a power in Iquitos. He is one of the leading merchants and, incidentally, your double landlord."

Tony Gembs, by way of explanation, pointed to the end of the wing that faced the waterfront. Fastened to one of the small balconies on the second floor was another shield bearing an eagle with outspread wings, and the legend: *Vice Consulate of The United States of America.*

Tony continued his explanation, "The street floor is occupied by the store of Israel & Company, Ltd.; the second, by our office, Don Victor's living quarters, and those of General Morla, the Commander-in-Chief of Peru's Jungle Division. On the third floor, you have the hotel."

Tony stepped inside the doorway and shouted up the staircase, "Joaquín! Baños! *Vengan abajo!* They'll help with the suitcases," he said to me. "There's no elevator and it's quite a climb to your room."

Joaquín, the Vice Consulate's office boy, was down in a flash. His broad Indian face opened in a smile as Tony introduced the new boss. Just as Joaquín disappeared with a couple of suitcases, a squat, barefooted man of middle age, with thin, graying hair and a snaggle-toothed smile, appeared. It was Baños.

We followed Baños up the staircase. The walls were lined with more glazed tile, but this time the motif was pink carnations. "Is his name really Baños?" I asked Tony. "Believe it or not, it is," Tony replied. "The name could hardly be more appropriate, for Baños is indeed Master of the Baths. But his authority doesn't cease with the plumbing facilities. He is Don Victor's maître d'hotel, manager, desk clerk, cashier, bell-hop, and chambermaid combined. A prodigy of a man, Baños! The only things he doesn't have to worry about are the meals and laundry. We eat out and track down our own laundress."

My room was clean, bright, and airy; and the view of the Amazon from the balcony was superb. The taut steel springs of the bed were a joy after Hope's hay-bellied affairs. It was cool that night; so cool that the cotton sheet was not enough, and Baños supplied me with a blanket. I had expected to find the bed shrouded in yards of stifling mosquito netting. There was none in the hotel, and Baños assured me that the window screens would keep out the few mosquitos that ventured up to the third floor of the building. "There is always a little wind off the river at night, *Señor CONsool*," he said.

I had a basin with running water in my room. The toilets and showers were located in an open portico that extended from the rear of the building. A large sign hanging over the entrance to this wing advertised: *Servicios Higiénicos*. Drainage tanks on the roof caught some of Iquitos' 105 inches of annual rainfall and guaranteed a cold shower without stint or proviso, and "chicagos" that flushed with enthusiasm. In such surroundings even Hope's blue angels would not have disturbed me.

Several minor features of the service, however, reminded the lodger that, even in the Gran Hotel Malecón Palace, life was not entirely a blissful dream. There was the matter of drinking water, a subject that invariably creeps into the limelight when outlanders penetrate the tropics.

"How about the water from the faucet?" I asked Tony. "Is it all right to drink?"

Tony replied, "That's a tough one. It depends on how thirsty you get at night. Baños always keeps your bedside decanter filled, but it's the same water that comes from the tap and that water drains off the roof. Of course, rain water should do you no harm, but those damn turkey buzzards always put me off. Our roof is the favorite roosting place of half the buzzards in town."

Later, Tony showed me the Vice Consulate and introduced me to the other half of his staff. I approved of Tony's taste in secretaries. "This is Miss Del Aguila, but you might as well begin by calling her Amalia. You had better be nice to Amalia, for she's the only English-Spanish steno in the Upper Amazon."

A formidable list of consular colleagues was in line for official calls—a veritable galaxy of international dignitaries. Our host,

Don Victor, a Maltese Jew, was Chinese Consul. Other members of the consular corps were the Belgian, Brazilian, British, Portuguese, and Swiss Consuls, and the Colombian Consul General. Cards were dropped also on many local officials.

"A number of my friends," Tony said, "are concerned over the scant titular prestige enjoyed by the United States' representative. Everybody else, they say, is at least a consul while the Colossus of the North dawdles around with a mere VEEsay CONsool. When you are confronted with this chatter," Tony continued, "don't write Washington requesting that Iquitos be raised to a Consulate 'in order to enhance the prestige of the United States,' because it won't work."

The Gran Hotel Malecón Palace once boasted a dining room. When I arrived, the dining room was still there, but it was deserted. Don Victor Israel had tried in vain to interest some stouthearted soul in operating a restaurant when he acquired the building. No one had a stomach for the undertaking. The task of scraping together enough food to serve meals day after day was so formidable that prospective candidates decided to eke out a living in less trying pursuits.

"The situation is very bad," sighed Don Victor from behind his massive ledger. "Why, do you know that Iquitos, in spite of its large Chinese colony, is the only city in the Republic that can't claim a single chifa! When the Chinos won't touch it, you may be certain the situation is tough!"

Fortunately, there was one rugged individual who refused to throw in the sponge. Don Martín, proprietor of the *Restaurant Unión,* should be classed as a public benefactor. Were it not for him, a number of homeless bachelors, including the Vice Consul Norteamericano, would have faced a lingering death from starvation.

No one knew very much about Don Martín. He was a Spaniard from Barcelona and had come to Iquitos before the turn of the century. He apparently had no family and lived in an inner recess of the restaurant. Don Martín remained strangely aloof from his clientele. His acquaintances were legion but friends he had none. He was never seen about the streets, at dances, or the cinema. The drab, windowless restaurant was his world in which he padded about in canvas, rope-soled slippers. His apparel did not vary, but always it was scrupulously clean and fresh: white duck trousers and a cotton-and-wool, long-sleeved union suit. He wore no shirt, but every button of his underwear was fastened right up to the neck. The skin of his face and hands was a bloodless white. His neat mustache and distinguished head were also white. His eyes behind round-rimmed spectacles were a washed-out blue. Don Martín was like the small, translucent lizards that clung at night to the walls.

The Restaurant Unión consisted of one long, rectangular room with a bare cement floor. Near the entrance was a bar and a few small, marble-topped tables. Beyond was the restaurant proper. A dozen tables with worn damask tablecloths were arranged along either wall. A grand piano with yellowed keys, covered with a faded, green plush cloth, stood on a low dais. At the far end of the room was a banquet table and buffet. A low half-wall separated the tables ranged along the left side of the room from an enclosure coated with the grime of years, where the rubber barons of a half century before had bowled for high stakes on waxed hardwood alleys.

Tony Gembs introduced me to what was called *la mesa de los solteros*—the bachelors' table—where a small group of men ate together.

Everyone made it a point to be on hand the moment that meals were ready, for food gave out with amazing rapidity. Don Martín prepared just so much and when that was gone there was no more. The bill of fare was entirely *a la carte*. We would scan the handwritten menu for one of Don Martín's scarce fillets of beef—the size of a silver dollar and no thicker. Unless we were fortunate, Julio and Emilio, the two waiters, would run a heavy pencil mark over the item and inform us that the last fillet had just been sold. If we came half an hour late the entire menu would be a blotch of pencil marks. However, among the deleted items, one could usually locate a portion of fried pork garnished with fried yuca (the potato of the jungle), rice, and beans.

The choice of dessert was as unchanging as Don Martín's

attire. Papaya, *guineo* (banana) , and *guayabada* (a tinned guava preserve from Brazil) are *muy sabroso* for the first week, but it is not long before your ingenuity at making combinations gives out. You can eat each separately; you can order papaya con guayabada; or guineo con guayabada; or you can fill the cavity of the papaya with sliced guineos. But no matter how you cut or slice or combine them, not many weeks go by before you eye the unholy three at the bottom of the menu with hopeless desperation.

The only condiments furnished by the house were cruets of olive oil and vinegar for each table. If you made the *faux pas* of asking Don Martín for a little catsup, Worcestershire sauce, mustard, butter, or salt and pepper to garnish your starch-heavy diet, he would inform you coldly, "Such things are not to be found here."

Local salt—mined near Yurimaguas—was a dirty rock salt about the texture of ice cream salt. I soon discovered that only the native *Iquiteño* could master the technique of sowing the five-carat crystals palatably throughout his scrambled eggs. Tony, however, was the proud owner of a bottle of fine, white salt that his wife had sent him by air express from Lima. I used to marvel at the lavish way he allowed his bottle to circulate about the table. When he left for Lima, I fell heir to the bottle.

Although Don Martín showed no particular affection for any person, he made up for his aloofness towards humans by his warm *cariño* for cats. They infested the place. As we sat down to order, they would stream out of the kitchen and besiege the table—cats of all colors, sizes, and personalities. Some would rub against your trousers while others would sit at a distance and eye you intently. There was considerable discussion about the mesa de los solteros as to the number of Don Martín's *gatos*. Finally, a tally was taken to settle the matter—the count totaled seventeen.

Considerable sentiment developed among some of the clients of the *Salón de los Gatos* to eliminate the cats or at least to exclude them from the dining room. Some sought to precipitate action by intimating that the cats enabled Don Martín to dispense with dishwashers. Others campaigned by pointing out that the big brindle cat with the nauseating red ulcer on its belly invariably arrived just as Julio brought on the chicken broth.

We finally got desperate enough to broach the matter in a gentle way to Don Martín. He shattered our crusade with the same devastating dispatch with which he handled all complaints about the service and bill of fare.

"If you don't like the conditions here, why not go elsewhere," he answered coldly from behind the bar where he squeezed countless limes for the gallons of *limonada* we consumed. "I am not asking you to come here. There are too many to feed as it is. I would be very happy if only a half dozen customers came for each meal." The cats stayed and so did we.

I shall never forget the crucial day of February 15, 1943. It was the day that Tony handed me the Vice Consulate. "She's all yours now," he said with a finality I didn't relish.

I felt my feet sink deeper into the jungle soil with each step of the transfer ritual. Tony got out from under several thousand dollars worth of consular fee stamps, records, correspondence, codes, seals, and office equipment. After all the forms were signed, certified, and sealed, Tony was a free agent.

Leaving no stone unturned to give the transaction every semblance of permanence, Tony sent Joaquín dashing about town with written notices addressed to the local authorities, my consular *compadres,* and the newspapers.

The flash was bruited the length of Jirón Lima by *El Oriente* and *El Eco,* the leading newspapers. In literal translation, Tony's circular letter read:

Pleasure is had in informing you herewith that I have today transferred the Vice Consulate of the United States of America in the city of Iquitos to Señor Henry W. Kelly who has duly assumed charge.

I avail myself of this opportunity to reiterate the sentiments of my most distinguished esteem.

ANTHONY GEMBS, American Vice Consul

There was no doubt about it—I was now in charge!

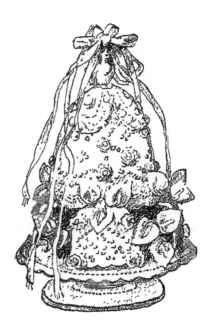

3

*A*FTER A couple of months, hotel life began to pall. Even the carnation tiles and the vigorous plumbing facilities lost their charm. When it became certain that Dot and I would be able to get married, I began house hunting in earnest.

It was then that I learned of a chalet for rent out Punchana way. The house belonged to *Teniente Comandante* Julio Oliart, a dentist in the Peruvian Navy, who, after years of service in Iquitos, was returning to the coast. He agreed to rent me his chalet, unfurnished except for a few basic items of furniture, at a modest rental, in spite of my nationality, principally because the chalet was separated from downtown Iquitos by a mile

Widney and Gidney Assist

of unpaved road that became a quagmire in the rain and a dust bowl in dry weather.

My friends thought my gentleman-farmer aspirations quaint but hardly practicable and tried to make me see my folly. "A few weeks of plodding through the mud every time you want to go to the office, to the movies, and to a dance will cure you, amigo Kelly." Warnings notwithstanding, I moved to the country in the teeth of the winter rains. With me went Pablo Fernández, a young Peruvian architectural engineer, who had arrived in Iquitos from Lima to supervise the construction of a large hospital in Iquitos.

Pablo possessed one of those personalities that is described so satisfactorily by the Spanish word simpático. The dictionary will give you sympathetic, which is hardly adequate. You can put your finger on no one word in English and say, "That's the meaning of simpático." Attractive, likeable, personable—all these, collectively, spell simpático. Pablo enjoyed all situations with a gay serenity that must have been acquired at home. Pablo's father married twice. His first wife bore him twelve children before she died. The second wife trailed by the narrow margin of two. As Pablo put it, he was "among the last of the first litter." In such an environment, being simpático is one's salvation.

Pablo entered into the readying of the chalet with as much enthusiasm as if he, and not I, were about to be married. His contribution ranged from designing furniture and selecting material for curtains in the Chinese shops on Jirón Lima, to wiring the house for additional lights and whitewashing yards of fence made of split balsa logs tied together with *tamshi* or jungle liana.

Without Pablo's imagination and savvy, Dot, on her arrival, would have found an empty shack instead of personable, if not wholly comfortable, Tacu Tacu.

The first and most urgent improvement that Pablo and I made was the amendment of the name of our chalet. The house was named for Comandante Oliart's wife, Piedad. Now *Chalet Piedad* is a passable name for a house. But the Oliart's spoiled everything when they strove for a cosmopolitan air by translating the Señora's first name into English. The sign on the veranda read *Chalet Pity*. Indeed, it was a pity!

We were hemmed in by cosmopolitanism. On one side august Chalet Crandall; on the other queenly María Antonieta. There was no alternative left us. Our chalet had to be of the people; it had to have roots in the Loretan soil. Señor Ortíz, the cabinet-maker-artist, painted the sign in red letters on a rectangle of cedar board. We installed the sign high on the porch so that all our barefooted neighbors could read CHALET TACU TACU as they passed. It would be a very simpático gesture, we reasoned, for tacu tacu is a traditional dish of the Loretan masses. It consists of boiled rice and beans, mashed together, then fried, and served in an elongated mound. Tacu tacu is inexpensive, plentiful, filling, and typically Loretano. It appeared on the menu of the Restaurant Unión at least three times a week—a huge kidney-shaped portion for sixty *centavos*. Si, Señor, the name was muy simpático.

Within a few days, the reaction of the reading public of Punchana became apparent. To our chagrin, our sign met with complete disfavor. An Indian woman passing by with a galvanized washbasin filled with oranges balanced on her head voiced the opinion of our neighbors. *"Ba! Qué feo!"* she grunted as she saw the sign. Tacu tacu was a prosaic word to her. It had nothing but humdrum associations. There was no escape and exotic appeal in something you ate every day. Now take Chalet María Antonieta. *Eso sí!* That was a real name—*Qué bonito! Qué simpático!*

The only people who considered our sign quaint and amusing were our prosperous friends like Don Carlos Echecopar, the prefect, and Ernesto Hoffman, who lived in town—people who didn't have to eat tacu tacu three times a week.

Our chalet appealed to us because it had a yard front and back. In Iquitos proper, the houses were all flush with the sidewalk in the style predominant throughout Latin America since colonial times. Our property was a rectangular plot about ten yards wide and seventy-five yards long. The house was back from the road and separated from it by a good picket fence set in concrete foundations.

To the rear we had a sizeable *chacra* or farmette. Here there was room for an irapai-thatched storage hut and a chicken roost. Beyond the hut, extending as far as a slough that marked the rear boundary of our domain, was a tiny plantation containing a wide variety of jungle trees—half a dozen *plátanos* or banana trees; two *limones* or limes; a tangerine; an *anona,* that bears fruit similar in appearance but far inferior in taste to the delicious *chirimoya* of the tropical uplands; a *sacha mango* tree, resembling in appearance only, the delicious mango; several *guabas,* that bear a string-bean-like fruit about two feet long containing large black seeds and an insipidly-sweet cotton pulp (the lower class Iquiteño walks about with an armload of these ropelike pods, littering the streets with the sizeable debris as he eats his way along) ; a dozen *piña* or pineapple plants that were kept in a constant state of shabbiness by the marauding hogs of the neighborhood; and, finally, two majestic *aguaje* palms standing guard over the slough as if to prevent the encroachment of the jungle that loomed beyond them in lush abandon.

Chalet Tacu Tacu itself conformed to the contour of the surrounding plot. It was simply a one-story, rectangular wooden box, roughly eighteen feet wide and forty feet long, set four feet off the ground atop concrete pilings. The exterior, once a canary yellow, had weathered to a dirty ochre. This expanse was adorned by stripes of russet-colored lath spaced about a foot apart and running vertically from the roof to the bottom of the wall. A galvanized iron roof, sloping gently up to a ridge, formed the lid to the box. Just under the wide eaves and around the entire house ran an open, screened strip about a foot wide. This strip was only the uppermost of Chalet Tacu Tacu's admirable lighting and ventilation system. Large windows opened out on all sides of the house. The windows were square, paneless apertures equipped with screens that could be pushed up and wooden shutters that could be bolted shut against a tropical cloudburst.

March and April found Iquitos bogged down in full-blown *invierno* or "winter" as the Iquiteño calls the wetter, cooler season. The skies remained a menacing lead; the Amazonas swelled day by day, meter by meter toward its crest; rain water lay about the city in vast puddles. Except for the paved Plaza de Armas, Jirón Lima, and Raymondi Street, the city was a fathomless quagmire. If you had the misfortune to fall into one of the open sewer ditches that ran down the middle of the side streets, you would have to swim out.

Disease followed in the wake of invierno. The chill, dank air (thermometer around 50 degrees F.), the sodden ground, the lack of sunshine primed the scantily clad populace for the plague of influenza that swept down the Ucayali River to envelop Iquitos. In a few days, *la gripe* had reached epidemic proportions. Schools closed, the streets were deserted. *El Eco* reported five thousand cases, then ten thousand.

In Iquitos, there was only one happy person. It was Don Martín, of the Restaurant Unión. Each day, his good humor increased as the rising tide of la gripe removed more and more of his clients from the chow line. *"Magnífico!"* he purred, surveying the empty tables.

The spunky LAN planes were the tenuous thread connecting the island community of Iquitos with the outside world. When the mail got through, the news coursed through the streets, giving new life to everyone. *"Llegó el correo!"* was the thrilling call. Flu-ridden Iquiteños would rise from their beds to besiege the post office. If the plane buzzed the Plaza de Armas in a roof-scraping, raspberry swoop, mail was aboard, but if it entered the Itaya demurely at the far end of the anchorage with no gymnastics, there had been no mail in Yurimaguas.

Air mail a faded memory, we Iquiteños fell back on earthbound mail. About once a month, a Brazilian or Peruvian steamer moored at the pontoon dock after fighting the swift current of the Amazon for twenty-five days and 2,300 miles. The Vice Consulate's mail from this source was usually distressingly official and belated. The Brazilian *Fortaleza* brought nothing more than a bundle of the *Federal Register* and some routine circular instructions mailed from Washington four months before. The Peruvian *Morey* arrived late in April bringing me a bit more cheer—three Christmas cards from the family.

Although the Atlantic mail was not timely, at least it was dry, which was more than could be said of the overland mail from the Pacific coast. It arrived not only late but sodden. It came by railroad from Lima as far as Cerro de Pasco, in the high Andes; thence by truck through Huánuco, down into the lush forests of the eastern slope over the unfinished Pucallpa Road, as far as the Aguaytía River, the farthest accessible point on the highway, 420 miles from Lima. The mail would then be lashed to balsa-log rafts or dumped into dugout canoes to shoot the rapids of the Río Aguaytía (not navigable for launches and steamers) for several days to its confluence with the Río Ucayali. At this point, the mail launch would take the canvas bags aboard for the final seven-day voyage to Iquitos!

The worst of the invierno's attendant ills was the lack of mail; specifically, mail from Dot. I was as far away and thrice removed as any G.I. squatted on a solitary coral reef. For me, also, mail was the nectar of life.

A break in the weather would bring a deluge of "Shanghai's" mist-dispelling numbers. They shrank the rain forest and leveled the Andes. They gave me an *esprit de corps*, a feeling of oneness and of belonging to an organization.

There was ample evidence in those of Dot's letters that succeeded in running the gauntlet of mountain, jungle, and weather that she was not pining away in my absence. I didn't expect "Shanghai" to limit her activities to the cloistered confines of the file room, but there were disturbing signs that absence makes the heart grow fonder—of the other feller.

There seemed to be an alarming number of fiestas at the girls' home—waffle breakfasts on Sunday mornings before the crowd of young things hied themselves to Herradura Beach; buffet luncheons after the swim; pick-up snacks, cocktails, the singing of Peruvian, Mexican, and American songs to Dot Jester's accompaniment on the piano; and finally, dancing to worn recordings of *Elmer's Tune* and *The Jersey Bounce*.

As I fumed in helpless isolation, storm-tossed letters my only weapon to beat the wolves from the door of Nicolás de Rivera 810, Dot wrote blithely that the fleet was in. The USS *Mac-Dougal*—one of the destroyers of the naval force that patrolled the west coast of South America—had dropped anchor in Callao harbor. Dot and other patriotic Embassy girls flocked to the Service Center to regale the cruise-worn sailors. There, Dot was charmed by the "most darling" of bell-bottoms, a radar technician, one Benjamin Franklin Sweezy, from Minnesota. Benjamin Franklin offered, in addition to his other charms, a moustachio that twisted at the ends. Thereafter, it seemed to me that Benjamin Franklin dropped his *MacDougal* into Callao every five minutes to enthrall Miss Smith with another tale of high adventure in the Coral Sea, over *Venturo* champagne at *La Cabaña*.

Of course, one could not discriminate between the services. While the fleet was away, there was always a lonesome aviator or two from the U. S. Army base at Talara, whose week-end in the big city had to be made agreeable. These lads, I read, though not endowed with the raconteur's charms of a Benjamin Franklin were not only "divine dancers," but were disturbingly addicted to bestowing their wings, bars, and other insignia on those who thought their dancing "divine."

Once again the situation demanded action. This time, however, I had to do it all by remote control. There could be no hikes around the San Marcos University or trolley car rides to La Punta pier to pave the way. I couldn't even telephone. The

Iquitos telephone service ended at the city limits. To talk to Lima I would have to go to Chiclayo, six hundred miles away. I took my pen in hand. My objective was to prevail on procrastinating "Shanghai" Dot to announce our engagement in the Embassy and to agree to a date for the wedding. This done, the seaborne and airborne wolves could howl themselves hoarse for all I cared.

I wrote and wrote. For the entire dreary, rainy month of April there was no answer; but at last, the great day came: a telegram from Dot advising that the lid was off and that Dickie Bird *et al* were delighted! The sun came out and shone once more on The Pearl of the Amazon.

I learned from the letter that followed that neither the Administrative Officer, nor the Ambassador were as smitten with the prospects of losing their capable file room chief as Dot's pollyannic telegram had indicated. "Why the devil," the Ambassador exclaimed in off-the-record frankness, "did he have to pick her!"

Such was the atmosphere when I wrote the Embassy requesting permission to proceed to Lima for the wedding in the early part of June. Before we could proceed with our plans, the Embassy had to obtain the Department's permission for Dot to resign and for me to leave my post and journey a thousand miles to Lima.

Mr. Boyce, before resigning himself to the loss of the Queen Bee of the file room, launched a subtle campaign to cause Dot to reconsider her rash decision to plunge into the *selva tropiCAL*. At odd moments, he depicted to her the grim realities of life on the other side of the hill. He spoke poignantly of hordes of mosquitoes, of heat, of beans and rice, of open sewers. Did Miss Smith believe that two could live as cheaply as one?

Dot more than weathered the barrage. Her years in China on the banks of the redolent Yangtze enabled her to match Dickie Bird's descriptives, insect for insect, stench for stench.

In view of Miss Smith's stubborn tenacity, there was nothing to do but draft the despatch to the Department and, in due time, the Department's instruction arrived, authorizing Dot's resignation upon the arrival of a replacement from the States.

The ensuing months were an ordeal for Dot. The wedding, when it took place, was to be in Lima. Dot leaped determinedly into the labyrinth of red tape and, by dint of much hoofing and research, the requirements were at last straightened out. First of all, one marriage ceremony wasn't enough; there were to be two. Peruvian law requires a civil ceremony without exception. The State does not consider a church wedding alone legal. The Catholic Church, of course, considers that a marriage is not a marriage unless performed under the auspices of the Church. Therefore, conscientious Peruvian Catholics do the thing up double.

Herewith is a sample of the *requisitos* for the civil ceremony of marriage in Peru:

> Birth Certificate—"legalized" by a Peruvian Consul in the United States and officially translated into Spanish by the Ministry of Foreign Relations in Lima.
>
> A certificate from the American Embassy stating that you are single.
>
> Health certificate.
>
> A certificate of residence.
>
> Personal data certificate signed by two witnesses.
>
> Publication of banns in the official gazette and on the blackboard of the city hall of San Isidro, the suburb where Dot resided.

Charlie Gidney, who had been my advisor and friend while I was training in the Lima Embassy, was the consultant on the civil ceremony. I assisted mightily by writing home for my birth certificate and by forwarding Dot my Washington Naval Dispensary examination record. There seemed to be no Peruvian Consul within a thousand miles of Santa Fe, New Mexico; so Mother sent the birth certificate with the notation: "Can't we skip the Peruvian Consul?"

The liaison officer between Baptist Smith and the Catholic

Church in Peru was Catholic George Widney, the Ambassador's trouble-shooting personal secretary. George arranged an appointment one evening with the parish priest of San Isidro in order to learn the requirements for the religious ceremony. "The Wid" accompanied Dot to bolster her hybrid Spanish and her morale. It was an audacious undertaking in orthodox Peru for a female Tar Heel to approach *la Santa Iglesia Católica* with the avowed purpose of making off with one of her faithful—especially one mysteriously buried in the depths of the montaña.

The padre, a massive Spaniard, received them in his office. He was seated behind a heavy carved desk. As he rose to his feet, a white, heart-shaped emblem surmounted by a cross—the escutcheon of the Passionist Order—shone on his breast against the coal black of his robe. "And so you are a Protestant, Señorita Smith," he said, after listening to the explanation. "That complicates your problem. You probably know of the Church's disapproval of 'mixed marriages,' " he added gravely.

The *Pasionista,* as it turned out, had a fair knowledge of English and the conversation lapsed from one language to another. He steered an aloof, and slightly hostile course for the first few minutes. "The Wid" turned the conversation to the Passionist Order. Was it a missionary order? Were there many Pasionistas in Peru?

Padre Vidurrizaga began to thaw. "Why yes," he exclaimed. "We Pasionistas work actively in the field. There are a number of us, Señorita Smith, working where, you say, your fiancé is stationed—in the montaña, especially along the Upper Marañón River. We do much work among the *Jívaro* Indians, the tribe that practices the art of reducing heads."

"Isn't yours a Basque name?" asked "The Wid," pouring more diplomatic oil on the waters. The padre's face brightened. "That's right. I am from Guipúzcoa on the Bay of Biscay."

"Oh, then you must be a Jai Alai player, Padre!" Dot said with enthusiasm. Padre Vidurrizaga's black eyes shone with pleasure. "Are you an *aficionada* of Jai Alai? There is no sport its equal! Ay, qué magnífico!" he sighed reminiscently. "But I didn't know you in North America played Jai Alai."

"I've never seen it in the United States," admitted Dot. "But the game was very popular in Shanghai. The players came from Spain under contract, and we used to go to the auditorium to watch them and make bets. They were amazing athletes!" The padre's head nodded vigorously and he repeated over and over "Qué magnífico!"

It was 10:30 p. m. before Dot and "The Wid" broke away from the sometime Jai Alai champion of Guipúzcoa.

Padre Vidurrizaga had outlined the requirements, and the outlook, though still formidable, no longer seemed hopeless.

The required documents were tracked down and forwarded to Dot and, escorted by "The Wid," she approached the Archbishop's secretary for the dispensations. The secretary turned his skeptical glance to Dot and began filling out a questionnaire with black ink, the scratch of his pen ceasing only long enough to ask the next question. The first few questions were innocuous enough. "Your full name, please. What is your birthplace? The date of your birth? Are you single?" Dot breathed more freely.

The scratchy pen worked industriously over the lined copybook paper. Then, without any warning and in the most matter-of-fact tone, "Are you legitimate, Señorita Smeeth?" Dot looked at "The Wid" in desperation. "Now don't get flustered and slap the man," he warned in a low voice. "That's a routine question." Dot nodded to the padre in the affirmative, her face a pink glow.

"Are you a Católica, Señorita Smeeth?"

"No, I'm a First Baptist!" came the almost defiant reply.

"Do you have a dowry, Señorita Smeeth?"

Two strikes and one ball! Poor Dottie, limp with embarrassment and indignation, turned tearfully to "The Wid." She had the wrong religion, no dough, and her Mama was in a Jap concentration camp. Her only asset was legitimacy.

The Archbishop's secretary suddenly ceased his inquisition. "Come back in two weeks for the dispensations," he said.

The marriage requirements of Church and State were at last

fulfilled; but still no word came from the Department about Dot's replacement. We charged off June and shifted our hopes to July.

We had originally planned a simple, informal affair, but upon investigation, it appeared easier to have the works. I asked Dot to examine the meagre supply of woolen suits that I had left behind in her care. She wrote back tactfully that the blue one was "very nice," but wasn't it a little on the blue jay side? Her appraisal was a masterpiece of restraint, for I had bought the suit on a dark day in a poorly-lighted haberdashery in the States. The first sunny day the stripes stood out like the slats of a picket fence. My family would wince when they looked at me and make cryptic remarks about "Harlem on a Sunday afternoon."

When Mr. and Mrs. Boyce offered their home for the wedding and reception, all thoughts of an informal ceremony were abandoned. Dot wrote me to come as I was; that I would be outfitted, somehow, in Lima.

The first of July found me still in Iquitos without an inkling as to when I might leave for Lima. Clear skies enabled LAN to deliver the mail twice a week, but the news I awaited did not come. Nine days passed in agonizing silence. On the tenth, a telegram in code arrived from the Embassy. I sweated out each word.

You are authorized to proceed to Lima any time after July twelfth stop Close office on departure stop Milton Wells, Third Secretary of Embassy, proceeding Iquitos as relief officer.

Norweb

An hour later, a telegram arrived from Dot. The wedding was scheduled for July seventeenth, but I must be in Lima by the fourteenth to secure one of the many dispensations; and please to bring as gifts for the Boyces "feather flowers and aromatic seeds!"

Those damn aromatic seeds! Leave it to "Shanghai" to pull something outlandish like aromatic seeds just as I was about to start on the most significant journey of my career! Neither Amalia nor Joaquín had heard of the seeds. "Maybe she's confused the seeds for gilded beetles' wings," Amalia brightly volunteered. "My aunt has a doorway curtain made of beetles' wings, and they tinkle like little bells when you pass through."

No one could help me with the aromatic seeds. As a substitute I picked out the largest and the least peppered with buckshot holes of a dozen jaguar skins in Don Victor Israel's warehouse.

My passage reserved and my errands done, I decided that it would be only fair to Dot to have a physical examination before leaving Iquitos. If I had developed beriberi, scurvy, or leprosy, she should know before the wedding.

The *médico*, personable Doctor Navarro, could find nothing amiss. He ended the examination with a stool analysis. "Congratulations, *cholo*," he said looking up from the microscope. "You are now a full-blown *Loretano*. You have intestinal parasites—the worm *askaris* to be specific. He is a long, white, spaghetti-like fellow, but, in spite of his size, he's really a very plebeian worm. But don't worry. They won't bother you unless they get crowded for space; and then they might startle you some fine morning by crawling up your throat."

"Do you think Miss Smith will have me now that I'm wormy? I'd better keep mum until after the wedding."

Doctor Navarro was very comforting. "Once she comes to Iquitos, cholo, you won't have a monopoly long."

The driver stopped in front of Dot's white modernistic house in Lima. I unloaded my dusty suitcase and the jaguar skin and stood hesitantly on the sidewalk. The door and the little pearl bell button looked strange. I felt strange—foreign. Yet I had been longing to push that little pearl button for many lonesome months. I had come a great distance in the last three days. In Pucallpa I missed the San Ramón plane by one minute. In San Ramón, plane service ceased because the Andes were too high for LAN's tiny planes. I took to the road. The hired car broke an axle. Back in San Ramón, I hired another. Lima was only 180 miles away—just over the mountain. It took the car ten hours to cross that mountain. The road climbed from hot-country San

Ramón to snow-blanketed, 16,000-foot Anticona Pass. Then it plunged with ear-popping abruptness to sea-level Lima, blanketed in the chill, depressing *garúa* of winter. In the rustic dress of another world—plantation straw, faded khakis, and run-down boots—I had dropped into the cold, sophisticated world of Lima.

I pushed the pearl button; Dot opened the door. The strangeness vanished and the world of Lima was good.

We had not looked forward to the civil ceremony. We were prepared for crumby surroundings and a perfunctory send-off by some threadbare officeholder. We could not have been more mistaken. Instead of a brusque, uninterested official, patently anxious to get home to his lunch and siesta, we were greeted promptly at the scheduled time by Señor Álvarez Calderón, a polished gentleman attired in a tailored, gray pin-striped suit. The *Alcalde* of San Isidro, scion of one of Lima's first families, had been educated in England and spoke flawless English.

The mayor stood before his desk as he pronounced the official words of the marriage ceremony in beautiful, measured Spanish. Gidney and Widney, our unfailing advocates, stood by to witness the culmination of their labors.

With one foot in and one foot out—a most disconcerting of situations—Dot and I, going our separate ways, spent the afternoon and evening preparing for the elaborate religious ceremony the following day.

The problem of the groom's formal attire was still unsolved. Mr. Boyce suggested that I go to Third Secretary Milton Wells for help. He was about my build. Milton gave me the run of his clothes closet, and, fortunately, his morning coat and striped breeches fitted like a glove. Milton's white shirt with stiff collar and pigeon-gray tie completed the ensemble.

"The Wid," graciously winding up his long ordeal, saw to it that I buttoned all the buttons and tied my shoelaces. He stepped back and surveyed his handiwork with a critical eye. "You'll do, I suppose," he admitted without undue conviction in his voice. "You were always given to optimism," I remarked, looking at my mirrored image.

As I eased my way down the stairs, I became keenly aware

of the sartorial contrast between the bridegroom and the best man. George, the louse, was the picture of *elegancia* in Ambassador Norweb's striped trousers and morning coat!

The ceremony went off without an untoward incident. Milton's seams held in all sectors. Dot was lovely. Mr. Boyce escorted her down the beribboned aisle to where Padre Michell stood in front of the fireplace. It was reassuring to be married, this time, in the good old American language. I remember that it took me ages to get the ring on Dot's finger. I had not laid eyes on the ring until just a few minutes before when "The Wid" handed it to me.

I had scoured the shops of Iquitos in vain for a ring. The only one I found was a dime-store affair in a Chino's shop for which the proprietor, José K. Wong, asked the barbarous price of ten soles. In my distress, I appealed to "The Wid." The only wedding rings available were the kind Granny wore—plain, broad gold bands. He prevailed upon Casa Kohler, one of Lima's most reputable jewelers, to make a platinum ring with hand-carved roses around the band. It was Kohler's first undertaking of this kind, and "The Wid" had rushed downtown to pick it up only a couple of hours before the wedding.

After the ceremony, our friends conspired to get rid of us. Dot and I wanted to stay and enjoy the party, but we were tolerated only long enough to cut the cake, sip fleetingly of excellent Chilean champagne, and take one mouthful of turkey a la king.

Two weeks later, the honeymooners were back in Lima, broke, and road-foundered after a two thousand mile trip through the wonderland of southern Peru.

As we entered Lima, the pink haze of honeymoon changed into the gray garúa of reality. Dot and I were faced with the immediate urgency of gathering together sufficient household supplies, in spite of wartime prices and shortages, to qualify as homemakers. Six months in Iquitos had convinced me that if we intended to have pots and pans, sheets for the beds, a reading lamp, and the many other possessions that, united, make up a home, we would certainly have to fly these things in from Lima, for they were not to be had in Iquitos. The two weeks following our return to Lima were a nightmare of hard pavements, aching feet, fruitless searching, and countless soles spent.

After tramping the streets for several days together without any notable whittling down of our long list of "musts" and "nearly musts," we realized that we had to divide forces if we were ever to assemble the required plunder. Dot and I, therefore, divided up the shopping list and went our respective ways, meeting every few hours to rechart our plan of attack.

I slipped some pretty nasty items into Dot's list. There was, for instance, an electric iron, a bathroom mirror, a smallish funnel, and some waterproofing compound for shoes and boots. Not even a reasonable facsimile of any of these articles was available in Iquitos, and each item was an assignment in itself in Lima. In several days of tramping, Dot found the iron and the mirror, but she began to take on a gloomy view of ever tracking down my "nasty little funnel and that darned old boot oil."

I tried to impress upon her the importance of these two items. "The funnel, Dottie, dear," I patiently explained, "will be the essence of your culinary happiness. Without the funnel you will be unable to fill the two Swedish kerosene burners that I bought from Tony Gembs. They are very handy to heat things in a hurry or to prepare tea. Without your burners, you will have to get the charcoal stove going—a messy job. Remember," I said, "just ask for an *embudo,* and tack the word *chico* on behind so they will give you a little one."

In a few more days, Dot proudly produced a funnel and it was an embudo chico! She had no intention, she said, of shovelling charcoal around at breakfast time.

But the boot oil was almost her Waterloo. She grew to loathe the thought of the greasy stuff, yet to find it became an obsession. She hunted with a vengeance. At tally sessions on street corners she poured out her frustration. "I've memorized the little speech you gave me till I repeat it in my sleep! Into every leather goods store, shoe shop, harness shop, and hardware store I walk boldly, look the clerk square in the eye and blurt in faultless Castilian,

'*Tiene-usted-aceite-para-hacer-impermeable-las-botas?*' Most of the shopkeepers simply stare at me in infuriating silence. A few smile and condescendingly explain that no one in Lima ever uses oil to make impermeable the boots for the simple reason that it never rains here. It makes me feel like an ass, especially when I can't tell them that in Iquitos there are 105 inches of rain a year, that mud rots untreated leather, and all that other fiddle-faddle you throw at me."

However, the persistence of the Turner Smiths is a force to be reckoned with. One afternoon we met at Amy Meredith's tea room on the *Pasaje Olaya* just off the Plaza de Armas. Both of us were laden with bundles, but the victor's gleam in Dot's eye told me that she was carrying something special. She sank into a chair, placed the packages on the floor, and came up with a heavy paper bag which she set triumphantly on the table.

There was a moment of silence. "This," she said with solemnity, "is *aceite de pato*."

"Aceite de what!" I exclaimed, extracting from the bag a liter-sized bottle of greenish-blue oil. "You heard me," was the tart reply. "I said aceite de pato, and I meant it. What's more, I know what it means. Pato means duck and the man said duck oil was *magnífico* to make leather waterproof. He spoke from experience, too, because he used to live in Cuzco, where it rains." The duck oil flew with us to Iquitos and was used, just once. Dot's fine feathered *Cuzqueño* had sold her a liter of number 30 motor oil!

My most difficult assignment was the solution of our transportation problem in Iquitos. I searched every bicycle shop in Lima for two British Raleighs. I did not succeed in locating a bicycle for myself, but I found a good second-hand ladies' model Italian Bianchi for Dot.

Before the wedding, the girls in the Embassy gave Dot a shower in the Hotel Bolívar, where she collected such domestic firsts as pyrex dishes, egg beaters, cookie cutters, a flour sifter, and a rolling pin.

Our wedding gifts were numerous and beautiful, consisting

mostly of exquisite platters, plates, trays, pitchers, knives, forks, and spoons, of 900-fine Peruvian silver, and a set of dozens in all sizes of stemmed crystal glasses.

All these gifts, together with the duck oil, the Bianchi, and the balance of our sundry purchases, we gathered in our room at the Country Club. The prospect of packing this mountain of possessions for air travel—light as possible yet secure from break-age—seemed hardly less formidable than the effort that had gone into amassing them.

The crystal goblets, with their slender stems, were the most challenging of all the articles to pack. Sliding them into my socks or wrapping them in Dot's slips obviously would not suffice. I had been down in the basement of the Club picking out wooden boxes for the overflow when I noticed a great many stiff card-board forms used to fit over champagne bottles to protect them for shipment. Eureka! These champagne covers saved the stemmed goblets. We cut off the superfluous cardboard necks, wrapped the goblets in tissue paper and thrust one into each form. We then pinched in the bottom of one cardboard form and shoved it into the open base of another making a hard-shelled cylindrical package. Thanks to the admirable consump-tion of champagne in the Lima Country Club, the stemmed goblets reached Iquitos without a single casualty!

At last our belongings were packed. Sixteen motley bundles —suitcases, wooden boxes, cardboard boxes, duffle bags, the burlap-draped Bianchi, and a case of ninety-six small tins of *Leche Gloria Evaporizada*—jammed our room at the Country Club. It was out of the question to fly to Iquitos with all our truck in the toy planes of the Faucett Aviation Company and the Línea Aérea Nacional, but the Ambassador broke the trans-portation bottleneck by arranging with Francis A. Truslow, Special Representative, in Peru, of the Rubber Development Corporation, to haul us and our effects over the hill in one of the RDC's huge PBY5A bimotored, Catalina amphibians.

4

S LIM" FAUCETT, managing director of the Compañía de Avia-ción Faucett, handled the flight operations and maintenance of the two Catalinas for the Rubber Development Corporation in Peru, thus giving them the benefit of the Faucett experience, airports, radio facilities, and other conveniences located through-out coastal and Andean Peru.

The Faucett Aviation Company, founded in Lima in 1928, is unique among airlines. Reputedly, it is the only airline in the world which builds and flies its own planes. The Faucett shops are located at the Company's airport at Lima. In addition, the Compañía de Aviación Faucett was the only completely unsubsi-

The Flight of the Oriole

dized airline in the Western Hemisphere. Its safety record could be envied by any airline in the United States.

The man for whom the company and the planes it manufactures are named was Elmer J. Faucett, its managing director, known throughout Peru as "Slim" Faucett. In 1920, at the age of twenty-nine, he shipped to Lima from Hammondsport, New York, as chief service man for the Curtiss Airplane and Motor Corporation. His job was to run a training school and to service the Company's planes sold to the Peruvians. In his first year and a half in Lima, he managed to sandwich in a few hours of solo flying experience between changing spark plugs and tightening guy wires. Slim wanted to fly and he realized that Peru needed airplanes and pilots probably more than most other countries in the world. Communication between communities scattered along Peru's fourteen hundred miles of coastal desert was carried on by sea. Thirty years ago, the only public paved road in Peru was Jirón Unión, a stretch of six city blocks in Lima's principal shopping district. Beyond the thick belt of Andean ridges lay Amazonian Peru—amounting to over one-half of the country's total area. This trackless region was Peru's only by remote control, certainly not by the bonds of modern transportation.

Slim's opportunity came, and he seized it. The Peruvian Government offered a cash prize of $4,000 to any foreigner and double the amount to any Peruvian for the first successful flight from Lima to Iquitos. Slim sought financial backing for a year before he succeeded in borrowing $8,000 with which he purchased a Curtiss Oriole biplane.

In comparison with today's stratoliners, Slim's Oriole was a whimsical apparatus that one would expect to find in the

45

Smithsonian Institution. The Oriole's bicycle-like tires seemed hardly capable of supporting the single 160-horsepower engine and its quaint radiator shaped like a stovepipe. The Oriole's ceiling was twelve thousand feet; twenty-two-thousand-foot Mount Huascarán, Peru's highest peak, was but one of a chain of sky-probing crags that blocked the way to the Pearl of the Amazon. Yet this was the plane in which the sometime New York farm boy and blacksmith set out, determined to be the first man to fly over the Andes to Iquitos. His five-hour flight up the coast to Chiclayo was uneventful. In Chiclayo, Slim spent twenty-five days overhauling his plane and avoiding arrest by suspicious authorities.

On October 5, at 7:00 a. m., Faucett lifted his dainty Oriole above the coastal desert and headed for the hazy battlements of the Andes. There were no maps or radio beams, but he was lucky, and, an hour after the take-off, he flew over the low, ten-thousand-foot Porculla Pass. Soon he spotted Bellavista, a small settlement on the banks of the raging Marañón River, and by eleven o'clock he was over the Pongo de Manseriche, the last Andean gorge through which the Marañón rushes out into the Amazonian flatlands. Slim followed the twisting Marañón, knowing that it would lead him to Iquitos.

As he passed the mouth of the Río Huallaga at noon, his good fortune was snuffed out like a candle. Behind him lay happy skies; ahead loomed sooty, wind-driven storm clouds, pregnant with the torrid fury of the jungle. The tempest that drove at him was too high to climb over, too wide to skirt. Slim dropped his Oriole to three thousand feet trying to get under it. He passed through two storms and reached the mouth of the Río Tigre, only twenty minutes flying time from Iquitos. Then the *chubasco* engulfed his toy plane with the fury that only a jungle storm can summon. He dropped below the level of the tree tops and followed the river, skimming over the chocolate waters.

It was no use. Had the Oriole been equipped with pontoons, the broad river would have offered a ready haven; but, to the bicycle-tired monoplane, the muddy waters were a last resort.

Back up the Marañón, close to the mouth of the Tigre, Slim spotted a sandbar. He circled, levelled off, and held his breath. The bicycle wheels touched, rolled normally for a moment and then dug into the loose sand. The wooden propeller chewed into the sand and splintered to bits as the Oriole stood on her nose. For an instant Slim felt that she was going on her back, but the fuselage settled to the ground and the plane rolled to a stop. Slim was not hurt, and the broken propeller was the only damage suffered by the Oriole.

In an hour, the storm had passed as suddenly as it arose. A benign sun smiled upon a sea of glistening foliage. At five that afternoon, Don Victor Israel's fifty-five-ton river steamer *Melita* slipped around the bend headed downstream to Iquitos from Yurimaguas. Slim reached Iquitos aboard the *Melita* the following noon, but left the same day with an officer and twelve men to rescue the Oriole. They built a raft and floated the plane to Iquitos, where they arrived on October 12, 1922.

Iquitos, Peru's jungle-bound stepchild, gave Slim Faucett a welcome that still made table talk when I arrived twenty years later. To the people of that lonely outpost on the Amazon River, Faucett's trans-Andean flight had a far more stirring significance than could have had Lindbergh's trans-Atlantic flight five years later. These Loretanos, burning with an intense national pride because of their very isolation, now had a real link with their brothers of the sierra and the coast.

Slim intended to complete the unfinished bit of his flight by flying from the sandbar at the mouth of the Río Tigre to Iquitos. He waited months for a propeller ordered by wireless from Lima. When it finally came, he shattered it when his plane struck a chuck hole in the cow pasture that served as an airfield. Seven months after his arrival in Iquitos the third propeller arrived, and Slim flew to the sandbar, landed, took off again and returned to Iquitos without any trouble. The trip had taken ten months.

5

*B*EFORE the reader was bundled off in pursuit of Slim Faucett's Oriole, Dot and I were about to depart for Iquitos in an RDC Catalina to set up housekeeping. Well, one August morning we did get aboard with all our sixteen bundles of chattels. Captain Biggs, a veteran Australian pilot, headed the plane up the coast beyond Chiclayo to Peru's great oil port of Talara.

Dot and I were the only others aboard besides the crew of four. We were really not passengers, for the Cats were cargo planes exclusively, and the only seats were those occupied by the crew. Even the bucket seats, with which Army transport planes are equipped, were not available.

At Home: Chalet Tacu Tacu

As part of the cargo, Dot and I moved about the fuselage searching for a perch among the rope-lashed crates and parcels. To the rear of the fuselage, near the huge cargo hatch, was a clear space of inclined flooring that looked more inviting than the sharp corners of the crates. We squatted on the whale-belly corrugations and tried, without success, to post to the uneven jounce of the ship's tail. We stuck it out for an hour and then decided that if we did not seek a new location our nether parts would bear the grill marks of the flooring permanently. I searched the plane for something softer to seat my bride upon. In the very tail of the ship, I found a coil of three-inch hawser and a sack containing a couple of vicuña robes. I moved these to our cleared space and arranged them on the whale-belly flooring, the robes padding the inside of the nest of rope. Dot was no longer mere cargo; she sat upon a fur-lined throne.

We reached Talara about 1:00 p. m. and had until next morning to explore the great oil port. Talara has no rainfall from one year to the next and not a single trace of vegetation except that nourished with water piped forty miles. Such is the importance of Talara that Peru permitted the United States to establish a military base there in the event that the then victorious Japanese fleet might attempt to blast the port off the map.

The PX was a cornucopia of delight, bursting with articles that had become dim memories of a peacetime past. We bought khaki shirts, toilet soap, liquid shampoo, American cigarettes, cartons of fine white salt (shades of Tony Gembs) , and, in deference to our benefactors, a copy of *See Here, Private Hargrove*.

Still not satisfied, we drifted over to the mess hall and had a talk with the mess sergeant. I told him how highly I esteemed the fat, brown loaves of bread baked in his oven. I spoke from experience. I told him about the flour situation in Iquitos—that the last sack of wheat flour had been consumed three months after I arrived there from Lima. The city's bakers depended almost entirely on flour shipped from New York to Belem do Pará for transhipment there to Iquitos in river steamers. Submarines and shipping shortages contrived to cut the flour arrivals to an occasional trickle.

Towards the end of the second month of this bread famine, a United States Army plane from Talara arrived in Iquitos on a photo charting mission. The crew lodged in the Gran Hotel Malecón Palace. The morning after the plane's arrival, I was going down the hall when I spied what looked like two loaves of bread on the tile floor just outside the room occupied by the pilot. Incredulously, I stared at the mirage. I picked up the loaves tenderly. Just then Lieutenant Groves, fresh and sleek from the flying fields of Texas, stepped out of his room. He looked at me with amazement. "Don't touch that bread!" he cried in alarm. "What do you mean!" I retorted, drawing away. "This bread is mine. I found it in the public hall."

"My God!" exclaimed the Lieutenant. "I don't want the damn stuff. I threw it out. Look, it is riddled with ants! They got into it only an hour after I unloaded it from the ship."

Relief swept over me. "Then, it's all right if I take it? Gee, much obliged. But please," I begged him, "promise me you'll never throw out any more bread just because it has ants. They're not big ants and you don't taste them at all. However, if you're squeamish I've found you can flush them out pronto by heating the loaf for a few minutes."

Lieutenant Groves backed nervously away from the American Vice Consul, a confusion of pity and consternation in his eyes. The next trip he would not provoke such upsetting incidents by bringing bread to Iquitos.

The mess sergeant at Talara was greatly moved by my tale. He disappeared into the kitchen and returned with two loaves of bread, still warm and aromatic. He handed them to Dot.

"You sure must be soft on that guy," he said with pity in his voice, "to go over there in the jungle where there ain't no bread."

The Catalina took off at seven the next morning for Iquitos. An early start might give us the chance of getting over the sierra before the weather set in. We were lucky and enjoyed contact flying all the way to Yurimaguas, although Biggs kept the Cat at an elevation of around fifteen thousand feet over the mountains. Beyond Yurimaguas, however, in the direction of Iquitos, storm clouds towered to eternity. Biggs decided to cut southeastward to Pucallpa.

He set the Cat down gently on the dusty Pucallpa field. Effusive Hans Hurlimann, a Swiss in charge of the RDC rubber gathering station, his cropped head parched like prairie grass and his prominent nose a tomato red, greeted us at the RDC staff house with lunch waiting.

More and more thick, pillar-like clouds crowded out the blue sky. Biggs announced in his gruff manner that if we didn't take off immediately it would be better to sit it out in Pucallpa until the following day. While we were at lunch, Hans had loaded a ton of crude smoked rubber aboard the Cat for shipment to the main warehouse in Iquitos. The rubber was in the form of balls, more oblong than round, about twice the size of a large medicine ball, each weighing from one hundred to two hundred pounds. Each ball had been cut in half—standard procedure, so that the quality of the rubber can be graded. Biggs wanted no more weight aft and had the halved balls stowed forward, a portion of them directly behind the pilot's seat.

In Pucallpa, we were joined by another passenger, tall, polished Jorge de las Casas, head of the *Corporación Peruana del Amazonas,* the Peruvian Government counterpart of the RDC. We three passengers were instructed by Biggs to gather in the fore part of the ship with the crew in order to take all weight possible off the tail section. Each of us settled comfortably on the rounded, yielding surface of a ball of *jebe fino,* the most elastic of the grades of wild rubber.

Biggs' concern about the mountainous cloud formations was

amply justified. The forest of clouds grew more dense as we neared Iquitos. Biggs had a strain of condor's blood in him, for he delighted in trying to get *above* cloud formations. Invariably grumpy and curt from sea level up to twelve thousand feet, above this a change came over him. The higher, the icier, the more rarified, the more bitterly cold, the more amiable he became. From twenty thousand on up, something about the air (or the lack thereof) made him positively exuberant. He would smile and bob his unruly red mop in sheer ecstasy.

Ironically enough, we climbed much higher over the flat, near-sea-level jungle than we had crossing the lofty Andes. I could read the altimeter over Biggs' shoulder—fifteen, eighteen, twenty, and finally, twenty-one thousand feet; and still the cloud columns soared above us. Biggs and the crew had gone on oxygen at thirteen thousand feet. The "cargo" had no masks. We were jazzed-up and headachy but none of us passed out. It grew bitterly cold. We pierced one cloud column after another. The Cat rose and dropped with acute suddenness. Ice formed on the windshield and on the skylight, and made a terrific popping, rending din as it broke off the wings and pelted the body of the ship. We feared that the Cat's wings would break off at any moment with the pounding the plane was taking. The radio operator removed his ear phones and handed a pencilled note to Biggs. Ice had broken our antenna. "Sparks" could hear Iquitos' nervous "I-say-are-you-there" but could not reply.

Dottie sat rigidly on her rubber ball. With one hand she grasped the cargo lashing at her side; with the other she clutched one of her precious pyrex baking dishes which we had no room for in the luggage. Her face was pale but the home-making gleam still shone in her eyes. Suddenly the plane bucked with unusual violence. Dot, given additional spring by her elastic seat, rose into the air at least three feet and struck her head on the ceiling. The pyrex slipped from her grasp and shattered on the floor. Fortunately, she was not hurt and seemed more disturbed over her broken bowl than her bumped head. Jorge de las Casas gallantly removed his sun helmet and offered it to Dot to protect her head. She wore it all the way to Iquitos and managed to stay in the saddle by "pulling leather" with both hands.

When our toes began to burn, we knew that Condor Biggs was reluctantly abandoning the stratosphere for the warmth of the jungle plain. The ship broke through the mist and Iquitos lay directly ahead. Condor Biggs had hit it right on the nose! We landed on the unsurfaced military airfield, the same field that had received Slim Faucett's Oriole.

Vice Consul Milton Wells, in his third week of relief duty, was on hand to meet us. "Am I glad to see you!" he exclaimed by way of a greeting. "I was beginning to wonder. . . ."

Milton, with great foresight, had hired three taxis. The Consular safari rattled off the field towards town, sending a spray of dust up through the flooring. Jungle Dottie was heading for her suburban home. In the lead taxi went her Bianchi; she rode in the second, clutching her two loaves of Talara bread; bringing up in the rear was her case of Leche Gloria Evaporizada.

The interior of Chalet Tacu Tacu was more than a match for the exterior. On Dot's inaugural tour of inspection, she was amazed to find that her rectangular box was a mansion of nine rooms, minute cubicles separated by parchment-thin partitions seven feet high. The narrow interior was halved lengthwise by a partition surmounted by a screen reaching to the ceiling, dividing the study, two bedrooms, dressing room, and bathroom, on one side, from the living room, dining room, and pantry, on the other. We eased our claustrophobia by knocking out the partition between the living and dining rooms thereby reducing our mansion to seven cubicles and one livable room in which you could execute a pirouette without banging your elbows against the walls.

The bathroom and kitchen were the only rooms not actually a part of the box. The bathroom was a cement attachment to the side of the building, the top section equipped with a tank five feet deep to catch the rain water that drained off the roof. The kitchen, also of cement, was an appendage to the rear of the house.

Before our wedding, I wrote Dot describing the efforts of Pablo and me at interior decorating. I mentioned how elegant Tacu Tacu looked with its gay red, white, and blue check calico curtains, hemmed on a Singer sewing machine by Isabel, a hippy little wench who lived in a palm-thatched hut nearby. (The fabulous Singer has worked its way into countless remote corners of the world.) As I, an artless yokel, stood by, Don Pablito and Isabel, amid a babel of artistic exuberance, ran bailing wire through the hems and hung the curtains by twisting the ends of the wire around nails driven into the walls.

Dot accepted the curtains gracefully and also the matching calico lampshades, designed by Pablo, to eliminate the glare of the electric bulbs dangling naked by a drop cord from the ceiling in the middle of each room. But when I described the color combination of the walls and furniture, her letters began to show concern and she tactfully suggested that I leave something for her to do. The interior of the walls had been painted a jungle green by the Oliarts, but much of the surface had become spotted with humidity mold. Paint was hard to come by, so Pablo and I limited our interior decorating to touching up the more unsightly blotches.

"Frankly," Dot had confided to me on our honeymoon, "when I read your description of the color schemes to the file room, the girls shrieked with laughter. Just imagine living amidst such a welter of clashing colors. To begin with, there was the bright foliage-green of the walls. Against this back drop I was confronted by a grass-upholstered couch with a bright blue cover piped in wine red and littered with a calculated variety of pillows—blue pillows with wine red piping, wine pillows with blue piping! Then there were the two orange stools—one with a tan pillow piped in yellow, the other with a yellow pillow piped in tan! To complete my gay living room, there was an ivory bookshelf, and table trimmed in dazzling orange. In this riot of color, my conservative soul found comfort only in the soothing red of the mahogany dining room furniture."

Fortunately, when Dot saw the ensemble herself, she admitted with a sigh of relief that Pablo's inspiration was alarming only on paper, and that Tacu Tacu, being a very special house, could tread on the fringes of garishness with impunity.

Iquitos was not the most ideal place in the world to set up housekeeping. Little by little, however, "Shanghai" Dottie equipped her chalet on Punchana Road with the trappings of "a representative American home," fulfilling, in spirit at least, the injunctions of the Foreign Service regulations. The furniture supplied by our landlord consisted of a small dining room table, four straight-back chairs, a chest of drawers, and two single beds, all of mahogany. The beds were built in the Iquiteño style—low solid bedsteads equipped in Spartan simplicity with closely-set slats. The only spring beds in Iquitos were those of the Gran Malecón Palace Hotel and of a few old-time residents who had imported spring beds and special mattresses from Europe or the United States before the war. Ninety-nine per cent of all Iquiteños manage to knit up the ravelled sleeve of care separated from bare boards by a thin grass-filled tick. The Iquitos mattress factories used sun-cured grass as a filling. Cotton or wool, if available, would be hot and disagreeable in that climate.

To the pampered outlander, these unyielding pallets, for the first week, are as painful as a Yogi's spike litter. The initial shock comes at the end of an enervating tropical day when you sit on the edge of the bed to remove your shoes. Instead of being greeted by a delightful sinking sensation, your posterior encounters the uncompromising rigidity of the slats. The school of hard knocks teaches you to lower yourself gently onto the bed.

Dot had more trouble than I had during the hardening-up period. She found that she could grab moments of sleep by lying squarely on her back or stomach. Sleeping on her side was an impossible feat of gymnastics. She came to the conclusion that to master the lateral position the more ample female pelvis required a hip hole in order to place the hips and shoulders on the same level. But try digging a hip hole in an Iquiteño bed! By the end of the first month Dot had modified her sleeping habits so that the positions prone and supine were adequate to give her a comfortable night's rest. Every half hour with clock-like regularity she would automatically execute a 180-degree flip.

When we became accustomed to our hard beds, the firm, level surface induced a relaxation that one can not obtain in a spring bed. We even tossed aside our balsa fluff pillows. On trips to Lima, where we again encountered box springs and overstuffed mattresses, the first few nights were so uncomfortable that we abandoned the beds for the solid comfort of the floor.

The balance of our furniture was made by Señor Ortíz, the cabinetmaker. Señor Ortíz was lavish with promises, but it usually took him months to deliver the goods. Tacu Tacu was in such dire need of furniture that I developed an unpleasant, though effective, technique in order to impress him with the urgency of the matter. I would drop by his house every evening on my way home to inquire how the work was progressing. Invariably, Señor Ortíz would be eating his supper. It was not long before he concluded that the lesser of two evils was the rapid completion of the Vice Consul's furniture. In one month's time, Señor Ortíz made us a mahogany buffet, a mahogany coffee table, a mahogany writing desk and chair, a cedar kitchen table, and cedar wall shelves. Mahogany and cedar were the only grades of commercial lumber produced by Loretan sawmills. Loretanos accepted mahogany as casually as we accept oak. The Astoria Importing and Manufacturing Company of New York, the largest mahogany producers in the Upper Amazon, whose mill was located seven miles downstream from Iquitos, cut up to twenty thousand board feet in a single day. Ed Hartman, the Tennessee mill superintendent, built his house entirely of mahogany, each board selected for perfection of grain. Over his mahogany floors he laid Sears Roebuck linoleum, on which he set gleaming mahogany furniture. Mrs. Hartman burned mahogany in her stove.

Prices of locally made mahogany furniture had soared along with everything else in wartime Iquitos, yet Señor Ortíz charged us only $50 for the mahogany buffet, coffee table, writing desk, and chair!

Loretan cedar, in a class with fir or pine, was still cheaper.

It contained too much sticky resin to make satisfactory cigar boxes and, consequently, the bulk of the production went to Lima, for cheap furniture and general construction.

However, the masterpiece of Maestro Ortíz was not the furniture, but a mahogany toilet seat and lid, whose arrival at Tacu Tacu was an occasion for rejoicing. I had searched in vain for the ready-made article. It seemed that most Iquiteños had no objection to the naked porcelain. But in Punchana, the nights were cooler than in town. I took my problem to affable Maestro Ortíz. "We will make the attempt, Señor CONsool," he courageously announced. Maestro Ortíz filled several pages with pencil sketches before we finally developed the desired model, complete with the best hinges available. "And with a light coat of varnish, Señor CONsool, to bring out the beautiful grain, the seat will be *muy elegante.*" And it *was* most elegant. There was no item of their household furnishings which Señor y Señora Kelly prized more than their "chicago's" mahogany seat.

Along with her household goods, Dot collected a staff of domestics. We were proud that Chalet Tacu Tacu was staffed entirely with Punchanaites, in fact, with members of one family. The keystone of the staff was Antonia Perez, cook and housemaid. Antonia was a property owner of Punchana. Her diminutive chacra, a hundred meters down the road, consisted of a three-room shack, a sow and piglets, three ducks, and a score of chickens.

We had spent several servantless weeks when Antonia appeared at the door. Her reference impressed us. She had cooked for General Morla. Antonia entered the living room and seated herself on an orange stool. The negotiations began. Both parties bargained with a wariness bordering on suspicion. Antonia had fortified herself for the interview by forcing her broad feet into high-heeled shoes and coating her cheeks with rouge.

I explained that we wanted a servant who would cook and perform all household tasks. For such service we would pay well. This requirement, we found out, ran counter to an ancient tradition of Iquiteño domestics. One is either a cook, a laundress, or an *arregladora,* never all three or any combination thereof. An arregladora is a species of domestic indigenous to Iquitos. Like other regionalisms, the term is not to be found in the dictionary of the Royal Spanish Academy. The common verb from which this noun is derived is *arreglar,* meaning "to arrange" or "to reduce to order." An arregladora, therefore, is a woman whose specialty is to arrange or reduce to order one's house. However, old-time Iquiteño householders had warned us that the run-of-the-mill arregladora was satisfied with merely "rearranging the dust" with a feather duster.

Negotiations had been under way for a half hour when the stubborn set to Antonia's jaw told us that we would have to compromise. We gave a bit and so did Antonia. Antonia agreed to serve as cook and arregladora for fifty soles ($7.71 U. S. currency) a month in addition to meals for herself and two children. Our Peruvian friends, already upset at the way the handful of Americans in town were running up the cost of living, were aghast at this arrangement. Washing was out; we would have to find a laundress.

When Antonia began her work the next morning, she was comfortably dressed in light cotton, the rouge was washed from her cheeks and she moved softly over the wooden floor in her accustomed bare feet.

Antonia's common-law husband was conspicuous by his absence. Antonia never volunteered any information about him, and when we occasionally inquired about his health and whereabouts she would evasively remark that he was away on business up some river. His river of commerce never seemed to get any closer to Punchana so, after a time, we dropped Señor Perez from the family circle.

Dot and I were eager to meet Señor Perez, for he must have been a remarkable fellow, judging by his offspring. Antonia was the regular Indian type of the region—sturdy, squat, broad features, high cheek bones, strong white teeth, dark brown eyes, and straight black hair falling to the shoulders. Her two children, whom she brought with her every morning to remain for the day, had the usual aboriginal build, but their eyes were gray and their hair light brown. Moreover, their names were foreign.

Petronila, aged twelve, and Walter, aged seven, soon became semi-official domestics. Petronila relieved her mother of the most burdensome of her tasks by setting off at dawn every day for the central market about a mile and a half away. The Iquitos market was so lean that probably more important than your cook's ability to cook was her skill and aggressiveness as a rustler of food. The most favorable hour for the shopper to obtain the day's victuals was from the opening of the market, at around 5:30 a. m., to 6:30 a. m. After that your chances decreased as the morning advanced. By 8:30, when the market was stripped clean except for undesirable odds and ends, vendors and customers alike would abandon the premises until the following dawn. Frequently on my way to the office, I would pass Petronila on Punchana Road returning from the market, her faded shopping bag hanging limply at her side. *"No hab-i-ia na-a-ada en el merca-a-ao, Señor Kehlee,"* she would call, to explain her empty bag, in her deliberate, doubly-accentuated speech.

The outrageous cost of food was chiefly responsible for making Iquitos such an expensive place to live, in spite of the low rentals, low servants' wages, and inexpensive mahogany furniture. The Embassy personnel received a liberal cost of living allowance because the Embassy Cost of Living Report showed costs in Lima to be far in excess of those in Washington, D. C. The Vice Consulate in Iquitos submitted its report showing that living costs were double those of Lima, but, like many small posts, got no allowance. If we had existed exclusively on beans, rice, yuca, bananas, oranges, chickens, and pork our food costs would not have been high. These staples were usually available the year round. But occasionally we longed for things unknown to the Iquitos market—things like asparagus, beets, cabbage, carrots, cauliflower, spinach, and tomatoes; apples, peaches, pears, plums, and strawberries. If we couldn't buy fresh food we bought the imported items that came up the Amazon from the States or from the Peruvian Andes. Here are sample prices Dot and I paid in United States currency equivalents back in 1944 for certain food items:

Local eggs, per dozen $0.95
Onions from the Andes, per pound .... .45
Potatoes from the Andes, per pound .... .40
Evaporated milk from Coastal Peru, per
    14 oz. tin . ... .30
Canned butter from Argentina, per pound . .   1.06
Tea from the United States, per pound 1.80
Canned tomatoes from the United States, per
    1 lb. 12 oz. .... .45
Canned peas from the United States, per
    1 lb. 12 oz. tin .... .67

If I hadn't salted away a few dollars in the Venezuelan oil fields, Dot and I would have eaten ourselves into the poorhouse. At the end of our first year of Amazonian diplomacy, we had spent $500 more than I had earned.

But back to the domestics of Chalet Tacu Tacu. As for Walter, he was mostly underfoot. At his worst, he littered the back porch, the kitchen, and pantry with the black seeds of the guaba, for which he had an insatiable passion, and bits of wood and broken roofing tile which were his toys. At his most helpful, Walter was a roving trouble-shooter. He would be assigned to perch on top of the gear box of the ice cream freezer, his bare feet gripping the wooden sides of the bucket to give it stability while Petronila cranked; or he would run down one of Dot's non-laying hens when her time of grace had expired.

Walter was most efficient, of course, in the job he most enjoyed—that of driving out predatory *chanchos* (Loretan razorbacks) from the yard. This task he performed with diabolic glee. From his perch on the railing of the back porch, Walter commanded the entire rear garden, fenced with woven saplings. Here the hogs could more easily force an entrance than through the fence nearest the house, constructed of split balsa logs bound close together. Walter would wait until the delegation of trespassers was well into the garden, rooting in blissful peace among the pineapple plants or at the base of the aguaje palms in search of its scaly, round, red-brown fruit. The stage set, he descended like a wrathful visitation upon the intruders, voicing piercing yells, hurling chunks of brick and tile especially prepared for the emergency, and brandishing a club for work at close quarters. For several minutes, the air was rent with a medley of high-pitched squeals and shouts. Then silence settled over the chacra and Walter would return to his observation post.

Walter's over-enthusiastic discharge of his duty often resulted in more damage to the fixtures of the estate than if the chanchos had been left to root at will. When Walter exploded in their midst they would scatter to the four winds in panic. The chanchos of Iquitos were razorbacks only in that their owners permitted them to batten at will about the neighborhood. They thrived on this promiscuous feeding. They were wild and fleet like razorbacks, yet as round and heavy as wine casks. A fence constructed of split balsa logs (the same wood used to build model airplanes) and secured with liana, in lieu of wire, constitutes only a psychological barrier to several hundred pounds of hurtling porker. The hogs collapsed section after section of our fence in their mad dashes for safety.

At times like this, or when the chanchos would hold a raucous caucus at dawn among the pilings directly under our beds, I wished heartily that I did not have to play the circumspect role of American Vice Consul. I envied our neighbor, Dr. Luis Felipe Morey. The Carachupa, too, had his afflictions. After the chanchos had rooted up his garden for the third time, the esteemed Justice took the law into his own hands. Dot and I were siesta-ing one sticky Sunday afternoon with the Embassy's fan turned on full speed, when a terrific blast rent the air. We rushed outside thinking that one of the gunboats at the Punchana Base had blown up. There in his front yard, dressed in undershirt, trousers, and slippers, stood the Carachupa blowing the smoke from the barrels of his 12 gauge shotgun. Nearby lay a large, black chancho, quite dead. At that moment, I longed to be a justice of the Superior Court of Loreto.

$\mathcal{S}$ UBURBAN Punchana had no monopoly on livestock. There was abundant evidence of animal life in downtown Iquitos. The American Vice Consulate was strategically located on the chief stock drive. Amalia, Joaquín, and I had ringside seats at the gladiatorial games presented daily in front of the Gran Hotel Malecón Palace. At the sound of approaching excitement, we would arise simultaneously from our respective desks in our respective offices and step out onto our respective silvered balconies to watch the passing of the porkers. When I had a visitor and failed to heed the signal, Joaquín would appear at my office door. *"Perdone usted,* Señor Kehlee," he would say to excuse the

The Poongaboom Folk

interruption, "but the chanchos are approaching." At that, I would invite my visitor to the balcony to witness the spectacle.

We were indebted to the pork-loving Iquiteños for our gladiatorial games. More pork is eaten than any other meat, because pork is one of the few items of food that is reasonably plentiful. The Restaurant Unión's menu afforded ample proof that the hog thrived better on the jungle forage than did either cattle or poultry. Dinner at Don Martín's featured, if little else, pork chop and yuca for eighty centavos and roast pork and lettuce for one sol. Nordics embarking for the tropics are told that hog meat is taboo because of the danger of contracting trichinosis. In Iquitos, unless you are a vegetarian, you eat great quantities of hog meat and are grateful to get it.

To satisfy this great demand for pork, an almost continuous column of chanchos passed to the municipal slaughterhouse along the time-honored route of the malecón or waterfront. The chanchos would make their appearance about mid-morning. From our balconies, we watched the sleek black herd approach at a fast trot, the flintlike feet beating a muffled roll on the hard-packed earth. The herd—sometimes as many as fifty hogs—moved in an amorphous troop, changing shape from one moment to the next like a flood of black water working its way through the dust. Some of the chanchos dragged a long rawhide leash from a hind leg. About the herd swarmed barefooted herders armed with long rods with which they kept the troop moving in the desired direction. Two huge dogs—one of German shepherd extraction, the other a short-haired mongrel—added their enthusiastic encouragement to the prodding of the men.

The ebony herd passed directly under our balconies, filling

the air with dust, basso profundo grunts, the shouts of men, and the bark of the pig-dogs. Just shy of the grocery store of my colleague, Don Gáspar Borges da Cruz, the Portuguese Consul, the herders brought the pigs to a halt, where a number were to be cut out and driven into the *proveeduria* or supply depot of General Morla's Jungle Division. Here the hogs to feed the approximately two thousand Peruvian soldiers stationed at Iquitos were inspected, marked, weighed, and then driven off to the municipal slaughterhouse.

The proveeduría stop invariably set off the fireworks. The entrance to the building was narrow, and there was no fence or chute to funnel the hogs inside. Hence, the herders had the problem of containing the hogs in the street in a compact herd—like cowboys holding a bunch of cattle—until they cut out the number destined for the proveeduría, one and two at a time, and drove them into the building. At this point, the regular swineherds were joined by a number of enlisted men from the proveeduría in faded khaki, some with shoes, some without. The cordon of herders ringed the nervous, bristling chanchos in close array.

When everything seemed to be going according to plan, some black monster would break through the ring and scamper grunting and squealing back down the malecón past the hotel. In hot pursuit went soldiers and dogs. Other chanchos found inspiration in the example of the leader. In a few seconds, the waterfront was a wild melee of fleeing porkers and pursuing men and dogs. Some pigs followed their gallant leader down the street; others dashed in the opposite direction; others fled up Putumayo Street towards the Plaza de Armas. The wiser hogs plunged for cover in the tall grass and undergrowth of the river bank. These were the last to be rounded up, for the herders thrashed helplessly about in the vegetation, hurling choice Loretano epithets at this or that *hijo-de-gran-puta* of a hog.

Only the dogs could flush the stubborn hogs from the undergrowth. They worked gleefully, those two, in the broiling sun, rounding up and rooting out panting, red-mouthed hogs. Never did their enthusiasm wane. They would overtake a fast-moving pig and run close to the flank, skillfully avoiding its savage bites. Just as the hog had completed a snapping backward lunge with its jaws the dog closed in and sank his fangs into the hog's ear. In this position, the hog wheeled and smacked his red chops to no avail. By the time he had dragged the stiff-legged dog a few yards, the chancho was exhausted and ready to stand and squeal. One of the herders would then grab a hind leg so that the chancho was spread-eagled fore and aft between man and dog until more herders arrived to drag him off to the proveeduría.

But the chanchos didn't lose their fight for freedom without inflicting losses upon their enemies. I watched the swineherds win many a Phyrric victory. An enraged hog hurtling along at top speed can throw as formidable a body block as an All-American halfback. Once a bandy-legged soldier attempted to turn back a chancho on the tile paving of the *Plazuela Ramón Castilla*, a small balustraded plaza opposite the hotel. The hog struck him squarely on the knees and sent the unfortunate jungle trooper into the air to land on the pavement head foremost. Blood from the soldier's split scalp smeared the red and white tiles at the foot of General Castilla's statue. His companions led the wounded warrior away, staining the sidewalk with a trail of gore.

During my eighteen months in Iquitos, I missed few showings of the tropical thriller *The Malecón Massacres,* and it was seldom that the protagonists failed to give a sterling performance. Apparently, it occurred neither to the swineherds nor the chanchos that a change in the routine would be much easier on everyone concerned. Racing around in the noonday sun only resulted in heat prostration and loss of lard for the hogs and rent clothing and broken pates for Morla's men.

While not sitting in on *The Malecón Massacres,* the American Vice Consul dedicated himself to his official duties. The "Bible" required the Foreign Service officer to keep an evaluating eye on significant political, economic, and social developments in his community. This obligation, in addition to keeping in touch with prominent individuals of the locality, naturally entailed a scrutiny of the local press for pregnant articles and editorials. Mr. Hull depended upon sound interpretive reports from the field upon which to base the foreign policy of the United States.

Toward this end, the Vice Consul set aside an hour each morning to comb the columns of Iquitos' two leading evening newspapers. The city had no morning news sheet, and there was little danger of falling behind the relentless march of current events by postponing the perusal of the evening papers until the following day. *El Oriente,* the self-styled dean of the Iquitos press, was a pretentious publication of four pages, whose circulation, according to Don Eliseo Salazar, the owner-editor, crowded three thousand. The rival *El Eco,* directly across the street, was also a four-page affair, whose owner-editor, Don Enrique Reátegui, stoutly maintained that the circulation of his *diario* equalled if not surpassed that of the dean.

The Vice Consul searched diligently in these two papers for momentous articles regarding the attitude of Loretanos towards the conduct of the war against the Axis; their opinion of the agreements made between the United States and Peru for the exclusive purchase of Loretan barbasco and rubber; sentiment relative to the liquidation of the powerful local German firm E. Strassberger & Compañía; the feeling of boundary-conscious Loreto on the progress of the boundary delimitation work along the Peru-Ecuador frontier; and whether Tío Sam was making enduring friends in the Peruvian Amazon by throwing heaps of money into a health and sanitation program for the montaña.

But the Vice Consul met with indifferent success in his search for the answers to these sixty-four-dollar posers. His failure to reap an abundant harvest of social, political, and economic tidbits for the Lima pouch does not imply a lack of journalistic stature on the part of the Loretan press. Rather, his meagre gleanings should be attributed to the Vice Consul's fledgling status and his undeveloped interpretive faculty.

Perhaps the difficulty also lay in that *El Oriente,* due to an acute shortage of newsprint, appeared month after month on green wrapping paper. Don Eliseo's tired type on that particular shade of green, over-absorbent paper made for poor legibility. This unfortunate condition prevented the Vice Consul from making much headway with weighty articles and limited his effective readings to the periodical fulminations against the continued disregard, by the owners of hogs, cattle, and other livestock, of the municipal ordinances prohibiting them the liberty of the city's boulevards and parks.

The subject of vagrant animals had long been a matter of the gravest concern to the city fathers and the public-spirited press. Such conditions were hardly in keeping with the "urbanity" (*urbanidad*) of the capital of the department. The kingdom of domestic animals seemed to have banded together with the purpose of appropriating the city for its exclusive stamping and foraging grounds. The chanchos formed the most numerous and powerful element of the confederation; second were the cattle; third, and least in the league, were the goats and poultry. The plazas' scanty display of grass, flowers, and shrubs was subjected to constant devastation by rooting hogs, munching cows, and nibbling goats. Joaquín called me to the balcony one day to point out six goats eating the flowers surrounding the monument of General Ramón Castilla. At night, in the poorly lighted sections of town or when the municipal light plant was on one of its recurrent binges, you were as likely to collide with a cow, planted squarely on the sidewalk placidly chewing her cud, as you were to bump into one of your consular colleagues.

The City Council rose to the emergency with characteristic vigor. A series of proclamations appeared in the newspapers, threatening dire action against the marauding animals and their owners. The usual decree reminded the citizens that the continued disregard of former decrees had forced the City Council to lose all patience with the offenders. The decrees ranged from moderate ones providing increasing fines for the first two offenses, to drastic proclamations that all "bovine and porcine livestock" found within the city limits after a certain date would be rounded up by the police and promptly slaughtered in the municipal abattoir. The slaughtered animals would be added to the city's meat supply and the owners would be reimbursed in the amount of the sale of the flesh "less expenses of slaughtering."

These decrees, escorted by appropriate editorials, blew up periodically like miniature, short-lived whirlwinds which dart through the streets raising dust and debris into the air, only to drop the mess shortly on the heads of the burghers who coughed and sputtered for a moment and then forgot the incident until the next gust of decrees.

One evening, Dot and I had dinner with the Prefect of the Department, Don Carlos Echecopar, and his charming wife, Betty. The dinner chatter was gay and scintillating, running the gamut from the rat that ate four holes in the Prefect's dress trousers, to Mexican hairless dogs, and the post-war outlook. After dinner, the men retired to their cigars and coffee. "What do you think, Señor Prefecto," I asked, "of the latest campaign against vagrant animals? Will it be more effective than the others?"

Don Carlos snorted good-naturedly. "It's already too effective to suit me. Do you know who the first victim is? Myself," he admitted with a grin. "Encarnación, our cook, announced this morning in a cascade of tears that the police had made off with her red milk cow, which they would not release until the fine of ten soles was paid. Encarnación is the finest cook in all of Loreto, so I paid the fine. The next time the cow is caught browsing on the ficus trees in the Plaza de Armas, it will cost me twenty soles," the Prefect sighed, "that is, if the crusading fever of the police burns that long."

If the grilled balconies of the American Vice Consulate were an observation post for the activities of the domestic animal life of Iquitos, the office proper became the clearinghouse for the wild life of the jungle. Hardly a day passed that some character didn't make an appearance with an exotic insect, reptile, or mammal. The idea was that if the Vice Consul wouldn't buy the cute *animalito* as company for his lonesome Señora stranded in Punchana, at least he would know of some other gringo who would pay a handsome price for the pet.

Writers describing the uncharted wilderness of the Amazonian jungle invariably have it reeking with fauna of myriad
types. Big or small, gorgeous or drab, dangerous or inoffensive,
these creatures fairly smother the hardy explorer as he hacks his
way through the rain forest. They are underfoot, all around, and
above him. Their cries are more incessant and overwhelming
than the din of a honky-tonk jam session. This is what I expected
and did not encounter when I made trips into the jungle. With
a few exceptions, I found the fabulous "Last Frontier" an empty,
silent tangle of vegetation. Even at tiny settlements on the banks
of secondary rivers, hundreds of miles from the metropolis of
Iquitos, the story was always the same. "And how is the hunting
hereabouts?" I would ask eagerly. "Very bad, Patrón, muy mala.
When I was young . . . Ay! then there was fine hunting, but
now there are too many settlements and the animals have moved
deep into the selva—allá, pa' dentro, Patrón—muy lejos," the old-
timer said, pointing into the distance towards that mythical land
of Poongaboom, the term coined by my Ozark uncles to describe
the fabulous, beckoning land always beyond.

If the all-engulfing jungle seemed bereft of the Little
Brethren, the American Vice Consulate was not. No wonder the
jungle was bare, for all its creatures converged on Iquitos to seek
diplomatic sanctuary on the second floor of the Gran Hotel
Malecón Palace. The present-day La Condamine, Humboldt,
and Darwin could have spared themselves the miseries of the
field by waiting comfortably in the reception room for their
specimens to come to them.

Out of the teeming womb of Madre Selva the Little Brethren
poured. There were the insects that arrived in bottles and on
the ends of sticks: the siquisapa, a large, cream-colored winged
ant, as succulent as its name, appearing from nowhere to blanket
the streets where barefooted people avidly snatched them up,
tore off their wings and popped them in their mouths like gum-
drops; gorgeous butterflies of all sizes and patterns; tremendous
beetles with horns like a Hereford bull; lightning bugs with
three times the wattage of their Missouri Good Neighbors; the

chicharramachacuy, an overgrown cicada wearing a mask resembling the head of a poisonous snake, actually harmless but universally regarded as deadly.

There followed the amphibians and reptiles—toads, frogs, and translucent lizards whose virtue is to cling to your lampshades and devour great numbers of nocturnal insects; the *charapa,* the giant river turtle; the *motelo,* the anti-social land tortoise; spike-backed iguanas; foot-long alligators; and baby water boas, striking in a mottled suit of black and orange.

Finally, into the tiled reception room trooped the lords of the jungle, the birds and beasts: parrots, from the vest-pocket *pihuicho* to the gaudy, outsized *huacamayo;* a host of spindle-legged, solemn-visaged wading birds; villainous bats, squeaking and baring needle-like fangs in protest against the blinding daylight; the *paujil,* the turkey of the jungle, attired in jet black plumage and a bright orange comb, like a fungus growth, atop his beak; assorted rodents from the rabbit-sized *punchana* and *añuje* to the pig-sized *ronsoco,* the largest of the rodents; the waddling *carachupa,* like a rotund knight in his armorplate; monkeys—from the *leoncito,* maned like an African lion yet tiny enough to conceal with the palm of the hand, to the gangling, gray *maquisapa* with the reach of a basketball center; spotted *tigrillo* kittens (ocelot); the *sajino* or black peccary, much more companionable that his redolent cousin, the *huangana* or gray peccary equipped with a fetid musk gland.

Such was the delegation of official visitors that, day after day and month after month, sought sanctuary under the shield of the Bald Eagle. Secretary Hull, perusing my quarterly administrative report, must have been amazed at the volume of business done by his two-bit Iquitos branch as evidenced by the statistics on "Visitors Received." I confess that I turned most of these callers away empty handed, referring them to the office of *La Rubber* where the per diemed RDC'ites were better equipped to accept boarders.

However, I occasionally succumbed to this constant barrage of temptation. Joaquín would be dispatched to Chalet Tacu

Tacu bearing a slight offering to the lady of the house with the compliments of her devoted husband. To my astonishment, I found that you have only to succumb once every fortnight before your distraught wife is the keeper of a zoölogical park.

The stress of entertaining her menagerie of uninvited guests at times put Dot on the verge of departing for the peaceful glades of the Poongaboom country. Fortunately, she was never pushed to that extreme, for a kind Providence kept her family at a bearable size. The turnover was large. Losses from disease, accidents, predators, and runnings away matched the new acquisitions.

Panchita, a rabbit-sized rodent known as an añuje, came to the office in the arms of a little boy who bargained like a river trader and walked away with my ten soles, leaving Panchita to deposit brown capsules on the tile floor. Dot really grew very fond of Panchita. She liked her clean, stiff gray coat; the tidy way she held bits of papaya between her paws. Dot refused to confine Panchita to a cage. She had the liberty of the house.

During the day, Panchita was a mirror of propriety, but, by night, she indulged her rodent passion with reckless abandon. Each morning, we would awake to find a new pile of shavings and tooth marks. The house itself and everything in it, except the kitchen stove and the toilet bowl, was of wood. Panchita was surrounded with a cornucopia of gastronomic delights, but her tastes proved not to be catholic. She gorged herself on mahogany only. Within a week, the four legs of the dining room table were elaborately carved from floor level to the limit of Panchita's reach. Next she dined on the chairs. When we confined her to the pantry, she almost succeeded in eating her way through the back door. A decision had to be made. Either Panchita had to be an outdoor pet or we had to resign ourselves to the inevitable outcome of her assiduous gnawings. Sooner or later, but as certain as the rise and fall of the Amazon, we would sit Joblike on the sawdust mound of our once quaint suburban home. Outdoors and free went Panchita. The first few days, Panchita came regularly for her meals, but soon the lure of the Poongaboom country drew her away.

The varnish had hardly dried on the leg wounds of the furniture when Tacu Tacu had callers. Doctor Morey, our neighbor, his wife and several small children arrived at the door bearing a gift. It was Christmas, and they had come to wish us *Felices Pascuas*. The Carachupa carried a small basket covered with a cloth. "Señora de Kelly," he said addressing Dot, "I have something, as you say in English, muy 'cute.' " The Carachupa then whisked out a small animal by the scruff of the neck with the flourish of a magician. We gasped. The Christmas present was a replica in miniature of Panchita. "An añuje!" Dot cried with thinly veiled dismay.

"Oh, no, Señora!" chorused the Moreys. "Similar, but *definitely* not an añuje. It is a punchana. Very appropriate, don't you think? Our suburb is named after this little animal. The punchana is *muchisima más simpática* and intelligent than the añuje. Sí, Señor, *muchisima más!*"

The situation demanded diplomacy. We accepted the superior pet. We kept Punchy barely long enough to give him a name. Intelligent and simpático Punchy might be, but he was clearly of the same ilk as Panchita. The only difference was that Punchy's sawdust was finer than Panchita's.

If Punchy's sojourn with us was brief, our next sylvan pet failed even to reach Tacu Tacu. Eugen Reis, a Czechoslovakian refugee and exporter of barbasco, had been presented by one of his up-country agents with a *sachavaca* shipped by steamer to Iquitos from the Upper Río Napo, near the Ecuadorean border. A sachavaca is a Loretanism for a tapir (*vaca* meaning cow and *sacha* meaning of the jungle). Reis' cow of the jungle was only a heifer calf weighing about sixty pounds. It had white spots and white stripes running along its back and down its sloping hind quarters.

When I remarked that it looked like an African hyena, Reis assured me that the adult sachavaca became a uniform blackish brown and, with a couple of hundred pounds additional weight, would present a much more favorable appearance. He kept the sachavaca in his patio and was delighted, he said, with the animal. "There is only one inconvenience," Reis admitted. "This sachavaca will eat nothing but peeled bananas, and I haven't the time to peel them for her. Just think—so much fine animal with only one small inconvenience! She's yours for twenty soles!"

The more I thought over Reis' proposition the more it appealed. "Just imagine," I rationalized, "a fine young tapir for only three dollars and eight cents! Why the St. Louis zoo would gladly pay a small fortune for one!"

There were other valid reasons why we should own a sachavaca. We were having trouble with our banana crop. When a stem was ready we would hack off the top-heavy mass with a machete and hang it in the palm-thatched storehouse to permit the firm green plátanos to ripen. Unless we were careful to wrap the stem in canvas the bats would eat the bananas as they turned yellow. We lost half a stem this way before Antonia told us what it was that could eat bananas suspended by a slender wire five feet off the ground.

We knew where the banana thieving bats were coming from. They hung up during the day in the attic of Chalet Crandall. They were the same terrifying jobs with an eighteen-inch wing-spread that swooped about the street lamps all night long, feeding on mosquitoes and other insects attracted by the light. They had the disconcerting habit of diving straight at your head in silent, ominous sweeps like a B-17 with engines cut. Just as you expected to have your scalp removed, the shiny black shadow would clear your head so close that your scalp tingled. I never learned whether these repulsive creatures were vampire bats. In any case, we were thankful that Tacu Tacu was well screened and that we had only rats in *our* attic.

The bats in the Crandall attic became so obnoxious with the chatter of their comings and goings and the debris they brought in to make nests, that the legitimate occupants of the chalet took up arms. One morning we heard a terrific commotion coming from Chalet Crandall—bangings, shouts, and curses. We watched intently. The chalet quivered with excitement. Dust seeped from the cracks and trap door of the attic. From the death trap, an occasional bat escaped into the overpowering sunlight. The din of battle continued incessantly for fifteen minutes. Then there was silence. Through the aperture onto the roof stepped Horace Tudor White and Hamilton Norton Conant, each armed with a club and flashlight. Ben Deveau followed carrying a frogging gig on the point of which was impaled a bat. All three were sweaty and grimy, but victory glistened from every pore. "We got fifty-three of the bastards!" yelled Ben Deveau, brandishing his gig aloft. The Crandallites found that fighting bats was much easier than fighting the Amazon.

But to return to the bananas. The entire stem of twelve dozen bananas would turn yellow at once. It was futile to prevent a colossal waste. We ate sliced raw plátanos with sugar, drenched in leche gloria; we ate them in a cocktail of pineapple, diced papaya, oranges, and taperibá; we ate them baked and stewed; we ate them cut in thin slices, fried and salted like potato chips. Desperately, working against time, we gave them away to Antonia and fed them to the pets, but still dozens rotted. Without a doubt, Reis' sachavaca was our only salvation! We could keep Walter and his guaba seeds out of the house by appointing him official banana peeler for the sachavaca. Then, when the sachavaca grew up, her diet would surely become more varied, and she would keep the rear garden cleared of fast-growing jungle growth and clean up the aguaje nuts that littered the ground. Chalet Tacu Tacu needed the sachavaca!

I should have had Joaquín herd the tapir to Tacu Tacu and presented Dot with a *fait accompli*. I made the mistake of consulting her beforehand. She threatened to abandon her country estate; to move to the most congested apartment on the Plaza de Armas, preferably one without a patio where there wouldn't even be room for a parrot on a perch. "But, *Dottie*," I protested, "a sachavaca is a gentle, sensitive creature. Besides, it's the nearest living relative to the horse and the rhinoceros; and think of the bananas . . ." I phoned Reis that the deal was off.

Dot and I did agree on certain pets that we did not want. Ocelots were out because they were as difficult to raise as a giant panda. They were always ailing and dying. Monkeys were out because they made such a mess. The nearest we came to harboring a monkey was the time that the Luis Felipe Moreys presented us with a monkey skin.

The monkey skin, like the punchana, was an expression of appreciation, we assumed, for little acts of neighborly assistance. The Carachupa entertained during his week-end visits on a scale far exceeding the size and facilities of María Antonieta. Those guests unable to squeeze inside drank their drinks outside. The Carachupa mixed a good pisco sour, but a pisco sour to be good must be well chilled. The Carachupa had no ice box. Consequently, his little girl popped over several times a day on Saturdays and Sundays for ice. Our refrigerator worked overtime to meet the Carachupa's rigorous production schedule. Then there were the dozens of oatmeal cookies that Dot passed over the fence to help out in a pinch. Finally, on Sunday evenings when the pisco sours and the guests were gone, the Moreys would drop over to struggle with our crank, party line phone to call a taxi to take them back to the city.

This was the background of the monkey skin gift. It was a good skin as monkey skins go—a full, brown pelt, untanned but well scraped and dried, measuring about a yard from head to tip of tail. Tacu Tacu was a tacker-upper's paradise. The wooden walls pleaded to have tacks driven into them. We had already tacked up the unframed enlargements of our wedding and honeymoon photographs, a pair of knitted llama dolls, Dot's red wool, flat-crowned Cuzco Indian hat, a head-hunting Jívaro's blowgun, complete with quiver and poisoned darts, a saw-toothed fish spear and my Iquitos-made guitar. There was one blank space left which had been bothering me for some time. Gleefully, I spread-eagled the monkey skin on the wall. Dot objected, bluntly remarking that she had not come to Iquitos to live in the Smithsonian. "Besides," she said, grasping wildly at any excuse, "my place at the table faces it squarely, and that rat-like tail nauseates me every time I look up from my plate."

We compromised. We exchanged places at the table so that

I faced the monkey and Dot had her back to it. The bare spaces were all filled, and everything was lovely until a few days later when I noticed that the skin was gone. No one knew anything about it—Dot, Antonia, Petronila, and Walter—all were in the dark. "Maybe the cockroaches ate it," Dot ventured brightly, after the dinner had proceeded as far as the dessert in complete silence. "They're getting awfully bold lately."

After this incident, if I wanted to see a monkey skin, I had to drop in at the *Casino Militar* where General Morla maintained an even more ambitious collection of the Amazonian fauna than we did at Tacu Tacu. The commanders of the General's far-flung garrisons kept the Casino constantly stocked with exotic animals.

The Casino Militar, the Officers' Club of the Peruvian Army, Navy, and Air Corps, was housed in a beautiful old home built in the days of the rubber boom. It was a single-story building with a tile roof, built in a three-sided square around a lovely patio. The Casino, finer than any civilian club in town, was equipped with a splendid ballroom, reading rooms, a bar, card rooms, a dining room under the portal, and a badminton court in the rear.

Also in the rear were the animals, chained to posts or ensconced on perches. On the highest of the perches sat a dignified sextet of flamboyant huacamayos, patently conscious of the brilliance of their red, blue, and green plumage. Below, at a safe distance, were a series of parallel bars to which were leashed several monkeys, the largest of which was a rangy, mouse-colored maquisapa. Beyond the monkeys were chained the tigrillos. General Morla saw to it that the animals were well cared for, but the attendants never could find a proper diet for the ocelots, which pined away to be replaced by others.

Achilles, the maquisapa, though, had a disposition as rugged as his constitution. Outdoing his Homeric namesake, he had no vulnerable spot. This horny old sinner ate his grub rain or shine and scoffed at the sickly carnivores. Achilles' abounding health was surpassed only by his capacity for devilment. He relished tormenting his guardians by slipping his bonds in Houdini's most baffling manner. Once free, he would embark on an orgy of indiscriminate transgression. Achilles was a one-man crime wave. He not only made it pay but had a helluva lot of fun while at it. This jungle Puck would begin his spree by hurling epithets at the tigrillos, chattering and bouncing just beyond the limits of their straining leashes. With the parrots, he was bolder. Once, before the club attendants could make their way through the blizzard of iridescent feathers, three huacamayos writhed in death with twisted necks and lacerated bodies. Eluding the cursing attendants, Achilles departed for greener pastures by way of the roof tops.

The maquisapa's escapades sometimes lasted for days before Morla's dragnet of a platoon of privates trapped him. Achilles had no desire to return to the Poongaboom country, for he could easily have disappeared into the jungle. Instead, he stayed within the city limits streaking over the roof tops, gleefully smashing roof tiles, pounding for all he was worth on the tin roofs and plunging suddenly into someone's patio to steal food. There was hardly a householder in downtown Iquitos whose tile roof was not reduced to potsherds by the rampaging monkey. They would shrug their shoulders in tired resignation. What could one do about it? The General's maquisapa, like bolts of lightning, fire, and flood, had to be accepted. There was no *remedio*. Achilles enjoyed the chase and gave himself up only when he was tired of the game, knowing that he could repeat the experience when life at the Casino again palled.

One of my fondest memories of Iquitos is a scene I witnessed one evening after work as I was bicycling through the Plaza de Armas on my way to Punchana. Strung out on the ridge of a roof in sharp silhouette against the setting sun were a half dozen shoeless soldiers making their way gingerly along. Well ahead, traveling at a bounding lope, was Achilles, the frayed end of his tether held defiantly high in the grasp of his supple tail so as not to catch on a projecting tile.

7

S COTTY LYONS, red haired and built solid like a hogshead, was the one to blame for Dot's start in the chicken business. It was Scotty who brought "Invasion Barge" Gertrude to Iquitos. But let me begin at the beginning.

Scotty began his explosive career back in 1916, when he had a British mine sweeper torpedoed from under him. He woke up in a hospital, the only survivor. Scotty left England, came to the United States, served in the United States Cavalry along the Mexican border, wrestled, boxed, married three times, and then departed for the oil fields of eastern Venezuela, where he and I were tenthouse mates in "Chancre Alley," the much maligned

Invasion Barge Gertrude

bachelors' section of the Gulf Oil camp at San Tomé. Scotty made a barrel of friends and sundry history all over Venezuela's uninhibited Guanipa mesa. When Nazi submarines forced a virtual shutdown of petroleum production, he joined the Rubber Development Corporation and ended up in the Amazon Valley as skipper of a flock of beat-up invasion barges.

In Manaos, Skipper Scotty received orders to transport a collection of bulldozers, scrapers, trucks, and other equipment to Iquitos for the construction of an all-weather airport. A bevy of *Brasiliera* hens were taken aboard the invasion barges to feed the crew. Among them was Gertrude, a voluptuous yellow-feathered wench, raised in the fleshpots of Manaos. The twelve-hundred-mile voyage should have taken two weeks under normal conditions, but circumstances stretched the voyage from fifteen to fifty days. The invasion barges had been banged around in North Africa and didn't run or keep out the water as they should have. The uncharted, buoyless Amazon is a river pilot's nightmare by day. By night . . . The flotilla was fortunate to lose only one barge when a huge snag pierced the hull one moonless night.

"Invasion Barge" Gertrude was not aboard the wrecked barge, but she would have perished at the hands of the famished, sun-parched, rain-lashed crew had she not found favor with Scotty. He kept her alive and uneaten during the whole ordeal. That was not easy. Scotty, himself, lost forty pounds between Manaos and Iquitos.

When Scotty recovered, we had a reunion at Tacu Tacu. He brought "Invasion Barge" Gertrude along in a box. She also had recovered—so well that she was sitting maternally on a clutch of nine eggs. "They're no ordinary eggs," Scotty announced proudly. He raised the protesting Gertrude. "Look—they're blue!" The eggs were blue, all nine of them—not a robin's egg blue, but the pale blue of much-washed denim overalls!

Scotty gave the fabulous Gertrude to Dot. Shortly, a half dozen ordinary chicks emerged. Gertrude, crushed that they weren't blue, too, turned sensationally harum-scarum. She trampled her babies by night and kicked them about by day. When a hawk circled low over the house she would run full tilt for the shelter of Tacu Tacu's pilings, leaving her chicks to shift for themselves.

Gertrude's crowning act of ignominy was her abrupt desertion of her offspring at the tender age of two weeks to embark on a purple-passioned affair with Chalet Crandall's sawed-off, black rooster. We could never fathom what elegant, fastidious Gertrude saw in that sorry *gallo*. His abnormally short legs even failed to give him sufficient elevation to keep his sickle feathers from dragging in the dust, and his crow was sadly ineffectual. He would start with great promise, but, as he reached the peak of an impressive crescendo, his aria would come to a sudden stop and trail off in an abortive gurgle.

However, the Crandall cock must have packed a punch crammed with tropical titillation, for Gertrude was completely oblivious of his shortcomings. When Dot threw out cracked corn, in the mornings, to Gertrude and her forlorn orphans, the Crandall rooster would appear on the top of the whitewashed balsa fence, survey the situation, and plop down to breakfast. Gertrude wouldn't eat until her gallo had had his fill. She would seek out choice grains and cluck until he came and ate them. Woe betide any of her babies who took a fancy to a bit of corn that Gertrude had earmarked for her paramour!

So complete was the rooster's domination that Gertrude veered giddily back to the throes of maternity. While her original brood still peeped and wore its fluff she began laying with fervor, intent on building up another clutch. When she had amassed a dozen eggs she abruptly ceased production, forgot her frivolous ways and sat in model broodiness. The Crandall rooster had done his formidable best: by candle test each egg showed the essential shadow.

The transgressions of Gertrude's youth were erased by this heroic display of productivity and devotion. We banished thoughts of chicken and dumplings. We felt that the folly of Gertrude's first fling at motherhood had passed.

"Invasion Barge" Gertrude did not disappoint us. She hatched out eleven of the twelve eggs and reared all the chicks with unmatched devotion to rugged adolescence. None were trampled and kicked about; none were left to cheep in troubled loneliness. When the shadow of the hawk moved over the white sand of the back yard, she would blow out her feathers, spread her wings and convoy her brood with watchful dignity to the protection of the pilings. In her excursions about the garden she located nutritious insects. With peculiar high-pitched clucks she taught her chicks to converge on the tasty morsel like iron filings to a magnet. The Crandall rooster now had to rustle for himself when Antonia stood on the kitchen steps, a machete in one hand and a yuca root in the other, and chipped off bits of chalk-white yuca onto the sand.

We determined to obtain a fit mate for Gertrude. It would be tragic for her to go through life with that dunghill chanticleer. The breeding and proportions of a pedigreed rooster blended with the stamina and resourcefulness of the jungle hen would produce, we reasoned, a perfect breed of chicken for Iquitos.

No such rooster was available in Iquitos. We would have to get him on the coast. Our friends shook their heads. "A blooded chicken will not survive the jungle climate a month." Don Victor Israel had gone to great expense to have a champion pair of Barred Plymouth Rocks flown from Lima, only to have them die shortly after their arrival. We conceded that it would not be wise to introduce a pair of imported chickens but held stubbornly to our plan of cross-breeding.

The opportunity of obtaining our gentleman rooster came in February, during our first "breather" in Lima. I had convinced the Embassy and the Department that it was essential to health and morale "to return to Peru" (as native Limeños, exiled in Iquitos, say to the infuriation of native Iquiteños) every six months for a combined consultation and vacation leave.

We found what we wanted late one afternoon in a poultry farm at Moche, a suburb of Trujillo, some five hundred kilometers north of Lima. The manager of the farm held up a large white cockerel for our inspection. "The White Jersey type," he said, "is creating a lot of fuss in your country now—a good layer and much body. The papá of this fellow," he added with pride, "came all the way from the *Estados Unidos* by airplane. A very fine gallo!"

The next morning, Dot and I boarded a bus for the long ride down the coastal desert to Lima. Moche, the rooster, rode on the roof in a huge basket. As we streaked southward over the Pan American Highway, Dot worried about Moche through every kilometer. "He'll catch cold in that terrific draft and die before we even reach Lima," she wailed. At the first stop, Dot had me climb up on the roof to see whether Moche had any feathers left. I peered under the burlap cover. He was comfortable and unruffled, but Dot insisted that the driver rearrange his cargo so that Moche's basket was surrounded by a windbreak of suitcases and boxes. The other passengers accepted the delay and the requisition of their effects with amiable resignation.

In Lima, we took Moche to our white stuccoed house overlooking the ocean. It wasn't really ours. We had swapped Tacu Tacu for it. It belonged to W. Stratton Anderson II, Third Secretary and Vice Consul at the Embassy, who had been assigned as relief officer in Iquitos during my absence.

"Here, at last, is the storybook personification of the career diplomat," I thought, as W. Stratton Anderson the Second arrived in Iquitos to assume charge. Son of true-blue Admiral Anderson, and Harvard "cum laude" 1934, he stepped from Biggs' Catalina onto the float at the Itaya Base. I introduced myself with a feeling of awe. W. Stratton Anderson the Second was over six feet tall and slightly pale, as a career diplomat should be. He wore round, steel-rimmed spectacles and a brown fedora set with proper restraint on his head. His white palm beach was rumpled just enough to indicate that he had crossed the mighty Andes. In one hand, he carried a well-nourished brief case, over the arm a raincoat, and, in the other hand, a first cousin of Neville Chamberlin's black umbrella. His feet were encased in rubbers. The rubbers seemed to disturb him. "I should really be wearing mosquito boots," he admitted apologetically, "but I lost my last pair on the Gold Coast. Accra was a ghastly place for mosquitoes."

I thought I would never succeed in turning the office over to Anderson. I had visions of my leave slipping away while he dug up a multitude of obscure regulations in the Black Book of Words (and some he admitted weren't there but should have been) relative to the proper procedure of the Transfer of a Consular Office. At first I protested, but, after an entire morning of protocol debate, I yielded to the superior mettle of careerdom.

Dot and I turned over Tacu Tacu complete with servants and livestock to Anderson. He entered the house, glanced quickly around, and exclaimed with genuine pleasure, "Why, it's so *clean!*" Dot tried to contain herself, but the temptation was too great. "Yes, isn't it, Mister Anderson," she carolled. "But you should have seen it yesterday before we ran the hogs out and swept the chicken droppings off the couch!"

Andy Anderson was a little baffling only on first acquaintance. As we got to know Andy, we discovered that he was not only a competent officer, but a delightful person whose sense of humor was as keen as it was subtle.

When Dot and I had unlocked the door of Andy's attractive California Mission-style house and peered into the tasteful interior, we suddenly realized that we had been looking at Tacu Tacu through the rose-colored glasses of isolation and adaptability. We felt like two trespassing clodhoppers as we explored the house—the kitchen with its gleaming white sink and factory-made gas range, a tiled bath with hot and cold water, and a sun terrace that looked down on the walled garden. And then, when

Emilio, the houseboy-cook, appeared, resplendent in a white mess jacket, black bow tie, and shoes, we almost crawled under the rug with remorse.

Such was the White Jersey rooster's first home. He was ensconced in the garden with all the scratch grain and lettuce he could eat, free to strut about the emerald green lawn and among the blood-red geraniums. He would have no geraniums, no velvety lawn, no commercial chicken feed, no healthful climate in Iquitos.

Yet, in spite of his ideal surroundings, Moche did not prosper. He began to droop. He squatted listlessly among the geraniums, his comb an anemic orange. Under the camouflage of his beautiful plumage, his body felt scrawnier day by day. His increasing feebleness certainly seemed due, in part, to lack of sleep. From dusk to dawn he filled the night air with a succession of prolonged mournful crows. The cries seemed to have difficulty in emerging from his emotion-choked throat, and, once out, were followed by a sighing intake of air.

His call had great carrying power, for all the gallos of Barranco, Chorrillos, and even those of San Isidro were kept in a state of perpetual alarm by his untimely and ceaseless bugling. In addition, the neighbors began to complain. It took them about a week to locate the source of the disturbance, for who would suspect discreet Meester Anderson of harbouring a rooster in his patio? The Colombian Consul sent his butler over with his card and a polite inquiry as to the possibility of silencing the rooster. After all, this was an elite residential district, not a country chacra.

In desperation, we sought a clue to Moche's strange insomnia, for, if an excess of grand opera didn't kill him, we certainly would be forced to do something equally drastic. At the eleventh hour plus, Dot broke the case. "We've been stupid!" she cried. "Why, of course, *poor* Moche couldn't sleep!" She pointed to the street lamp that projected over the patio wall. "That lamp keeps the garden in perpetual twilight! It *never* gets dark!" Dot was right. Valiant, misunderstood Moche, in a marathon of self-immolation, had been dutifully heralding rosy-fingered dawn all night long!

We put an end to Moche's bootless heroism by confining him at night to a light-well between the kitchen and the living room with a broom for a perch. It worked. Ear-splitting silence reigned all night.

By the time we were ready to board the RDC Catalina to return to Iquitos, Moche had caught up with his sleep. His impending ordeal would test the virility of his Yankee daddy. Once again, we were flying with Condor Biggs. We were almost left behind. When we arrived at the Santa Cruz airport in the inky morning, everyone was aboard, and the Cat was poised for the take-off, growling and shaking with impatience. We were barely able to fling ourselves, Moche, and our luggage aboard before the Cat began moving down the pitch black field.

We found that the rugged old Cat had become a pantywaist. It no longer was exclusively a rough, tough freighter. Instead of a coil of rope and balls of rubber, four seats for passengers were arranged behind the control compartment. Even more, each seat was equipped with an oxygen tube! Since our last flight seven months before, the RDC had authorized Faucett to take general passengers and freight aboard the two Cats in order to cut down on the terrific cost of operation. RDC freight, of course, still rated top priority.

If Condor Biggs' plane had abandoned a bit of its austerity, Condor Biggs had not. In fact, he had grown grimmer. He no longer wasted time in beating his way as far north as Chiclayo to take advantage of low passes in the mountains. Instead, he bee-lined for Iquitos, hedgehopping the highest damn ridges in the Peruvian Andes. That day, he gave the frozen fingers of Huascarán (Peru's loftiest peak—22,051 feet) a hasty manicure in passing.

Goaded by Dot, I staggered back to the tail periodically to see how Moche was enjoying the exhilarating mountain air. When we piled aboard, we had time only to dump him, sewed in a burlap sling, near the cargo hatch and rush to our seats.

When I checked him at ten thousand feet he seemed quite comfortable, resting quietly on his side. At fifteen thousand he still lay quietly, breathing regularly but, this time, white eyelids filmed his eyes. On my third and last visit at twenty-two thousand feet, just as we were avoiding the clutching fingers of Huascarán, Moche looked twice as bad as I felt. My head was splitting and a deadly nausea had settled like a stone in my stomach. As sorry as I felt for myself, I felt sorrier for Moche. "Dot's chicken is a goner," I thought. He lay on a canvas tarp, a limp mass of feathers, his once proud comb a droopy, gangrenous purple.

Back at my seat, I gulped down oxygen like a man dying of thirst. Dot sensed that all was not well. When she refused to believe my shouted assurances over the roar of the engines that Moche was all right, I told her the worst. She yelled at me that if I didn't bring Moche forward where she could pour oxygen down his throat she would go get him herself. I didn't budge. I had had enough high-altitude hiking to last me a lifetime. Dot attempted to climb over me to the aisle, whereupon I plopped her back in her seat with the shouted suggestion that she stuff the heroics.

That settled it. Moche was left to die while we huddled in icy truce with rubber tubes clamped between our teeth. The passengers weren't troubled with complicated oxygen masks. There was a little pet cock beside each seat to which was attached a length of rubber tubing. It was simple. You put the tube in your mouth, turned on the gas and blew yourself up like a blimp. When you felt sufficiently inflated you removed the tube and burped.

This cycle of inflation and deflation continued until the lessening cold told us that Biggs was dropping on Iquitos. At twelve thousand feet, I felt capable of making a final trip aft to inspect Moche's remains. To my surprise, Moche, the rugged son of a Yankee, was very much alive! His eyes were bright and his comb no longer looked as if amputation were imperative. If we garnered no other kudos, the distinction of being the first Foreign Service couple to fly a purebred rooster into the Upper Amazon at twenty-two thousand feet was glory enough to last for many a rise and fall of the river!

In Iquitos, Moche fulfilled our fondest expectations to the chagrin of the gloom-mongers. He took to his duties with a will. He weaned his harem away from an exclusively starch diet of yuca, rice, and corn, and taught them to eat banana leaves and scrap lettuce; gurgled a proper warning when a hawk appeared; became adequately flustered when Dot pursued his women, scissors in hand, to clip their wings; and, apparently, kept the black Crandall rooster on his side of the fence. For his devotion to duty he was rewarded once a month with a bath in Lux Flakes (at 75 cents U. S. a box) and a thorough drying with my bath towel!

On the great day that Moche's first batch of superior offspring broke their shells, we were completely befuddled to find "Invasion Barge" Gertrude sitting demurely on a dozen cheeping lumps of coal—not a blonde chick in the lot!

8

𝒞 HE BLACK Book of Words, in one of its early chapters, en-
joins each consular officer "to cultivate friendly social relations
with the members of the community in which his post is located." This instruction is unique in the "Bible," for it gives
the officer, in a few succinct, proviso-shy words, a rare opportunity to unleash the latent initiative, resourcefulness, and imagination with which he is supposed to be liberally endowed. Paced
by Dot, I plunged into the Iquitian social whirl.

Social life centered in the clubs, the Plaza de Armas, and the
cinemas. The most select clubs in town were the *Club Social
Iquitos,* the *Centro Internacional,* and the *Casino Militar.* Mem-

. . And the Band Played on

bership in the Casino was limited to officers of the Peruvian Army, Navy, and Air Corps. Of the two civilian clubs, the Cloob SoCIAL Iquitos was, by all odds, the most fashionable. Its membership boasted the four hundred—every merchant, politician, professional man, and military and civilian official of consequence. Admission was freely granted to foreigners on the same modest basis that applied to Peruvian members—ten soles per month ($1.50).

The club occupied the second, and top, floor of the most distinctive building in the Upper Amazon Valley. Probably one of the earliest examples of prefabrication, the building was constructed entirely of iron trusses and sheets bolted together and painted from ground level to roof a dazzling silver. According to the story, a Loretan rubber baron took such a fancy to one of the exposition buildings of the Paris Exposition of 1898 that he purchased it. In true Ghost-Goes-West style, he unbolted the metal palace, loaded it on a steamer, and shipped it across the Atlantic and up the Amazon to Iquitos, where the sections were again bolted together on the Plaza de Armas. This rubber baron was not as lucky at cards as he was at collecting black gold, for he forfeited his collapsible palace to settle his gambling debts. The building passed from one owner to another in a series of card games and other exchanges until the upstairs became the club, and the ground floor, site of *El Patito* (The Little Duck), the grocery store of Alfredo Ochi, leader of the local Japanese colony.

From mid-morning to mid-afternoon, the fierce equatorial sun beat upon the burnished armor of the Cloob SoCIAL Iquitos. You could squint at the sun with as much success as you could at the club. Although an egg dropped on the roof would have been carbonized in a moment, the interior of the club was surprisingly cool.

A deep veranda extended the length of the second floor. The veranda opened into a ballroom, used between dances as a reading room. The reading matter consisted of a dog-eared, antiquated collection of magazines and newspapers scattered about the top of a large table. A few wicker rocking chairs were lost in the large room. An upright piano on a small dais in one corner and a series of huge, yellowed mirrors hanging on the bare metal walls completed the furnishings of the club's most elegant room. In an adjoining room was a ping-pong table, the club's only rug, a radio-phonograph, and a half-dozen rocking chairs. Beyond was a pool room containing one small pool table whose cloth was faded and nicked. Although gambling was illegal, a roulette wheel was installed on the pool table several nights a week. The police could determine, by standing in the middle of the street and looking through the open window, exactly who was playing. If, in the intense huddle around the pool table, they picked out the Prefect, the Mayor, members of the City Council, prominent merchants, army officers, or members of the consular corps, they would refrain from making a raid that would be embarrassing only to themselves. Occasionally, when the glare of the dangling, green-shaded lamp revealed only smaller fry, they would screw up enough courage to enter. For several nights thereafter, club members would content themselves with pool, and then out would come the roulette wheel once more.

In a dark rear room, a dingy bar and a few marble-topped tables completed the facilities of the club.

It was pleasant in the early evening to pull your chair close to the edge of the veranda, prop your feet against the iron railing, and, drink in hand, watch the sights in the Plaza de Armas. The Plaza de Armas in all Peruvian cities is the principal square of the community. It would be as unthinkable to name the principal square of a Peruvian community anything but the Plaza de Armas as it would be to name the principal square of a Venezuelan community anything but Plaza Bolívar. In the case of Peru, the name originates from the custom of using the main square as a parade ground for troops, while in Venezuela it is a sign of the intense veneration for Simón Bolívar, the Venezuelan-born liberator of five South American countries.

The Plaza de Armas of Iquitos, a large rectangle hemmed about by one- and two-story buildings, was a place of sun, silence, and solitude in the daylight hours. At dusk, when people no longer plotted their way about, hugging the shady side of the street to avoid the wilting sun, the Plaza de Armas came into her own. She was a nocturnal creature like the translucent lizards.

The first to arrive were merchants and store clerks, who gathered after closing hour around the little tables at the two sidewalk kiosks. If there were canned milk in town, they ate *imperiales*, the local name for vanilla ice cream. They drank tall, ice-packed limonadas (made with the best limes in the world) for ten cents U. S., or Callao beer, bitter with arsenic preservative, for forty cents U. S.

Iquitos beer came overland from coastal Peru. The Lima-Pucallpa highway was completed as far as the Aguaytía River, about one hundred miles short of Pucallpa. At this point, the sacks of beer, lashed to the heaving platform of a balsa, shot the rapids and spun about in the whirlpools of the Río Aguaytía until they arrived, soaked and battered, at the Río Ucayali, where a steamer picked them up. After such a trip, it is small wonder that those green bottles that survived arrived rusty capped and labelless. Considering the exorbitant freight and mortality rates, it is surprising that a bottle of beer cost no more than it did. But once you paid your two soles sixty centavos, you were still not sure of your glass of *cerveza*. The first hurdle was to pry off the rusty cap without breaking the neck. A newcomer to Iquitos immediately gave himself away when, with an oath, he put aside the shattered bottle. But as you learned that there was a remedy for ant-infested bread, so you learned that beer seasoned with glass splinters was potable. The experienced toper would whip out his handkerchief, arrange it in the mouth of the glass and expertly remove all foreign matter by filtration.

The bottle opened, the next step was to determine whether your beer contained an overdose of arsenic. The experts would tell you that an abundance of foam spelled a carefree *"salud!"* while a flat amber spelled certain death. In great thirst I have taken them foamy and I have taken them flat. Always I have walked away from the table.

As the flamboyant colors of the sunset faded out over the jungle and the tropical stars pricked the sky, releasing the cool night air, the Plaza de Armas would fill with promenaders. Around and around they would go, two concentric circles, one moving clockwise and the other counterclockwise. In this way, everyone got an eyeful of everyone else. The men were walking tributes to the heroic washwomen of Iquitos as they paraded along in glazed, highly starched whites. Probably the predominance of the military affected the civilian element, for the amount of starch in men's suits was fantastic. They walked along crackling at every step, as stiffly as if they wore steel braces on their trunks and limbs. Once home, they had only to emerge from coat and trousers and leave them standing in readiness for the next promenade. The women, hatless and in silk prints or fashionable black silk, flowed gracefully along at the side of their straight-jacketed men.

The carriage of the Loretan women, whether rich or poor, is queenly—back and shoulders wonderfully erect, head held high, Bali-like breasts thrust forward. The Indian and mestizo women owe their enviable posture to a lifetime of balancing water jugs and market basins on their heads. The daughter of the prosperous Iquitos merchant never carries a thing on her head, not even a hat, yet her carriage is as erect as if she secretly practised walking every day with a book on top of her head. Mere association with a city of erect people causes the humpbacked, slump-shouldered foreigner to straighten up involuntarily. Iquitos may not be a health resort, but if you wish to cure yourself of curvature of the spine, go to the Pearl and devote a couple of months to the nightly promenade around the Plaza de Armas.

Promenade etiquette was strictly observed in Iquitos. On the first two times around the cement track, you were required to salute each of your acquaintances verbally, accompanied by a dignified nod of the head. *"Buenas noches, Señor Múnoz,"* you would say in passing. *"Buenas noches, Señor CONsool,"* was the polite rejoinder. If your acquaintance was accompanied by his wife and children, addressing him, as head of the family, was sufficient. A nod and mechanical smile took care of the group. By the third time around, unless new faces appeared on the scene, the nod and smile (by now more of a grimace) were sufficient. After the sixth lap, all authorities agreed that you were free to proceed oblivious of your surroundings—free to look blankly through, over, or away from the constant stream of revolving acquaintances.

The promenade gave everyone an opportunity to get caught up with current events. If you had heard Comandante Pinto's wife was once again "that way," you could make sure during the promenade. If, after the first time around, there was still divided opinion, you were sure to agree by the second or third lap.

Three nights a week you could strut to the music of the Jungle Division Band. It entered the plaza punctually at eight, stepping smartly to a martial air, and would take its place under the cupola of the frilly bandstand. The band then put aside things military and gave forth an unadulterated flow of lilting criollo waltzes, melancholy *huaynitos* of the Sierra Indians, and pulsating Brazilian sambas. At least once during the two-hour program, the band played its repertoire of cosmopolitan numbers: *The Dark Town Strutters Ball, You Are Always in My Heart,* and *Profundamente En El Corazón de Téjas* which those living deep in the sovereign heart of Texas would have recognized as their national anthem.

At this time of the evening, especially on a Saturday night, Iquitos assumed its most metropolitan air. On all sides there was sophistication—the starched, groomed promenaders; the sidewalk cafe society spooning its imperiales and sipping pink cola; the music; the orange moon; and the sensational neon sign, Iquitos' first, about which *El Eco* had devoted two columns. At such moments, the Pearl had great luster—Sí, Señor!

Our hearts always went out to General Morla's band. If among its members there were those with artists' souls, life, at times, must have been unbearable. Just across the street from the bandstand was the Casino Militar. The officers' lounge was equipped with a powerful radio and loud-speaker, so that music and news broadcasts could be blared all over the Plaza de Armas. The band had occasional moments of unchallenged glory, but it spent most of the evening locked in a bitter struggle of conflicting harmonies with the loud-speaker.

The battle for supremacy between General Morla's loud-speaker and General Morla's band continued unabated during our entire stay in Iquitos. Band never threw in the towel, although Loud-Speaker won round after round by sheer aggressiveness. Loud-Speaker's most staggering punches were the right counters of BBC's Big Ben from London and the left hooks of Radio Berlin's *Voice of Culture*. Seated in an armchair in the plaza under a ficus tree was General Morla himself, cool and unruffled in his braided cap, white uniform, and glistening boots. Night after night, he took up his position between Band and Loud-Speaker as though he were a referee bent on keeping the two contenders from tearing one another asunder.

At 9:10 o'clock, a most amazing thing happened. In an instant, the promenaders and the cafe society disappeared, leaving Band and Loud-Speaker to continue their struggle in an empty plaza, the orange moon the only spectator. Even the General had gone. It was like pulling the plug in a wash basin. Now, it is full; whoosh, and it's empty. The entire plazaful of people had decamped with the speed of thought to the *Alhambra* theatre for the 9:15 movie. The heroic musicians, their spirits hardened by a thousand such rebukes, played on according to orders until ten o'clock. Then they marched out of the deserted plaza to a martial air, their heads held high, leaving Loud-Speaker and its *Voice of Culture* temporarily in possession of the field.

Iquitos had three moving picture theatres—the *Teatro Alhambra*, the *Excelsior*, and the *Bolognesi*. When I first arrived, only two were in operation; and both of them had such dilapidated projection equipment that the sound emerged badly blurred. The films, mostly American and Mexican, with a scattering of pre-war British and French productions, were flown in from Lima after they had made the run of all the cities and hamlets of coastal and Andean Peru.

Fortunately, when Dot arrived, the wartime boom occasioned by Uncle Sam's heavy purchases of Loreto's jungle products enabled the local movie magnates to remedy the sad condition of the projectors. Don Joao Pinto, an energetic Portuguese who owned the city's only ice plant and had imported the famous neon sign, was also the owner of the Excelsior and Bolognesi. He obtained new projectors from Lima for both theatres. The Excelsior reopened after a complete remodeling that featured huge murals of jungle scenes executed by Señor Ortíz, the versatile creator of Tacu Tacu's mahogany toilet seat, and a crimson curtain on which were sewn thousands of sequins to form a gorgeous butterfly.

Not to be outdone, Don Carlos Bonilla, owner of the Alhambra, bought a new projector and completely remodeled his theatre. If we movie-goers drew in our breath at the splendors of the Excelsior, we ceased to breathe when we entered the new Alhambra. Here was a superb example of Loretan craftsmanship and ingenuity. Everything but the new projector was made locally of regional products. Far more thrilling than the bold geometric designs on the walls and ceiling was the seating arrangement. The gradient of the main floor had been increased. There was no peering around the person sitting in front of you. The chairs were constructed of mahogany, with cool wicker backs and seats and space enough between rows to stretch your legs. Don Carlos proudly remarked that he could have installed two hundred more seats on the main floor if he had cared to cramp the legs of his patrons. As it was, the theatre had a seating capacity of a thousand. Down the center aisle ran the finest carpet in the Amazon Valley, approximately four feet wide, woven entirely of the fibre of the *chambira* palm and dyed attractively in alternate strips of red and black.

Lima's movie theatres are flea-ridden. In the cheaper theatres, the *pulgas* are as thick as lottery ticket vendors in the Plaza San Martín. In the finer theatres on the Plaza San Martín, you may think for a few minutes that there are none; then, the hairs on your legs begin to tickle, and you know that the pulgas are on their way up. Iquitos is blessed. There are neither lottery ticket vendors nor fleas. Not even the barefooted cholo in the top balcony has to share his bench with the pulga.

Iquiteños are the world's most fervent movie fans. In their isolated, swamp-bound island, the movies are their only form of canned diversion. They are starved for the wondrous gadgets of the twentieth century and experience them vicariously by going to the movies.

The favorite type of film is the musical comedy. Most Iquiteños have a bellyful of worms, but all, without exception, are shot through with rhythm and music. After every musical film, adults and children alike push their way into the street whistling or humming the melodies of every song on the program.

Strangely enough, Westerns were not popular; at least, they were seldom shown. Their place was taken by serial thrillers. Frequently, all three theatres showed nothing but serials. The *estreno* or debut would offer the first four chapters of a serial, the balance to follow in similar installments. Then, as an irresistible *re-estreno* or debut No. 2, the public-wise management would place large canvas posters on the street corners offering all twelve spine-tingling chapters of *El Avispón Verde* (The Green Hornet) for sixty centavos! The following week, the posters were changed to advise the public of the *despedida* or farewell showing. The despedida usually lasted for several days, and, if foul weather continued to hold the new picture in Chiclayo, the same serial was held over in a *grandiosa despedida final* —a farewell showing to end all farewell showings—for forty centavos!

December ninth is Peruvian Army Day. The army is very important in Iquitos, so the American Vice Consulate paid its respects by closing up shop along with the rest of the town. The following morning, I arrived at the office to find Joaquín sitting at his table in the reception room, with bloodshot eyes. He arose groggily from his seat as I entered. "What the devil did you do yesterday?" I asked. "Na-a-ada, Señor Kehle-e-e, fuí al ci-i-ine no ma-a-as," he replied. "No movie can pack a wallop like that," I thought.

I questioned Joaquín further. It was as he said. He had *only* been to the movies. In the morning he had gone to the Alhambra to see *Flash Gordon y la Conquista del Universo, twelve* harrowing chapters of the conquest of the universe, beginning with *Purple Death* and closing with *The End of the Dictator.* Joaquín had then staggered across town to the Bolognesi for the matinee, featuring *fifteen* chapters of *Rinty and the Horse Rex.*

I do not wish to intimate that the legitimate theatre did not reach Iquitos. It did—once during our stay. To Don Carlos Bonilla's Alhambra came the Fakir Aben el Kadi, who amazed us by frying eggs with his flaming breath and lying stripped to the waist on a bed of broken glass while Princess Zamarcanda, in pink pajamas, squatted on his chest and poured molten lead into his mouth.

9

*I*quitos is a city with a garish past and an unpredictable future; a city of glazed tiles and open sewers; a city buried in the heart of an empty wilderness yet peopled with cosmopolites; a city of mud and dust; of blazing sun and torrential rain; of despondent lethargy and unbounded enthusiasm. The one unfailing source of energy and joy is the dance. The dance is the great, fraternal bond of all classes and nationalities. He who dances finds the real Pearl of the Amazon; he who does not dance finds only the mud, the stench, the isolation, the leanness, and the boredom of a tropical hole.

The *raison d'être* of any social gathering was always, and

The City of the Samba

designedly, the dance. The dance might enter dressed as Army Day or as the anniversary of the glorious Boundary Treaty with Ecuador, or as Loreto's patron Saint John. If no official pretext for a dance was at hand, a pretext was devised. There were dances of *bienvenida* to welcome the arrival of a prominent visitor, and dances of despedida upon his departure; there were fiestas to celebrate the crest of the Amazon and fiestas to celebrate the low point of the river.

An indication of Iquitos' cosmopolitan society and that the city faces eastwards toward Europe despite its political ties with the Pacific Coast was the Gallicism used to refer to a dance. For every time the Spanish word *baile* was used, the French derivative *danzant* appeared twice. The danzants were variously combined with food and drink. There were té-danzants or tea dances, cocktail-danzants, and *comida* or dinner-danzants. In every case, the danzant was the important and constant element. The té-danzants and cocktail-danzants were supposed to begin at six and end at nine o'clock. They invariably began at nine and lasted until two in the morning. The comida-danzants began about ten o'clock and broke up at dawn.

Because of the high cost and scarcity of food and the modest size of most private houses, few people were able to entertain on a large scale. As a result, fiestas were held in the clubs and organized by a quota subscription. For instance, several people would decide that a cocktail-danzant should be given as a birthday surprise for one of the gunboat commanders. A list bearing the names of potential subscribers would be drawn up with the blue typewriter ribbon that is so popular in Latin America. This list, preceded by a short statement of the "why" of the

party and the amount of the individual quota, was carried by
a messenger from office to office to garner the cash contributions.
If you didn't want to be involved, you had the unconvincing
choice of jotting "previous engagement" or "out of town" by
your name. Either of these was a feeble out, for Iquitos society
kept close tab on itself and getting out of town was a major
undertaking, involving the use of an airplane or a steamer.

There were no regular caterers in town. The bakeries could
occasionally be prevailed upon to supply a little pastry, but
nothing adequate. Consequently, the ladies on the list were assigned cakes, cookies, puddings, sandwiches, and hors d'oeuvres,
while the money donated by the men paid for the whisky, beer,
cola, ice, the orchestra, and the use of the club. Sometimes the
fiestas were organized with several days' notice; other times the
list would circulate only a few hours before the party. The first
few occasions that Dot was requested to whip up a batch of
brownies in five minutes she would fume with indignation.
But she became resigned to the fact that most fiestas sprang out
of thin air, and, stoking up her two-by-four charcoal stove, she
would somehow have her contribution ready in time.

The dances of the Cloob SoCIAL Iquitos, in spite of its
austere and dog-eared furnishings, had a certain gay abandon
that those of the other clubs seldom attained. For one thing,
the music was always tops—nothing less than the *Gran Orquesta
Jazz Band Bolognesi*. This legend appeared on the head of the
bass drum, but Bolognesi was not the name of the leader of the
Grand Orchestra Jazz Band. He was more; he was its inspiration.
Colonel Francisco Bolognesi, one of Peru's heroes, died glori-
ously in combat on June 7, 1880, with all eighteen hundred of
his men defending Arica against the sea-borne invasion of six
thousand Chileans. Unlike us of the United States, Peruvians
do not restrict the tribute paid their heroes to cities, parks,
streets, and public buildings. They also proclaim their patriotism
in the names of their soccer teams and jazz bands.

Each member of the Gran Orquesta Jazz Band Bolognesi,
from the piano player to the *maraca* rattler, was bursting with

the heroic spirit of the gallant colonel. Each was a man of iron, each was indefatigable. There were no lulls between dances. Hardly had the dancers quit the floor when the music would begin again. Even when the fiesta had dwindled to several sweaty, groggy couples, the band played on. The contagious glee and enthusiasm of the musicians, playing because they loved it, so infected the dancers that they stomped, shuffled, and spun with rapturous delight.

The party was marked as a failure if the dancing did not cause the floor of the club to pitch and heave in vertical vibrations. A rumba or tango seldom produced the desired effect. It took a heated samba or criollo waltz to make the steel girders under the rough flooring really undulate. Then we dancers, very pleased with our accomplishment, would laugh and call to one another that some day the floor would collapse, and we would all end up in Ochi's grocery store, below. Although newcomers manifested alarm over this phenomenon, and some even abandoned the tossing deck for the safety of the bar, the floor has never yet collapsed under the strain.

In spite of the heat, Iquiteños would tolerate nothing but spirited, fast-moving dances—dances that permitted a maximum of twirling, scooting, sliding, and stomping. Iquiteños could claim no dance that was indigenous. Instead, they borrowed from East and West and produced a delightful blend of their own. The sultry, sensuous samba of Brazil came upriver to join the more restrained but light-hearted criollo waltz of coastal Peru. These two were the perennial favorites, eternal as the Amazon herself. There were many other dances. The orchestra leader put up a cardboard sign announcing: *The Conga, The Tango, The Viennese Waltz, The Blue, The Fox,* and *The Swing.* But the blood of their virile parents stood out all over these half-breed children. No matter how hard the orchestra tried to play and the dancers tried to dance a lilting, smooth, full-skirted Viennese waltz or an American swing-time number, the black-eyed samba or the choppy, head-wagging vals criollo would cut in and steal the show.

Iquiteños not only danced with every ounce of their rhythm-packed bodies, but they sang as they danced. One of the favorite song-dance pieces was a conga entitled *El Alacrán*—all about a scorpion who spent his time cutting sugar cane. When the orchestra launched into El Alacrán, the crowd went wild. The baile rushed to its fulfillment. The rhythmical stomping made the floor rise and fall like a dory in a choppy sea. The dancers sweated and steamed in full-blown ecstasy, their faces flushed as they shouted:

> *Oiga, compadre, no te asombres cuando veas*
> *El Alacrán cortando caña . . .*

The women's flimsy dresses were plastered to their bodies in soggy intimacy, accentuating the contour of breast and thigh. Dot once rashly wore a green crepe dress which by midnight had shrunk to above her knees. The men sweated through their shirts and white coats so that the starch oozed from the fabric and was slimy to the touch, while the dye from their partners' dresses left rainbow patterns on their white sleeves and other points of contact. These by-products of the baile tropiCAL disturbed you at first and you held your dripping partner at a discreet arm's length. But, by the third fiesta, you clasped your lady to you in sticky bliss and shouted El Alacrán with the best of them, assuring your friend, in the words of the song, not to be alarmed when he sees the scorpion cutting cane, because it's just a custom of your country:

> *. . . El Alacrán cortando caña*
> *Costumbre de mi pais, Hermano,*
> *Si, Si Cortando Caña . . .*

Several times I launched a one-man campaign to prevail on the men to remove their sticky coats. They thought my suggestion interesting but hardly practicable. Whoever heard of dancing in shirt sleeves! "Why, Señor CONsool, you wouldn't attend the cinema without your coat, would you?"

During the brief intervals between dances, everyone rushed

to the bar to gulp down *whiskeycito* after *whiskeycito* and glass after glass of pink cola to stave off complete dehydration. The amount of liquid refreshment consumed by both sexes was fantastic, but only the handful of non-dancers got drunk. The rest of us sweated it out as fast as we drank it down. We moved out on the veranda with our drinks to seek the cool breeze off the river. As we panted, drank, and mopped our faces, the conversation would trip brilliantly along like this: "*Qué calor tan formeeDAAbleh!*" you would observe to Señorita Calixto. "Si, what heat!" she would agree, as if we had done nothing to make us wringing wet. "*Qué fiesta tan animada!*" "Yes, a very lively party," she would echo.

The lassies of Iquitos are not noted for their brilliant conversation. They grow up with far more satisfying graces. They are pretty, often beautiful, gay, and they dance and sing like the books say tropical señoritas should dance and sing. With them, rhythm is a stronger instinct than self-preservation.

Among the crowd, there was always a sprinkling of colorful individualists who pointed up the essentially cosmopolitan character of Iquitos society. There was, for instance, Luis Mairata, a quiet little man in his sixties, who was Secretary of the Chamber of Commerce, distributor for Argentine radios, and one of the leading exporters of peccary skins. Señor Mairata, like Don Martín of the Restaurant Unión, was one of the senior members of a once numerous and flourishing Spanish colony that had come to Iquitos from Spain in the fabulous days of the rubber boom.

Señor Mairata attended all the dances, though he seldom danced and never drank. No one would accost him with the incredulous remark usually reserved for male wall flowers: "How dry your coat is! *What*, not dancing! *Qué te pasa, cholo*, aren't you feeling well?" Throughout the years, people had grown accustomed to Señor Mairata not dancing. He invariably wore a dark wool business suit, and who could be expected to cultivate the dance seriously in a wool suit? Señor Mairata, therefore, was privileged to move quietly and unmolestedly about the club.

He would stand against the wall watching the dancers, an inscrutable expression in his watery eyes, all the while fan-
ning himself briskly with a large, black Japanese fan which
he manipulated with the dexterity of Koko, the Lord High
Executioner.

My colleague in the *cuerpo consular*, Ernesto Hoffman, Swiss
Consular Agent and head of the French import-export firm of
Kahn y Cía., was no wall flower or teetotaler. Ernesto came to
Iquitos from Switzerland when he was twenty-one, and grew
up with the firm. In his forties, he married Lucha Pinasco, one
of the beautiful brunette daughters of a prominent Italian merchant. Ernesto was a good six feet tall and his girth was that
befitting a prosperous merchant of the *tierra caliente*. Intensely
blue eyes shone in a handsome face, florid from good eating and
drinking.

Ernesto was the most copious sweater on the floor. His immaculate white duck suit, starched like the headgear of a nun,
was as slippery as a fish by the second dance. Salty drops glistened all over his face, ran in streams down his cheeks, and
dripped from the tip of his prominent nose. For all his resem-
blance to a garden sprinkler, Ernesto missed few dances. He
would keep one handkerchief handy in his side pocket for quick
mopping and another tucked bib-fashion into his collar to keep
the freshet from pouring down his neck. Ernesto had his own
style of ballroom technique. He may have developed it because
he towered over most of his diminutive partners or because he
had never become reconciled to soggy bodies in intimate contact. In any case, he scooted about the floor with a flat-footed
shuffle, grasping his partner's fingertips and resting her hands
on his stomach as he pushed her about like a baby carriage.

Ernesto and his business associate, Gaston Kahn, were among
the few private individuals who entertained on a large scale in
their own homes. In New Mexico, rural merchants live in the
rear of the store to protect their merchandise. Iquitos merchants
protect their goods by squatting on them. They reside on the
floor above the store. So it was that the Hoffmans' home took

up the entire floor over Kahn y Compañía. Gaston Kahn lived with the Hoffmans, for his wife, like those of many Iquitos merchants, lived almost constantly in Lima "for reasons of health." Don Victor Israel's wife never once came to Iquitos during our stay. Don Victor's former partner, Sam Harris, hardly saw his wife from one year to the next. She lived in England and would send him food parcels at Christmas and Easter.

The huge rectangular Hoffman living-dining room was the scene of some of Iquitos' gayest parties. It was especially difficult to tear yourself away from Casa Kahn fiestas. Perhaps the most potent reason was that the bar was located at the head of the entrance stairs. Don Ernesto and Don Gaston provided a fabulous bar. Whisky from the United States and England rivalled the Amazon in volume. The mob at the bar completely blocked the approach to the stairs. If you succeeded in fighting your way through and reached the door at the foot of the stairs any time before 3:00 a. m., you would find it locked. Both Ernesto and Gaston became so distressed when people came to say goodnight that they saved themselves considerable grief by simply locking the guests in until three. After that, you could go home if you insisted.

Most members of our consular corps made use of a neat formula to avoid giving an official reception on their country's national holiday. Who could blame them? Except for the Colombian Consul General and myself, the corps was composed of business men whose consular rank was only incidental to their business. For instance, a couple of days before the Double Tenth, China's Fourth of July, Don Victor Israel, the Chinese Consul, would write Mr. John Wood Massey, the British Consul, requesting him, as Dean of the Corps, to circularize the colleagues. Each Consul would then know that "the worthy Consul of China respectfully requests his colleagues to honor him on the tenth of October, the day of independence of his *gloriosa* fatherland, by joining him in raising the flag of the glorioso country that he represents. The worthy Señor Cónsul de la China," employing the formula, then "advises that there will be no official reception at this time." In this way, the unsalaried diplomats contrived to honor the nations they represented at no greater cost than the pole and cord with which to run up their flags.

The Vice Consul of the gloriosos *Estados Unidos de Norte-américa* resorted to the same penny-pinching device for the Fourth of July. My three hundred dollars a year representation allowance enabled us to give two or three very modest dinner parties a month. A blowout worthy of the Fourth of July would have knocked the representation allowance into a cocked hat for the balance of the fiscal year.

One of the consular corps, however, was no tightwad. He was Gaston Kahn. Gaston was a Frenchman, a *Free Frenchman* he was careful to insist. He was small and slight, with straight, jet-black hair, heavy, black eyebrows, and black, tortoise-shell glasses. One day in June, Gaston appeared at my office. "I have not come on commercial matters," he announced in his nasal Spanish. "This is an official call. I have just been appointed French Consul by General de Gaulle." I gulped and almost yelled for Uncle Charlie. Here was a situation! I had just finished reading an instruction from the Department, advising its Embassies and Consulates all over the world that the United States Government did not recognize De Gaulle's attempt to convert the French Committee of National Liberation into the Provisional Government of France. I explained to Gaston that my instructions prevented me from congratulating him in any but an unofficial and personal capacity, but that I hoped soon to make my congratulations official.

Evidently Gaston took no offense, for, on July 14, Dot and I were included in the Bastille Day fiesta at Casa Kahn. As we climbed the stairs, mindful of the Department's instruction, I made a mental memo that my attendance was purely unofficial; I added a mental ditto when we first toasted our ally, the gloriosa *República Francesa*. But by the time we were all bellowing the *Peruvian National Anthem*, the *Marseillaise*, and the *Star Spangled Banner*, the Department's instruction was in the wastepaper basket. Between renditions of *Somos Libres . . .*, *Allons*

Enfants . . ., and *Oh Say* . . ., there were fervent manifestations of fraternal *cariño* with much back-slapping, much embracing, much patriotic shouting. *Viva el Peru! Viva la Francia! Viva Los Estados Unidos!*

Commodore Wilke, another notable of the Club Iquitos dances, was employed by the Rubber Development Corporation to supervise and maintain its sizeable fleet of river craft—knockdown barges of plywood, invasion barges, diesel-powered tug-barges, and launches. He also operated the two powerful new river tugs of the Ganso Azul Oil Company, the *Dorothy* and the *Jean,* making trips hundreds of miles up the Río Ucayali into the Río Pachitea to haul back drums of oil and gasoline to power the RDC airfield equipment.

The only thing phony about the Commodore was his rank. He had commissioned himself after his first trip to the Blue Goose oil field. The Commodore's dress befitted his rank. He wore a white shirt and trousers, black shoes, and a black silk tie studded with a collection of campaign ribbons and decorations for valor, both American and Peruvian. The overflow, consisting of civilian emblems like the *Loyal Order of Moose,* spilled onto either side of his shirt front. The Commodore spun such wondrous tales about each of his decorations that, in time, you half believed them. The most convincing article of the Commodore's attire was his cap—the regulation cap of an officer of the Peruvian Navy, which had been bestowed upon him with many a fond *abrazo* early one morning by one of his many drinking *compadres.*

Although the Commodore's tongue could not twist itself around a single Spanish word, he gathered in friends like *tagua* nuts wherever his tug nosed into the bank. Possibly, some of his following may have been drawn to him by the complete abandon with which he tossed his salary and per diem about. Otto Losa, the local RDC chief, used to worry about Wilke's family. "He spends every cent he earns, and he has a wife and a bunch of kids somewhere along the Mississippi."

I registered the Commodore on the official Foreign Service

Form 177 for registration of citizens residing abroad, as I did all Americans in the locality whom I could corral. The form asked a lot of personal questions. The Commodore was vague about his family. All I could glean was that his wife "was the sweetest lil gal in the world" and that he had "several kids." Form 177 is stuffy about things like dates so I was forced to insist that he try to recall when his children were born. The Commodore thought hard. "It's no use. Best I can tell you is 'proximately how many years old each kid is. Take Bessie, she was about fourteen when I left home. Tom, he oughter be crowdin' twelve now. Jane must be around ten. And, hold on there!" said the Commodore excitedly. "Believe I can narrow it down on Jane! She musta come in winter 'cause the woman that was hepin the lil wife had me haul a lot of water from the well, and I remember it was as cold as charity outside . . ."

Commodore Wilke might have doubled for Captain Hook, for "onc't on the Río Mississip" he lost the entire thumb and three fingers of his left hand. His index finger was all that remained, but, with years of use, it had grown uncommonly long, thick, and dexterous. The Commodore could perform any task with his supple, hooklike finger. On the dance floor he was more Iquiteño than the Iquiteños. His lean, wiry body was capable of sustaining perpetual motion without a trace of perspiration. The Commodore introduced a whirling, hopping Bayou Stomp that was both the fascination and bewilderment of the local belles. He cut a devastating swath about the ballroom, dropping partner after exhausted partner in rapid relay to search for a fresh filly. It was not only the Commodore's killing pace that left the ladies limp after one round. His cozy, gap-toothed smile was neither here nor there, but the hook . . .! The hook was tipped with a long, razor-edge fingernail which the Commodore whipped about like a scimitar. During the Commodore's blackout spins, the scimitar swished in a menacing arc before the lady's nose, and, while the Commodore sprinted to the opposite wall, the scimitar's point was held an inch from her windpipe as if poised to administer the coup de grâce.

Although only in his early thirties, Edward Christopher Anthony Saint George Drewry, universally known as "Baron," was on his way to becoming an institution in Iquitos society. Baron Drewry, a subject of His Britannic Majesty, left London in 1937 to become sawmill foreman of the Compañía Maderera Loretana, manufacturer of mahogany and cedar lumber, located a few kilometers down river from Iquitos. The sawmill belonged to a slick Frenchman, named Emil Chennivesse, who had arrived in Iquitos years before with a group of Polish colonists. The colonization program rotted in the jungle, but not Emil Chennivesse. He bought up some stranded mahogany logs and started a sawmill. He thrived. By the time I reached Iquitos, Chennivesse's mill, next to the powerful Astoria mill, was the biggest sawmill in Loreto, and the United States Government snapped up all the mahogany he could ship.

After a year's work, Baron wrote Peggy, his pretty red-haired fiancée, to say good-bye to her London home, take a boat, and hie herself off seven thousand miles to Iquitos to set up housekeeping. Peggy departed amid screaming headlines telling the islanders that "Beautiful Girl Abandons Home and Family to Wed Man She Loves in Amazon Village Beset with Head-Hunters." Baron and Peg were married and spent a cozy honeymoon in the prefabricated metal house of John W. Massey, agent of the Booth Steamship Company. Peggy not only eluded the head-hunters and gave successful birth to a son (of the two feats, the latter much the more difficult for a Nordic in Iquitos), but she became the toast of the town.

After six years in the deadly Amazon, broken only by one short trip to the United States, the Drewrys were as fresh and lively as a pair of week-end *turistas*. Baron probably owed his immunity to the implacable hand of tropical enervation to his innate love of physical exercise. He was "frightfully keen on sports, you know" and, in proof thereof, did a lot of running around in the noonday sun. He was champion badminton player of Iquitos, strong at baseball, basketball, canoeing, cycling, soccer, swimming, and tennis. When the rain prevented outdoor sports, he repaired to the Club Iquitos and took on all comers at pool and ping pong. Dancing was the only form of physical exercise that Baron could not master. When he embarked on one of his rare duty dances, it was plain to see that his feet were performing a routine drill, painfully concentrating on keeping out of the way of his partner's.

Peg was physically indolent except in one sport. She was as keen on dancing as Baron was on badminton. She danced beautifully and with every inch of her shapely body. Were it not for the dances, Peg would have gone to pot in the jungle.

So Peg and Baron were musts on everybody's dance list, and they stayed until the last vals criollo was played. While Peg was swept from one partner to another, Baron took his stand at the bar, engaging in heated arguments in fluent but hybrid Spanish and working up green-eyed animosity for the hordes of General Morla's starched officers who embraced his wife so ardently as they glided about the floor.

Membership in the Casino Militar was naturally restricted to the military, but General Morla was generous in making the club available to civilians. In fact, General Morla was the most lavish and hospitable host in town. He could afford to entertain well, for the army controlled most of the local supply of food, manpower, and other resources. Although the parties at the Casino did not always reach the apogee of enthusiasm that they did at the Club Iquitos, the Casino had an air of sophistication that the civilian clubs lacked.

The Casino's biggest fiesta of the year was held on Army Day, the ninth of December. The Day arrived, and the General, who had flown to the remote Department of Madre de Dios, a few days before, still had not returned. It was reported that bad weather was holding him in the Department of Mother of God, but he surprised everybody by arriving at the dance looking his usual natty self. He walked with a slight limp that did not, however, interfere with his dancing. "Did you hear that the General was in a plane crash?" "It's a miracle he's still alive!" "What a host, to arrive on time after all that!" The reports were correct. The General was taking off on the Río Madre de Dios, when the pilot spied a log. To avoid striking it, he had to lift the plane off the water before it had sufficient forward speed. At this point, the river curved sharply, and the plane crashed into the sandy bank, where it turned over three times and ended up on its back. Miraculously, no one suffered more than slight injuries although the plane was a total loss. The three crash victims were picked up by Condor Biggs and flown to Iquitos. The General was certainly the complete host.

With the crash as a stimulus to his sense of the dramatic, the General dominated the tango that evening as never before. In Peru one does not perfect a dance step, one learns to *dominate* it like a good bullfighter dominates a bull. The General was very proud of his tango. He danced *el tango legítimo*—the real thing. "After all, Señores," he would explain in quiet dignity, "I learned it in Argentina." The General was convinced that only one woman in Iquitos could do justice to his tango. That woman was Dot. Not even *La Generala*, the General's Du Barry, could properly interpret the lights and shadows of the tango. Iquitos society used the designation *La Generala* only in the privacy of their homes, for Clarita was the General's lady's name. Clarita was a school teacher in Iquitos, attractive and ladylike. Because Señora de Morla remained considerably in Lima and the General threw swish parties, Clarita was accepted by all the *alta sociedad* with the exception of a few prudes.

Dot had danced few tangos before coming to Iquitos. I certainly had given her no help, for my Washington lessons had stopped short of the tango. The only explanation for her favor at court was her uncanny ability to follow any dance step from the very outset. Before long, the tango of the General and la Señora de Kelly became a tradition of Iquitos dances. The General subscribed to the praying mantis school of the tango—a style of classic stiffness, statuesque poses interjected with twenty-yard dashes. His body, spare as a praying mantis, lent itself to the tango. The General cut a fine figure on the dance floor. His tube boots shone like the legs of a mahogany table. His crisp white uniform was cut just so and set off by a sky-blue sash and red and yellow epaulettes. Between tangos, the General danced infrequently—now and then with Clarita. He would sit, watching the dance, puffing his cheeks out like a child blowing up a balloon as he exhaled the smoke of his cigarette.

On the evening of the Army Day dance the two gringas, Dot and Peg, stole the show. But let *La Dama Tapada,* the mysterious veiled lady who once walked the streets of colonial Lima but who now writes the Society Column of *El Oriente,* describe that night of nights in her own incomparable Latin imagery.

A thousand diverse sensations still course through my mind . . .
Last night's memories remain inconstant and elusive . . .
Multi-colored serpentines tossed from the diaphanous
   hand of a fairy bear brief messages such as these:

> Cascades of light on the inky cloak of night . . .
> Promises slipping from hesitant lips . . .
> Dilettante union of arpeggios in the flowing rhythm of a
>   waltz . . .
> Precious hours frilled with romance and frenesí . . .
> Symphony of colors—in gowns, in eyes, in lips . . .
> Rustle of silks—captivating bubbling of champagne . . .
>
> Oh, Dorothy, thou made the evening thine!
> Like a Lily of freshness wafted by the evening breeze . . .
> But newly wed, by Love thou art intoxicated,
> By Love thou art garbed in Love's own caprice . . .
> A rose in thy burnished hair . . .
> Décolleté blouse . . . a gauzy illusion of pale rose . . .
> Black froufrou taffeta skirt clasping thy Terpsichorean
>   waist . . .
> Charming, Dorothy, Charming . . .
>
> Peggy, estupenda as always! Exquisite in a Heim cre-
>   ation . . .
> Full black satin skirt . . . bodice of blue lace . . .
> The Queen of the Waltz . . .
> Your ecstasy takes us back to those happy nights
> Of Peace in los Halls de Piccadilly
> And los Dancings de Trafalgar Square

Rendezvous of Love! Noche de Casino!
Bravo, Gentlemen-at-Arms! Another Social Triumph!

"Who is La Dama Tapada?" We lay awake nights in speculation. We made inquiry in the club, in the Plaza, at parties, everywhere. There were a hundred surmises, but nothing definite. One day Baron burst into the office. "I've found her!" he cried. "Found who?" "The Dama Tapada—and she's no lady." "What do you mean, no lady?" I asked. "She's no lady 'cause she's a guy. She's Cristóbal Sotomayor, the warden of the city jail! The same character who plays right field in our softball games."

The normally intense social life of Iquitos whirled even faster during Carnival time. *Los Días Carnavales* are national holidays—a marathon of festivities lasting from the Saturday evening preceding Lent through Shrove Tuesday. The word *carnaval* comes from the medieval Latin *carne vale*—a farewell to flesh—on the threshold of forty days of self-denial and penitence. The spirit of Carnaval is openly one of "Eat, drink, and be merry, for tomorrow is Ash Wednesday."

The Carnaval opens Saturday at dusk. Down Jirón Lima comes a horde of costumed figures swarming about a makeshift band and a truck bearing the huge, grotesque figure of *El Carnavalón*, the spirit of carnival. Leading the parade are the *Mamarrachos*—a dozen droll figures with massive heads and torsos and shrunken limbs. With the official sanction of El Carnavalón, an orgy of merrymaking begins, to last four nights and three days.

Dozens of dances break loose all over town like a string of firecrackers. Light, laughter, and music pour from the windows of every club and from between the chinks of cane huts along Punchana Road. People dress *de comparsa*, in masquerade. Those who have no costumes at least wear masks.

At every carnival dance, you encounter the *chisquete*, the most fiendish invention of the Latin mind. This little instrument is a glass vial the size of a laboratory test tube, containing several fluid ounces of perfumed ether. The chisquete works like a siphon bottle. You can squirt a lethal stream for several yards by a push of the thumb. The idea is to catch your victim unawares and administer a love potion where it will cause most discomfort. The eye is the most delectable of all targets. On the dancé floor, you maneuver until you approach your choice from the rear. Then, from close range, you play a stream directly on her eyeball.

The pain is excruciating—the sensation, one would imagine, of a hot needle thrust into the eye. The uninitiated thinks he is blinded for life. He gasps with pain, screws his eye shut, and thrusts his fist into it. He eventually learns that this procedure only prolongs the agony. Fortunately, ether is highly volatile, and leaving the eye open is the quickest way to find relief. Although you hear wild tales about people being blinded for life by chisquetes, the worst that befalls you is momentary pain, and a set of bloodshot eyes.

Carnaval is no place to indulge your ill humor. You must accept whatever comes your way with smiling grace and fight back in the same gay spirit. The only hope of relief from the dread chisquete that Dot and I could see was that, if the war lasted several years longer, the price of chisquetes—imported from Lima and Brazil—might rise so high that their use would be restricted. Relief never came.

Carnaval precludes onlookers. You either throw yourself into the fray or remain safely at home for three days. The onlooker who ventures out into the streets is courting disaster. People throw dirty water from windows. Roving mobs of unsightly carnivalites, their hair matted and sticky with flour, pelt you with dried corn, rice, flour paste (food scarcity notwithstanding) , and indelible dyes. If you appeal to a policeman, he will only shrug his shoulders and say, "Thus, is carnaval."

Carnaval is essentially a democratic institution—a great leveler. Differences of rank, caste, and economic position, for three days out of the year, are washed away in a great heaving of liquids and solids. The masked cholo in rags and bare feet can, with impunity, heap refuse on the head of the merchant prince, and vice versa. Men who would never remove their sweat-sodden coats at a dance for comfort's sake, dance coatless and even shirt-less during carnavales. Señoritas are momentarily free to cease being ladies, and, under the approving eye of parents and friends, to douse and be doused, to roughhouse, to be dunked in rain barrels, and to dance a hip wagging, erotic samba, clad in drenched slacks. The last day of Carnaval, Pablo Fernández, Dot, and I sought escape from the vals criollo, the chisquete, and the dye slingers. We took a dugout canoe at Moronacocha, an abandoned oxbow meander of the Nanay River, and paddled for three hours in a circle: along one prong, out into the swift black waters of the Nanay, downstream, and back along the other prong of the oxbow to our starting point. We were never more than five kilometers from the capital of Loreto, yet the Nanay swept silently along between walls of matted jungle as untouched as if we were floating down some remote back-country river a month's voyage from Iquitos. A river otter thrust his bullet head above the surface, flipped his whiskers, and disappeared into the depths. Two pink-faced *bufeos* or dolphins flashed across our prow, startling us with their noisy exhalations.

There was no visible sign of man, yet the sound of his cele-bration seeped through the curtain of verdure and reached us across the waters. These were the carnaval sounds of the true Loretano, the lean, barefooted Indian and mestizo, who hacked down the jungle to plant his field of yuca and bananas and moved silently about his flooded homeland in a dugout canoe. This Loretano was not dancing a sophisticated tango in a starched coat to the music of the Gran Orquesta Jazz Band Bolognesi. He danced barefooted, in his shirt sleeves, on a dirt floor. Be-tween dances, he drank fiery *aguardiente* instead of whisky. His dance was the sedate huaynito of the highlands Indian; his music, the thin, plaintive trill of a reed flute and the rhythmic pom pom pom of a drum. The primeval tone poem overwhelmed me. The river, the green wall . . . from beyond the wall, the flute, the drum pom pom pom, and, as we floated around the bend, the great silence of the jungle. Then, once again from another hut lost beyond the green wall—the flute, the drum. Carnaval!

10

*I*QUITOS and its environs are pinched into a narrow, swampy peninsula about sixteen miles long and from a mile to three miles wide. The rivers that make the city almost an island are the Amazon and the Itaya on one side, and the Nanay on the other side, flowing roughly parallel to each other. In the less wet season—July through January—when these rivers are shrunk in their channels, a maximum of the low-lying peninsula is above water. A vertical fluctuation of thirty feet in the water level, between high and low stage, spells the difference between dry land—land on which the harassed Loretan farmer can raise crops and pasture livestock—and devastating inundation. When you

The Green Cockroach

consider that Iquitos, although 2,300 miles up the Amazon from its mouth, is situated in a forested plain only 350 feet above sea level, it is not difficult to realize that a great amount of land is subject to inundation by the swollen rivers for three to four months out of the year. Every bump and knoll that assures the house owner a year-round margin of safety is at a premium.

The prolonged annual inundation of a great part of Loreto is the chief reason for Iquitos' lack of a land connection with Coastal and Andean Peru. A road from Iquitos to any point would have to be constructed as an almost continuous viaduct elevated high above the swampy ground. The cost, of course, would be prohibitive.

In the "summer" season of less rain and low water, we could drive a car, cycle, or walk over rough, unpaved roads a maximum of seven miles along the Amazon in one direction, from the Plaza de Armas as far as the mouth of the Río Nanay, and nine miles in the opposite direction, to a lake called Quistococha, between the Itaya and Nanay rivers. The mud and inundation of the wetter season cut our effective range roughly in half.

In Iquitos, there was no golden mean. Everything happened in extremes. There was either deluge or drouth; quagmires or dust. One hundred and five inches of rain a year is much water in any man's language, especially to a New Mexican who gets along on fifteen. During one cloudburst, Dot and I got an idea of how much water can cascade from the Amazonian sky. We put on bathing suits, dashed out into the cold, pelting flood, and emptied the rain barrel placed under the three-inch spout that drained one-half of Tacu Tacu's roof. The fifty-three gallon oil drum overflowed in sixty-six seconds!

Iquitos receives about half of its annual rainfall in the "winter" months of February through June and the other half during the remaining seven months. In August and September and again in November and December there are periods of intense "summer" when, for as long as two and three weeks at a stretch, not a drop of rain falls.

Despite abundant rainfall, the Loretan sun burns so fiercely that two clear days sufficed to turn the red gumbo of Punchana Road to choking dust, ankle deep. In four days, the sun toasted the lush green grass, carpeting many of the secondary streets, to a straw color. After a week, the Pearl reeked with the stench of open sewers and accumulated refuse that was usually swept away quickly into the Amazon by the terrific downpours. To make matters worse, everyone's rainwater tank went dry.

Without a municipal water supply and sewage disposal system, people became desperate. At such times, even the huge rain storage tank on the roof of the Gran Hotel Malecón Palace would suddenly go dry. We would advise Baños that the toilets wouldn't flush and the shower wouldn't shower. A couple of days later he would connect the hose, one end in the empty tank, its patched length emerging from a window on the third floor and running down the front of the building and down the embankment to disappear into the river. After coaxing the pump for a day the first muddy stream would reach the tank.

But Tacu Tacu had no pump. Neither did we have a well, as some did. Windmills also were out. Except for occasional violent and brief squalls ushering in a cloudburst, there was not enough wind to operate a windmill. The only recourse left was to haul water in five-gallon gasoline tins from the Amazon, two hundred yards away. Even rugged Aurelio, our yardman, struggling six hours at a stretch between the house and the river in the prostrating sun, could haul barely enough water to take care of a minimum of washing and cooking. Dot and I showered by pouring a pitcherful of water over one another. But a pitcherful of water only tantalizes. Afterwards, the stickiness, the dust, the tense electric feel of the air settled once again upon you.

About once a month, the thousand and one little things that made living a constant struggle piled up so that you were frantic to get out of town for a change of scenery. Yet you couldn't jump in your car, hop a bus, mount a horse or bicycle, and escape to the nearest town on Sunday to see new faces and new surroundings. Of course, there were opportunities for river excursions by launch or canoe, but the rivers and the flat, viewless jungle are the same at Iquitos as they are two hundred miles away. You were stuck on a small island in a sea of changeless green, where you marked the passing of the seasons by the proportion of mud to dust and by the slow rise and fall of the Amazon. When the murky waters crept up the tree trunks, it was "winter." When the sandbars appeared, it was "summer."

Between the semi-annual breathers in Lima, Dot and I made the most of the meagre travel routes and transportation facilities of Iquitos. When I first arrived, five buses and about twenty decrepit taxicabs made up the public conveyance facilities of the city. There were also a few trucks and about a dozen privately owned automobiles. To have owned an automobile would have been frustrating. There was no place to go in your car; the few brief roads were riddled with chuck holes and quagmires; there were no spare parts and no regular servicing facilities. Most people in Iquitos walked.

Each of the five buses had its name painted on the side. There was The Little Bee (*Abejita*), The Beehive (*Colmena*), The Condor, The Rápido No. 1, and the Rápido No. 2. They ran along a single route, about three miles long, extending from the Itaya Base through town as far as Punchana Plaza. When the wetter season set in, the buses curtailed their operations to avoid bogging down, venturing only as far as the abattoir, a good kilometer shy of Tacu Tacu. By the time Dot arrived at Iquitos, The Little Bee and the Beehive had given up the struggle. The bedraggled Condor and the two non-rapid Rápidos were left to drag their weary, creaking bodies across town.

In the good old days before the war, the omnibus company offered its stoic passengers something to take their minds off the unpadded wooden seats and the teeth-rattling jolts. Ensconced near the driver, a three-piece orchestra pounded out vals criollos and sambas as the bus lumbered along. Many people who had no place to go rode back and forth between the Santa Rosa Hospital and Punchana for hours at a time enchanted with their musical excursion. Unfortunately, the orchestras disappeared from the buses of Iquitos a short time after I arrived, thus eliminating most of the appeal of travel by bus.

Prior to about 1933, Iquitos had no bus service. But it had something more exciting. It had a railroad! The railroad belonged to the then Prefect, who maintained his monopoly on public transportation by blocking the establishment of a bus service. The equipment consisted of fourteen kilometers of track, two tiny French locomotives, one German locomotive with a swollen smoke stack, a few passenger cars, and a dozen flatcars. Most of the railroad's revenue came from hauling freight from the customs warehouse to business houses around town.

The railroad also ran Sunday excursions to the boat club on Moronococha, and served the municipal cemetery. After the funeral services in the church in the Plaza de Armas, the coffin would be loaded onto the train, along with the bereaved, and accompanying friends. The funeral cortége would then stoke up and snort down Jirón Lima towards the cemetery. Music was always taken aboard for holiday excursions, and you can imagine how gay it was on the Iquitos Limited.

John Wood Massey, the British Consul and veteran agent for the Booth Steamship Company, was one old-timer who did not grieve the passing of the railroad. One day I was at his office, a tiled building bearing a huge shield with rampant lion and located only a block from the customs warehouse. I broached the railroad, saying how much I would have liked to see it. "Good riddance, m'boy, good riddance," he announced, peering over his black-rimmed spectacles and clicking his false teeth at me. "The blasted engine used to stop right in front of the office to stoke its furnace. The engineer would throw on a couple of logs and wait until the contraption accumulated enough steam to pull the rise up Raymondi Street to the Plaza de Armas. In a few minutes, the old boy was whistling to be off and vomiting a deluge of sparks from its stack. That bloody engine burned up a half dozen of my awnings before it quit running."

In 1937, when Baron Drewry arrived in Iquitos, the railroad was burning its last firewood and awnings. The following year it went bankrupt, and Baron's boss, shrewd Emil Chennivesse, bought the rails and rolling stock for a trifling ten thousand soles. Baron showed me the three whimsical little engines parked in one of the sheds of the Loretana mill. Chennivesse used one of the engines to haul firewood from the Nanay River to the city light plant, which burned wood to generate electricity. He had the contract to supply electric power to the city, and the plant was conveniently located alongside his lumber mill. With scrap steel at a premium, Chennivesse had sold over fifty thousand soles worth of rails alone and had plenty yet to spare.

The defunct railroad and the buses offered no solution to Dot's and my transportation problem between Iquitos and Punchana. Taxi service to and from the suburbs was hardly more dependable. The range and rates of the taxis varied with the moment to moment condition of the roads, the hour, and the mood of the driver. In dry weather, we taxied to Tacu Tacu for as little as two soles (30 cents U. S.). In rain storms, we paid as much as a dollar. Frequently, the driver would agree to take us only part way to Tacu Tacu—to the bottom of a soapy, clay rise a few hundred yards from the house—or would refuse to undertake the expedition for any amount.

You couldn't blame the cab drivers for trying to limit their trips to the paved streets or at least to those in which the proportion of sand exceeded that of clay. Without spare parts and tires, their jalopies had depreciated to the point where they ran on nerve. Tires were down to the fabric and displayed an impressive patchwork of boots held in place with iron bolts. Hopes ran high in 1943 for a shipment of tires from Brazil, which was sent to the bottom of the Atlantic by a U-boat just outside the mouth of the Amazon.

On Raymondi Street, between Massey's office and the Plaza de Armas, there is a slight rise; the same "hill" for which the locomotive used to prime itself. The hill is paved in large, rough squares of gray granite brought from Europe in the rubber days as ballast for a steamer. The rugged granite, exiled in a stoneless jungle, has withstood the beating of traffic and cloudburst year after year, in marked contrast to the worn brick sections adjoining it on either end. This block-long section is the only bit of paving stone in town. The nearest outcrops and gravel deposits are at least 325 airline miles away at Borja, where the first Andean foothills rise from the jungle plain.

Dot and I generally agreed that life in the suburbs was worth the trouble. The few available houses in town were flush with the sidewalk, crammed between their neighbors, poorly lighted, and stuffy. However, the difficulty and cost of transporting supplies from the city through the Punchana gumbo often made us wonder whether our choice was rational. First of all, we had to purchase a large amount of tinned food to make up for the many times that Petronila returned from the Central Market with a lean shopping bag. None of the stores had a delivery service. You carried your parcels yourself or hired someone to do it. More troublesome than food, because of bulk and weight, was charcoal for the stove, kerosene for the refrigerator, ice for the icebox when we had to return the refrigerator, and drinking water.

Before our transportation problem began, we had problems of supply. Joaquín was invaluable on both counts. Charcoal, with which most of Iquitos cooked, came to the city in dugout canoes from nearby chacras. The *carboneros* sold their *carbón* by the sackful either at the river bank or in the streets. The farther the charcoal got from the canoe the more the middlemen ran up the price. Joaquín would buy directly from the canoes and have the sooty carboneros deliver the charcoal to the office. A gunny sack full cost from thirty cents to a dollar U. S., depending on the supply. In dry weather, charcoal was fairly plentiful and inexpensive. But, during the soggy winter months, cutting

firewood, burning, and transporting charcoal was especially difficult, and the supply dwindled.

The price, f. o. b. the office, included the charcoal only. The
carboneros insisted on keeping their sacks. I, therefore, had to
supply my own sacks. To freight less than two weeks' supply of
charcoal (or anything else) over the bottomless Punchana Road
was foolishness. Dot's little stove devoured charcoal at an alarming rate, especially on bread-baking days. Five sacks of solid,
chunky *capirona* (the best in charcoal from the tall, smooth,
steel-blue capirona, as hard as ironwood) lasted a scant two
weeks. As a special favor, Don Victor Israel let me have five new
gunny sacks for seventy-five cents apiece. Joaquín would spread
out the sacks on the rear portal of the hotel and supervise the
transfer of the charcoal.

This messy business of charcoal would have been unnecessary
if I could have exchanged Dot's ridiculous stove (about the
size of a table radio and fashioned from cast-off ship's plates,
brick, and mud) for an electric model. There were two new
Westinghouse stoves on display in the downtown office of Emil
Chennivesse's *Empresa Electrica*. We used to run our hands
admiringly over their immaculate finish, but the stoves were not
for sale at any price. Emil, as Westinghouse agent, was not
opposed to a good sale; but Emil, as supplier of electric power,
had to say no. His overtaxed dynamos at the sawmill were on the
verge of collapse under their present load. In fact, every few
nights they would throw up their weary hands and leave the city
in darkness. One more electric stove on the line would have
brought on a complete breakdown.

High on the transportation priority list was kerosene for the
refrigerator. There were no refrigerators for sale in Iquitos,
but the United States Health and Sanitation Mission had a
warehouse filled with kerosene-burning refrigerators destined for
hospitals and dispensaries projected and already under construction throughout the montaña. Rather than have all these units
mold in their crates, I arranged to rent one until its dispensary
was built. We bought Blue Goose kerosene from Mr. Massey,

who distributed *Ganso Azul* products in Iquitos. Like the charcoal vendors, Mr. Massey sold his product without the container. (In fact, the Iquitos shopper had to supply all of his own containers. At the market, if you forgot to bring a bit of paper or a palm leaf, you carried your gory hunk of beef home in your bare hands.) Therefore, in order to buy kerosene, I bought two empty five gallon gasoline tins for five soles apiece, and paid a tinsmith another two soles each to equip them with mouth and cap.

The weather affected the supply and price of kerosene as forcefully as it did the supply of charcoal. While wet weather put out the fires of the carboneros, dry weather plugged up the kerosene at the Ganso Azul refinery six hundred miles away on the Río Pachitea. The Pachitea, in summer months, dropped so low that launches were unable to reach the refinery. Rain or shine, Iquiteños had their shortages.

The frige had an insatiable thirst—five gallons of Blue Goose juice a week. Its overindulgence brought on intestinal complications: its pilot wick and main burner wick were always clogging with carbon. If the burners went out during the night, the food was spoiled by the time we discovered the trouble the next morning. Then it would take another gallon of Blue Goose to put the frige in a refrigerating mood, and, by that time, the carbon crusted the wicks again. So we did not grieve when word came that the frige was needed at the newly completed hospital at Pucallpa.

Our frige gone, we attempted to keep fungus off our food by cramming a locally-made icebox with huge slabs of ice for which we paid two dollars a hundred pounds. We purchased ice in large quantities so that there would be something left by the time the slab reached Tacu Tacu.

The last item to be gathered in the Vice Consulate for transport to Punchana was drinking water. One hundred and five inches of rainfall a year and not a potable drop in the home! In short, there was no municipal water system. Iquiteños obtained their water in the time-honored way. The barefooted women of the cholo class hauled their household water from neighboring springs and bayous and from the Amazon, balancing pottery jars and gasoline tins skillfully on their heads. The middle class bought their drinking water from public water carriers, who delivered unfiltered spring water to the door, in large metal cans carried by emaciated horses, at a cost of four cents a gallon.

The most popular public spring of Iquitos was *Sachachorro* (Jungle Spring). The waters of Sachachorro were celebrated for their magical attributes. A jungle maid suffering from unrequited love might fill her man with devotion by having him drink from Sachachorro. Outlanders who drank enough of this water were supposed to become so enamored of Loreto as to lose all desire to return to their birthplaces.

I always suspected that an overdose of Sachachorro water might give the foreigner a physiological rather than a sentimental reason for not leaving Iquitos. In fact, an iconoclastic few, like Señor Sánchez, the head engineer of a projected water supply program, openly condemned Sachachorro as polluted. "Did you know," Ingeniero Sánchez told me one day as we passed the famous spring, "that the drainage feeding Sachachorro runs off from the municipal cemetery?" Whether or not the waters of Sachachorro picked up noxious salts as they passed over the bones of the dead, I do not know. If they did, the solution must have been mild, for in all the months that I drank unboiled, unfiltered Sachachorro water from the red pottery decanters in Don Martín's Restaurant Unión, I never once experienced any ill effects.

In Punchana, the conflicting opinions on Sachachorro were neither here nor there, because the water horses didn't service our district. Rather than drink rain water from our roof, which is supposed to lack nutritive salts, Dot and I accepted the helping hand of Don José O'Neill, head of the Astoria Importing and Manufacturing Company. Don José, or Don Pepe as he was called by his intimates, is a peppery Puerto Rican, who spends six months of every year in Astoria's New York office and six months during the sawing season in Iquitos. Don Pepe had a fine, pure spring at his sawmill, located seven miles down the Amazon River from Iquitos, at the confluence of the Río Nanay and the Amazon. The Astoria launch shuttled daily between Iquitos and the sawmill with commuting personnel, so Don Pepe offered to supply the Vice Consulate and Tacu Tacu with large glass demijohns of his spring water. I have never tasted water so soft and sweet as the Astoria spring water.

Buses, taxis, and mule-drawn tumbrils might be cowed by Punchana Road, but our bicycles seldom were. Shortly after our arrival, I matched Dot's Bianchi with a brand-new British Raleigh. There were several establishments where bicycles were rented by the hour. Cycling was so popular that bicycle shop owners did a rushing business on rentals and had no desire to sell their equipment. The owner of *La Miniatura,* the bike shop on the Plaza de Armas, had received twenty new Raleighs from England at the outbreak of the war. He kept his treasure concealed in a rear room and assembled a new bike only when an old one was worn beyond repair. After a month of constant negotiations, he agreed to part with a new Raleigh for nine hundred soles, the equivalent of $140. There was no argument about price. I did not endanger the sale by pointing out that the pre-war price of a new Raleigh was around $40.

Joaquín had not cleaned the Punchana clay from the mudguards a dozen times before my Raleigh was stolen from Tacu Tacu. One morning I found the neatly etched tread of the tires and the imprint of bare feet extending from the storehouse, over the white sand carpeting the back yard, to the front gate. The theft was a heavy blow—equivalent elsewhere to the loss of an automobile or a good horse. I was afoot. I threw every bit of my Vice Consular weight around. I did my best to make the theft a national disgrace. The prestige of Peru in the eyes of the United States Government hung on the recovery of the bicycle. Comandante Briolo, the Chief of Police in Loreto, assured me that every step would be taken and that radiograms would be sent to the sub-stations in the towns of Requena and Contamana, on the Río Ucayali.

Everyone was very sympathetic. The news of the tragedy raced through the city. Friends consoled me as if I had lost my wife. They all warned me to organize my own search. "Who ever heard of the *policia* recovering anything!" they said. "The bicycle will be smuggled out of Iquitos and sold up the Ucayali River, or up the Huallaga, or down the Amazon at Leticia, Colombia. You must spread the warning along the rivers for hundreds of kilometers." Dozens of friendly hands helped spread the net. The Administrador of Customs promised to have outgoing steamer cargo watched closely; Alejandro Navas, the Colombian Consul General, sent a coded message thousands of miles, via Lima and the Ministry of Foreign Relations in Bogotá, to the Colombian Commissary in Leticia, three hundred miles downstream from Iquitos; Ernesto Hoffman wired the representative of Casa Kahn, in Yurimaguas, to keep an eye open for the Veesay CONsool's *bicicleta;* Otto Losa used the RDC transmitter to tip off Hans Hurliman, in Pucallpa; in Iquitos itself, the chief of the Yellow Fever Control instructed his agents to watch for a blue Raleigh while they contaminated people's water supply by pouring kerosene in the domestic water tanks. The net was laid. The most extensive hunt in the Upper Amazon swung into action.

A week passed. Then, one morning the office phone rang. Joaquín informed me that the *Capitán* of the Guardia Civil would like to have me drop over. When I reached the station, I could tell by the look on the Capitán's face and on the faces of the many policemen gathered about that this was a red-letter day in the annals of the much-maligned Iquitos police. In a rear room sat the thief, a very ordinary cholo in patched cotton trousers, surrounded by a motley display of booty. The cholo had aroused the interest of a policeman by staggering down the street at two o'clock in the morning with a sewing machine in his embrace. Questioning revealed that the cholo merely did the dirty work for a merchant who handled hot merchandise.

The merchant's storeroom contained the plunder of a score of unsolved thefts among which was my Raleigh, unscathed and shiny. The Veesay CONsool's bicicleta emerged from hiding dragging behind it two sewing machines, a portable radio, a typewriter, a folding cot, three wrenches, two hammers, and a trunkful of clothing. From that time on, the Bianchi and the Raleigh spent the nights in the living room of Tacu Tacu.

In time, Dot and I became skilled cyclists, but we served a hard apprenticeship. By day, in the black of a moonless night, in gumbo or dust, in the wilting sun, in the driving rain, we challenged the cunning of Punchana Road in its multiple disguises. We learned to assay the texture of Road's varied wardrobe of mud. A glance, a sample dab rubbed between thumb and forefinger, gave us a good idea of Road's battle plan for the day. A greatcoat the consistency of heavy paste meant that the "fly paper formula" was likely to prevail, designed to ball up your tires until they locked to your mud guards. It was far better to walk than to be forced to dismount and carry your bike with your shoes growing to the dimensions of snowshoes.

The "deluge formula" was Road's most spectacular battle attire. He spread a thick cloak of water over his red hide. This was his form of psychological warfare. The cyclist was supposed to take one look and decide that he was marooned in his stilt house for lack of a canoe. Actually, once he set out, the abundance of water kept the mud sufficiently diluted to prevent the wheels from locking.

The "banana peel formula," one of the Road's most treacherous devices, was harder to distinguish. Road's attire, in this case, was neither the stiff greatcoat nor the watery cloak. But, if Road's attire was nondescript, his formula was not.

These were Road's choicest surprises for the traveller. Should any cyclist have the misfortune to contend with a road similar to ours, here are a few *always* and *nevers* plucked from the mire of Avenida Coronel Portillo.

Always roll up your trousers knee high, especially if you are biking to a dinner dance in your best white suit. *Always* bring your own shoe rag or put a change of shoes in your basket. *Always* bring slicker and hat. It will be pouring after the dance.

If you are a female and are wearing a formal, your problem becomes complicated. Of course, the conservative thing to do is to travel in an old dress with your evening gown crammed in your handlebar basket. If you are a reckless soul, or have no basket, you must put your trust in the concealing shadows of the poorly lighted road, brazenly gather up your skirts and throw them over your shoulder.

If a car has made a set of ruts through the mud, you are in luck. Pick your rut and stay in it. *Never* leave your rut for what you judge to be a nicer rut on the other side of a mud ridge. If the ridge of mud doesn't throw you, you will not be happier in your new rut. Once you decide on a route, *never* slow down or vacillate. Hit 'er hard and keep a'pumpin'.

If your road is as sparsely lighted as Punchana Road and you are not certain of a full moon, *never* try to muddle through without a flashlight. On a dark night, only an owl can distinguish between one shadow and another, between the shadow of a dry chuck hole and a bottomless puddle, between an empty bog hole and one containing a napping hog. Hogs are rough deals when they rise up suddenly under your front wheel, squealing like murder and heaving their weight around. If you aren't sent sprawling, you are scared so badly that you forget to cuss the goddam country for not having any rocks to heave.

It was essential to be able to tell when Road had served up such an insidious mess that we were licked from the start. Then, instead of trying to bully through, we walked or stayed at home —or rode in a weapons carrier. We had been invited to a formal dance at the Casino. It had rained in gray curtains all day, and Road had prepared an extra special brew. Clearly, biking was out. Just for the record, we phoned the three taxi stands to hear the confirmation of what we already knew. "Tonight! Not for one hundred soles, Señor CONsool." We had almost decided to pass up the dance, for neither of us felt like hiking in that mess. "How about Brooky and his Command Car?" exclaimed terpsichorean Dot, hopefully.

Brooky Brookshire, tough as the high-heeled boots he wore

and only half as high, was an old hand in Spanish America. He landed with the Marines at Vera Cruz in 1914, punched cows in Mexico, built airports in Bolivia and Peru in the pioneer days of Panagra, and was now in charge of the construction of the RDC airport in Iquitos. Brooky's weapons carrier truck, that had come up from Manaos in Scotty Lyon's famine flotilla, was the sensation of Iquitos. It dominated the Loretan mud with defiant ease. But that night it went down to its first defeat. Brooky's horn sounded out in front of Tacu Tacu shortly after we called him. I yelled from the front door that we would be right along. "No hurry," answered Brooky, "I'm stuck in your damn bog hole." Brooky had pulled a Navy truck out of the mud, but got stuck himself in the process. The next two hours were spent with flashlights, routing out sleepy sailors from the naval base, gathering planks and shovels, pushing, digging, cursing, floundering in the bottomless morass. It was midnight before we arrived at the Casino—in style, riding a weapons carrier.

And there were the times that I underestimated the mud. It was on Mother's Day that I insisted that the Road had prepared an innocuous variety of the "deluge formula" through which we could bike to church with ease. I was wrong. It turned out to be an off-breed "banana peel" to which Dot's Bianchi had a strong allergy. The result was that Baptist Dot (in her freshly washed white piqué suit and wearing a red feather rose under her black lace mantilla), on her way to pray among Papists for her Jap-imprisoned mother, was spread-eagled in the rust-colored mire. Mongrels barked, barefooted cholos laughed, and Dot lay in the mud and wailed. I tried to be helpful and consoling, but Dot emerged from her wallow in full war paint and stomped off to Tacu Tacu, leaving me standing helplessly in the road with two bicycles, in the midst of a pack of smirking natives and sniffing dogs.

Another disastrous misjudgment of mine occurred when an afternoon thunder shower interrupted a badminton game at the downtown home of the Brazilian Consul. Dot and I rushed to the bicycle shop on the Plaza de Armas, where we had parked our bikes. A debate ensued. Dot was for playing it safe and walking home—slow but sure. I maintained that there was so much water falling that the mud would be well lubricated. Dot reluctantly gave in. Again, I was wrong. About halfway home, we hit a "fly paper" section which gummed up our wheels so that we could neither pump nor push. I made a sheepish offer to carry Dot's Bianchi to Tacu Tacu and return for mine. She responded with a wilting look, picked up her Bianchi and strode away at a tremendous pace. I didn't even try to keep up with her.

Our isolation and battles with Road were nothing compared to what Baron and Peg Drewry had to contend with. They lived at the Loretana sawmill, about five kilometers beyond Tacu Tacu. Their cottage was cool, well screened, and roomier than ours. In addition, they had a fine lawn and flower garden in the English style and a badminton court set up on the lawn. During low water, the Drewry's place was heart's desire. A colonnade of majestic breadfruit trees lined the road in front of their garden as if standing guard on the boundary between the sweeping Amazonas and the little patch of England transplanted to the tropics.

In mid-winter, though, the Drewry's home became uninhabitable because of the rising waters. The waters would climb up the concrete pilings under their house and engulf the lawn, the flower beds, and the badminton court. Most of the road from the drop-off at Punchana Plaza to the sawmill would disappear under several feet of brown water. Consequently, around the end of March every year, as the river approached its crest, the Drewrys would migrate to town for several months.

During the flood season, Baron was busier than ever, because the first booms of mahogany and cedar logs would be arriving from upriver to inaugurate the sawing season and his daily trek between home and work was novel. From town to Punchana Plaza, Baron bucked the mud in his 1929 Chevvy, the *Cucaracha Verde*. Parking his Green Cockroach under a palm tree in Punchana Plaza, Baron descended the embankment and climbed into a slender, temperamental dugout canoe moored to the trunk of a swamped *cetico* tree. Paddling with the swift current, it took Baron less than a half hour to reach the mill. The return in the evening, even though he hugged the bank to avoid the full sweep of the current, was back-breaking work—steady paddling for an hour.

Late one afternoon, Dot and I were chugging upstream to Iquitos with Don Pepe O'Neill in the company launch after a visit to the Astoria sawmill. Just before reaching Punchana Plaza, we passed Baron's canoe. We waved and shouted. Baron was paddling stern and one of his mill hands squatted in the prow. The rounded bottom of the canoe between the two paddlers was filled with a mass of brilliant zinnias—yellow, orange, red—which Baron had picked, wading knee deep in the garden, before their bright heads disappeared under the brown blanket of the Amazonas.

While the Drewrys lived at the mill, they would often save us a treacherous bike ride by stopping for us on their way in to a dance. Baron would squeeze the Cucaracha's bulb horn to announce their arrival at the gate. Then he removed a bed sheet from a bag and spread it over the back seat to protect madame's gown.

The Drewrys and we had an invitation one noon to luncheon at the Prefect's, a block from the Vice Consulate. Luncheon was to be at 12:45. Baron and Peg were to pick up Dot at Tacu Tacu, and I was to wait for them in the office. One o'clock came and still I waited. I tried to phone Tacu Tacu, but the line was out of service.

An hour later, the Cucaracha klunked to a stop before the Malecón Palace. Baron, sweaty and covered with that good old Punchana gumbo, was not in a jovial mood. "Sonafabitchin road!" he roared with un-English un-restraint. "Got stuck three times, and that goddam bog hole in front of your house was the worst of all—broke the pole I always use to pry up the hind end of the Cucaracha to goose it out of a hole. They can take this Amazon Valley and stuff it—imagine, two hours to drive four miles!"

The ride must have been rugged. Baron's change of "clean" clothes which he put on in the office was spattered with mud, as was the "clean" white shirt Dot brought to me. "What the hell, Mister Veesay CONsool," said Baron, surveying his spots, "let's go eat before Mrs. Prefect throws out the yuca and beans."

$\mathcal{T}$ HE FEAR of sickness was probably the greatest worry of the small colony of Americans on wartime assignments in Iquitos. In Washington, I had asked Mr. Ferris, of the Division of Foreign Service Personnel, what I should do in the event of serious illness while in Iquitos. Mr. Ferris was as much in the dark about the darkest Amazon as I was. In his ignorance, he played safe and recommended that I drag myself to Lima for treatment, but not, of course, before the arrival of my replacement.

Mr. Ferris had made a far more educated guess than either of us realized. Although the native citizens of Iquitos went about being born, giving birth, contracting and surviving serious ill-

The Armadillo Plays Medicine Man

nesses, and undergoing operations with complete nonchalance, we finicky outlanders prayed that our plagues might coincide with our rare trips to Lima, where one could rush to the hygienic arms of the Anglo-American Hospital. Iquitos' Santa Rosa, compared to a modern first-rate hospital, had few more sanitary and surgical facilities than a medieval castle. The new hospital of the Health and Sanitation Mission was still a full year from completion at the time Dot and I left Iquitos.

Despite their supposed handicaps, the local Loretan medicos performed major operations with an impressive percentage of success. You would read in *El Oriente* that Señor Fulgencio Ortíz "finds himself delicate of health." A day or so later, you would read that Señor Ortíz "has been subjected to a surgical intervention (*una intervención quirúrgica*) with splendid results." A week later, the social column would announce that Señor Ortíz was fully on the road to recovery.

These tributes to the skill of Iquiteño doctors did not allay the fears of the squeamish Americans. They remained adamant in their determination not to be subjected to a surgical intervention if they could possibly avoid one. The two American doctors of the Health and Sanitation Mission were confined by instructions to administrative functions, although they would treat Americans who requested their help. The only serious operation that the American Mission doctors performed was an emergency appendectomy on an American tractor operator of the Rubber Development Corporation. The doctors, having no surgical equipment of their own, performed the operation at the Santa Rosa Hospital. The ordeal lasted about three hours and was packed with all the improvising drama of the appendectomy aboard the movie submarine *Copperfin* in the bottom of Tokyo Bay. The patient recovered, but none of us envied his fame.

The Peruvian montaña is not a healthy place. The fact that the Peruvian Army required of its personnel no more than two years of continuous service in the Jungle Division speaks volumes for the perils to health in the jungle. One was subject to the momentary onslaught of biting, burrowing, and drilling insects, sundry intestinal worms, grippe, pneumonia, tuberculosis, amoebic dysentery, gaseous stomach and other intestinal disorders, yellow fever, malaria, and leprosy. Fortunately, in Iquitos proper, yellow fever and malaria were only potential menaces. At my desk in the Vice Consulate, I was punctured a dozen times a day with impunity by the feathery-legged *stegomyia fasciata,* the carrier of yellow fever. There just happened to be no yellow fever around to transmit.

In view of the abundance of stagnant water out-of-doors, the earnest efforts of the *Servicio de Control de Fiebre Amarilla* to fight the yellow fever mosquito within the home alone seemed rather strange. The Yellow Fever Control Service was an entity financed by the Peruvian Government. The Servicio apparently had funds and plenty of investigating technicians who were authorized to enter any building at will in search of the breeding grounds of fasciata mosquitoes. The yellow fever boys would arrive at your house, laden with flashlights, cans of kerosene, and stepladders. The emblems of their rank were yellow arm bands and a little yellow flag which they displayed on your front door to tell the world that the Control de Fiebre Amarilla was engaged in official business within.

A yellow fever *técnico* entered Tacu Tacu once a month without so much as a knock on the door. Fortunately, Dot always managed to save her precious horde of water by assuring the técnico that we had just scrubbed out the concrete tank and that there couldn't possibly be any bugs in the water. Fearful that he had compromised his professional integrity, the técnico would prowl the balance of the house with special zeal, playing his flashlight about the sun-lighted rooms. He was unusually suspicious of Dot's two silver flower bowls containing hibiscus bells. Although Dot assured the técnico that she changed the water every day, he would poke an inquisitive flashlight among the flowers and gravely announce (as though he had found the nesting grounds of an entire generation of stegomyia fasciata), "Señora, the condition of your flower bowls is very serious. I request that you change the water immediately. If not, it shall be my duty to administer kerosene."

Although many settlements on the river banks of Loreto were ridden with *paludismo* or malaria, Iquitos was remarkably free of this plague. Every now and then you would discover an anopheles mosquito poised on your arm in its characteristic dive bomber position. But the puncture of an anopheles only itched— like that of his lowbrow cousin. Dot and I never got around to taking the atabrine tablets in the jungle kit sent by the Embassy "for the official use of the consular establishment in Iquitos."

Spared from yellow fever and malaria, we were attacked by a plethora of commonplace insects. We defended our home and persons as best we could, but the insect world of the jungle was overwhelmingly numerous and constantly on hand to catch us off guard.

If we forgot to seal up the bread box with adhesive tape, we found our bread and cookies teeming with minute café au lait ants. When it came to sugar, these little ants could work their way into any jar no matter how snugly the top screwed on. To keep the café au lait ants and their big black cousins from climbing the dinner table, Dot set each table leg in a tin can filled with water. The moat defense was effective; only a bedraggled handful reached the table top. These tireless scavengers were as swift and meticulous as a Dutch housewife. Whether it was a bit of food on the floor or the remains of a cockroach smashed with a well-aimed shoe, the ants, big and small, sprang from ambush and hauled away every bit of the débris. We found that the only complete, but hardly practicable, defense against ants was to keep no food in the house.

Cockroaches abounded. These tough, slippery characters,

three inches long, carried on their nefarious activities in my wardrobe, where they glutted themselves in particular on my dwindling collection of neckties.

There were moths, too. The Drewrys lost all their woolen clothes, in spite of sealing them in a tin box well stocked with moth balls. Dot decided on different tactics, seeking to keep our idle woolen clothing of Lima days intact by daily brushings and sunnings. This procedure postponed but did not prevent eventual disintegration. Dot's bitterest defeat occurred the day that her woolen Cuzco hat and Sierra Indian dolls, tacked to the wall of the living room on either side of the blowgun, fell to the floor in shreds.

The most repulsive of the insects that devoured our goods was the *comején* or termite. The comején builds his moundlike nest of a brown, crispy substance resembling dry breakfast cereal. We found one huge nest in our attic and another clinging to the rafters of the chicken house. The comején sneaked about his destructive ways within tunnels made of the same crispy material as his nest. Break the tunnel, and he would emerge into the light, revealing a loathsome maggot body and a shiny, polished turret head that turned in nervous, light-blinded jerks. Our most effective offense against these stealthy saboteurs was to chop open their nest with a machete and sprinkle it liberally with powdered arsenic.

The Amazonian mosquito is called a *zancudo* (after *zanco,* meaning stilt) in deference to his stiltlike legs. The zancudos did not dull their lance tips jousting with our household effects. They made straight for succulent Dot. As long as she was in the vicinity, I enjoyed comparative peace. For the first few months, Dot suffered a great deal from zancudo bites. Her legs became a mass of livid bumps, which she scratched until the blood ran and the bumps became scarred pits. We bought liter after liter of camphorated alcohol to alleviate the incessant itching. The treatment brought sweet but fleeting relief. In a half hour, Dot was again tearing her flesh with her long nails. "Don't worry, Señora," her friends would assure her, "in time you will become *acostumbrada* to the zancudos." Becoming acostumbrada indicated that some sort of relief was in store for the sufferer. It was never clear whether the relief was to result from the acute indigestion of the glutted zancudos or their inability to find virgin tissue to puncture. Dot was the exception to the rule. She never became acostumbradaed to zancudos.

Dot's zancudo ordeal reached its peak shortly after her arrival at Tacu Tacu. The house was carefully screened and, in addition, the bedrooms were screened off from the rest of the house. As an extra precaution, we would spray the bedroom before retiring, until we gasped with the fumes. Yet, Dot would awake in the morning with a new crop of welts. The situation became unbearable. There was no refuge either indoors or out. We examined the screens and searched the house for hidden apertures. There seemed to be no place for a zancudo to enter, yet they were getting in. We were about to admit that there might be something to the flower-bowl theory of the yellow fever técnico, when we solved the mystery. Our bathroom, a cement structure surmounted by the water tank, was attached to the side of our boxlike house. One evening, as I entered the front gate, I saw a strip of light coming from inside the house extending from the floor to the ceiling at the joining of the bathroom with the house proper. It was no tiny crack through which a zancudo would have to cramp his legs and wings. It was a boulevard twelve feet long and tapering from one to three inches wide! We spent the evening patching the narrower sections of the crack with adhesive tape and plugging the wider sections with wads of Lima's *El Comercio*.

If Dot was the delight of mosquitos and chiggers, she was able to scratch her bites raw without once bringing on infection. On the other hand, if the great mass of insects considered me not sabroso and therefore not worth biting, I could ill afford the pleasure of scratching my few bites. The *isango* or chigger, of the Amazon, delights in digging in where your clothing hugs your body. The waist and ankle are favorite spots. Two days after your most fleeting contact with grass, shrubbery, or any kind of vegetation, you begin to itch with exquisite intensity. It is useless to resist the urge to scratch. There are few sensations as satisfying as a well-scratched isango bite. But after you have scratched once, you must scratch again and again. That is what I did with an isango bite on the instep of my foot. Three days of fingernailing, topped off with an afternoon of heated badminton, blew up my foot to the size of a papaya. With the infection came the usual fever.

Dot cranked Tacu Tacu's party telephone for fifteen minutes before she reached Doctor Fischer, head of the Health and Sanitation Mission in Iquitos. He recommended prolonged immersion in a warm solution of epsom salts. The road was dry, and Dot set off on her Bianchi to the *Farmacia* Loretana to buy the salts. She returned in an hour with a large bag of the stuff. She was in a great hurry as she poured the hot water and the salts into a basin and thrust my foot into the bath. "No time to waste," she said. "Better get as much good as you can from the epsom before the Carachupa arrives to subject you to his medicine man treatment."

"What's the Carachupa got to do with my foot," I asked. "He's a judge, not a medico."

"That's what you think," replied Dot, adding so much epsom that the solution became supersaturated. "He claims he's the best *brujo,* or witch doctor, in Loreto, and he's coming here this afternoon to cure you. He waddled in to the Farmacia, and his curiosity was aroused at my difficulty in obtaining a kilo of *sulfato de magnesio.* The druggist must have thought we kept a constipated cow, because he simply refused to concede that anybody could want a whole kilo. He kept dealing it out to me in tiny packages. Fortunately the Carachupa came to my rescue, and in no time the druggist coughed up the remaining eight hundred grams."

"The Carachupa's fee for professional services," Dot continued, "was a full explanation of why I had cornered the sulfato de magnesio market. His face registered what he was too polite to say. He was clearly disturbed over our American medico's ignorance in treatment of an infection in the tropics."

"Well, what did the Judge prescribe," I interrupted, "a liter of his pisco sours?"

"No, he was serious," Dot replied. " 'Señora de Kelly,' he cautioned, with genuine concern in his voice, 'in the tierra caliente, an infection may be very serious. Promise me you will forget this sulfato business, for a *purgativo* will not cure the foot of Señor CONsool. I am no mean brujo, and I will go to Tacu Tacu this afternoon and cure him personally.' So that's why," Dot concluded, as she poured more hot water into the basin, "you'd better sulfato while you can, for nothing will keep Medicine Man Morey from restoring you to health."

Rather than sit in uneasy fear that the Carachupa would surprise me with my foot in the forbidden sulfato de magnesio, Walter was posted at the front gate with instructions to sound the alarm the moment he caught sight of the approaching medicine man. While we waited, Dot feverishly plied my foot with fresh portions of hot water and salts, as if repeated changes of the sulfato bath would accelerate the healing process to meet the shortage of time.

Dot had used up a pound of the sulfato when Walter swarmed up the front steps and pounded on the door with fists and feet. "*Ja-a-a vienen, Señor Kehlee, ja-a-a vienen!*" he shouted so that all Punchana could hear. Dot swept the bowl from under my foot and dashed with it to the kitchen. Returning, she snatched a pillow off the couch, plopped it on top of a wastepaper basket and set my bloated limb upon it. The Carachupa did not come alone. In trooped his two children, his wife, and lastly, the Carachupa himself, bearing in an upright position, like a gigantic bouquet, a large cactus bush. The long arms of the bush filled half the living room. Each arm bore a number of fleshy, oblong leaves with crenelated edges and bristling with spines.

There followed a moment of stunned silence as Dot and I shot bewildered glances from the cactus bush to one another. The Moreys seated themselves, and the Carachupa cleared his throat by way of a prologue to his dissertation. "Señor CONsool," the Carachupa began in his husky voice, "as your *estimada* Señora has no doubt advised you, I have come to alleviate your sufferings, to banish your fever and the infection from your leg. I carry with me a marvelous plant, a plant whose curative powers are beyond belief. Be not skeptical, Señor CONsool; neither be alarmed by its appearance, for these very leaves beckon you back to health."

The Carachupa cleared his throat again. The culmination of his remarks was at hand. His audience was transfixed. Even his two little girls sat frozen in their chairs, with wide, awed eyes. "Señor CONsool," entoned the Carachupa, "I give you the *shucucuisacha.*" With that, the Carachupa arose from his chair and thrust the trunk of the cactus tree into my hands.

I flashed an agonized glance at Dot. She returned it unchanged. *"Muchiiisimas gracias,* Doctor Morey," I stammered through the shrubbery, "but . . ."

"Do not be alarmed, Señor CONsool," soothed the Carachupa. "The preparation of the shucucuisacha is very simple. Your Señora has only to cut off one leaf, remove all the spines, wash the leaf thoroughly, and chop it up on a clean cloth. Be sure to chop it well so that the curative juice oozes out. Then, tie the poultice on the foot so that the chopped shucucuisacha comes in direct contact with the infected wound. When you desire a fresh poultice, chop up another leaf. The cure will begin immediately. By tomorrow evening, you will have no fever and the swelling will be gone."

The Carachupa's eyes burned with crusading zeal as he related the wondrous cures of the shucucuisacha (pronounced, if you care to give it a whirl, Shoo-koo-kwee-sah'-chah). "I have seen persons," he said, "in the last stages of torture, racked with fever, abandoned by the doctors. To such people, I have administered shucucuisacha and brought them back to health. Once, there was a woman on the Upper Río Ucayali who was caught by an alligator while washing clothes in the shallow water. People came to her rescue and dragged her screaming to the bank. Her leg was horribly mangled. Infection set in, and she was consumed with fever. The padre was called; people prayed about her deathbed. I was in that village on business and was allowed to treat her with shucucuisacha that I found growing wild near the house. Before I left, a week later, the woman's fever had gone and the leg was healing rapidly." After a half dozen similar accounts of his shucucuisacha cures, the Carachupa and his family departed for Chalet María Antonieta, promising to drop in frequently over the week-end to check on my progress.

I was trapped. The Carachupa's prestige would suffer a staggering blow if he popped in and found my foot in the sulfato de magnesio. The Carachupa was a loyal friend, but a vindictive enemy. Moreover, he was a judge of the Superior Court, a person of consequence in Iquitos. It behooved me to use the cactus.

In the mid-afternoon, as I was sitting in the living room staring at my propped-up foot, wondering if the curative powers of the cactus poultice were at work, or whether that cool, slimy pulp was deadly poisonous, callers appeared unexpectedly at the door. It was Doctor Fischer, my official physician; Doctor Westphal, Chief of the Health and Sanitation Program for all of Peru; and Doctor Herdener, a new medico whom Westphal had brought from Lima. They had dropped out to see how the patient was progressing under the epsom bath treatment. The cactus intrigued them. It might be perfectly harmless, but it would be well to get back to the epsom right away, they said, with quiet finality. They also promised to be back to see how I was getting along.

The next two days were a nightmare of uncertainty; of lightning switches from sulfato de magnesio to shucucuisacha and back to sulfato, depending on which of my attending physicians appeared at the door. On the third day, Dot could stand the strain no longer. She pronounced me cured and sent me biking back to the sanctuary of the American Vice Consulate, pumping my Raleigh with one foot.

Everyone in Loreto has intestinal worms. Some have more, some have less; some harbour a wide variety while others specialize. But everyone has at least *some* worms. Worms are so prevalent as to constitute the greatest threat among many to the health of Peru's jungle citizens. Worms are more abundantly found among the poorer classes, who seldom wear shoes and who have no sanitary facilities. Every health program undertaken in the Amazon, whether the independent efforts of isolated foreign missionaries or a broad health and sanitation program, must place the battle against *parásitos intestinales* at the top of its list.

In our desire to become genuine Loretanos, Dot and I did not draw the line at Loreto's intestinal parasites. We did not go out of our way to acquire them, but we decided that life was too short to attempt to live in a vacuum jar. We relaxed and ate what Iquiteños ate, drank what they drank, and even walked home barefooted through the mud of Punchana Road to spare our irreplaceable Stateside shoes. We paid the wages of relaxation. We contracted every worm in the book.

I was wormy at the time of our marriage; but Dot, as Doctor Navarro had assured me, broke my monopoly soon after she settled in Iquitos. In fact, she had rubbed elbows with worms long before I had ever heard of Iquitos. While a grammar school student in one of Shanghai's private schools, she disgraced her family by contracting worms. The family wept a collective wail for the family name when the school health report was read. Cassie, Dot's mother, wept; Kitty, Dot's sister, wept; Harry, Dot's brother, wept; and wormy Dot wept. But Dot's family survived and so did Dot, to get them again another day.

We first contracted the plebeian askaris, or roundworm, which, if well-nourished and given time to develop, grows to the length of six inches and the thickness of a pencil. Then, we were promoted to the *agchylostoma,* or hookworm, of the United States. Finally, we graduated to the high-toned *trichocephalus,* or whipworm. As long as we remained in Iquitos, there was no point in taking pills to kill the worms, because they would come back within a few days. However, when we stepped aboard the

Cat for the last time, on our way to Chile, we popped some huge red pills in our mouths. The pills knocked out the roundworms (the ones that scared you the most when you saw them), but failed entirely to disquiet our hookworms and whipworms.

In Santiago, Chile, we consulted Doctor Hugo Hochschild, reportedly the brother of fabulous Mauricio Hochschild, the tin Croesus of Bolivia. Doctor Hochschild prescribed arsenic pills. Daily doses of Doc Hugo's "rat poison" for several months discouraged the hookworms. The aristocratic trichocephalus alone clung relentlessly to his domain.

When we returned to the States, we went to a highly-rated clinic in St. Louis in a final attempt to get rid of the whipworms, which we blamed for our chronic gastro-intestinal discomfort. The medicos of the clinic were so impressed with our rare worm that we were sent to consult Dr. Tsuchya, a Japanese intestinal parasite specialist in the Washington University School of Medicine. Dr. Tsuchya found our case "very, very interesting," because he had never before encountered the trichocephalus within the continental limits of the United States. He also told us what we were beginning to suspect—that the trichocephalus was a very tenacious fellow. "Your only hope," he informed us, "lies in repeated draughts of the sap of the bastard fig tree. Unfortunately," sighed Dr. Tsuchya, "such a tree is not to be found in the Mississippi Valley." Hoping against hope, Dot and I stalked Forest Park, the Busch Gardens, and every other botanical park in Greater St. Louis, tapping knife in hand, ready to bleed the first bastard fig tree that lay in our path. But, alas, there was none, and we were to harbour the trichocephalus for a long time.

In the reception room of the Brazilian Consulate in Iquitos, there hung a sign, in Spanish, which read: Please Do Not Extend the Hand. Pablo Boner, a Swiss engineer engaged in the extraction of wild rubber, made a fetish of not shaking hands. When you met him on the street and inadvertently extended your hand for the accustomed hand shake (Peruvians, like other Spanish Americans, shake hands at the slightest provocation), Boner would pump his clenched fist in the air safely beyond your grasping fingers. His maneuver made one feel silly, yet I could never remember not to lead with my right. The Brazilian Consul and Pablo Boner were, however, an insignificant minority among a city of avid hand shakers. The rugged individuality of these two rebels was a faint recognition of the prevalence in the montaña of the world's most dread disease—leprosy.

According to an official of the *Servicio Nacional Antileproso*, an entity of the Peruvian Government, leprosy worked its way into the montaña from Brazil in the first years of the twentieth century. The quest for rubber, with its swarm of adventurers flocking to Loreto from down the valley, helped spread the disease into the headwaters of the Amazon. The affliction took hold most sensationally in the populous valley of the Río Ucayali. By 1944, the incidence of leprosy in the montaña of Peru was estimated at 1½ per cent, among the highest in the world.

The Servicio Nacional Antileproso maintained a leprosarium at San Pablo, on the Amazon River, about two hundred miles downstream from Iquitos. Reports that reached Iquitos of conditions at San Pablo were often sensationally bad. They painted San Pablo as a place of horror and death—a concentration camp where the unfortunate wretches were doomed to die a lingering death from their disease or a more rapid death from starvation and insufficient care. Other reports, while admitting that conditions were not satisfactory at San Pablo, emphasized the splendid work of the Servicio with the meagre funds at its disposal. Apparently, there was room for improvement at San Pablo, for a delegation of lepers started paddling for Iquitos in a dugout canoe to protest conditions at the colony. After journeying for several days, they were halted at the Peruvian garrison of Pijuayal and sent back to San Pablo.

Whatever the conditions at San Pablo, it was certain that it had facilities for only a small percentage of the lepers of Loreto. In 1944, the Servicio had records of eighty lepers (among whom some thirty were suffering with a contagious form) running loose in Iquitos for lack of space at San Pablo. One of these contagious lepers earned his living by selling bread, while another whittled sticks for *raspadillas,* the frozen sherbet suckers that Iquiteños devoured by the thousands every day! After hearing of the leprous whittler, Dot and I lost our stomach for raspadillas and squeezed what comfort we could from the thought that leprosy is not easily transmitted.

But Ray and Lib Russell were not perturbed by the story of the leprous whittler. They and their small children, Betsy and Billy, continued to devour aguaje and pineapple raspadillas by the gross. The Russells thought it hardly consistent to balk at contaminated raspadillas while they lived in the one-time home of a leper.

Ray, alias "Iron Man," Russell was the chief field technician, in Peru, of the Rubber Development Corporation. He came to Iquitos from Firestone's rubber plantations in Liberia early in 1942 to lay the groundwork for RDC's program of reviving Peru's long-dead wild rubber industry. Except for a half dozen Protestant missionaries and Don Pepe O'Neill, Ray Russell was the dean of the American colony from the point of view of length of residence in Loreto. But "Iron Man" Russell won his name not merely because of his staying power. His ruggedness, strength, and endurance during his prolonged field trips brought him his greatest renown. Ray would disappear into the jungle for months at a time, nosing his dugout canoe up remote tributaries or hiking through the *monte* by canopied *trochas* or trails, naked except for boots and a pair of blue trunks. Ray ate everything in the bush—from stringy barbecued monkey to thick *masato,* the yuca beer of the montaña—without so much as a gastric twinge; he brushed ants and winged insects from his hairy torso with as little concern as if they were rose petals; he paddled the arms off his stoutest *bogadores* and walked the legs off his most rugged *trocheros.* "Iron Man" Russell was *muy macho* by any yardstick.

Between one bush Odyssey and another, Ray would return to his Tar Heel wife, Lib, and his two children at their suburban estate, *Chanticleer,* located about as far outside Iquitos as was

Tacu Tacu but in the opposite direction. Chanticleer was once the pride of Kurt Riess, a German national, an officer of the powerful German firm of E. Strassberger and Cía., and German Consul in Iquitos. The house was hidden from the road by a nine-foot wall behind which rose two beautiful specimens of *Hevea brasiliensis,* the finest type of Amazonian wild rubber tree.

The house was a masterpiece for tropical living—a long, single-story, rectangular building with connecting rooms. Every room opened onto a wide, cement-floor portal extending around the entire building. The plumbing and household fixtures were the best that German industry produced. The roof was a vast expanse of galvanized iron which caught enough water to fill a number of cisterns. During the short but furious drouths, when the rest of Iquitos had empty water tanks, and parched householders struggled through the dust with gasoline tins from Sachachorro Spring, the Russells enjoyed abundant water.

The house was surrounded by twelve acres of productive land crowded with every type of palm and fruit tree of the region. The Russells kept a cow in a rear pasture, pigs, chickens, and turkeys in pens nearer the house.

Disillusioning as it may seem to those accustomed to thinking of the Amazon as a region of tremendous fertility, actually much of the arable land of Loreto is very poor crop land. One cannot raise a vegetable garden simply by throwing out the seed, grabbing a machete, and harvesting the crop before it grows out of sight. It is true that lush, fast-growing jungle vegetation covers everything, but these plants have adapted themselves to a soil that is largely leached out to an impervious clay by the heavy rains. In this barren soil, bananas, yuca, and beans—the traditional trinity of the Loretan diet—manage to grow with surprising success, but if your temperate clime vegetables push above the surface at all, they will emerge shriveled and tasteless.

"Why not fertilize the soil?" you ask. An excellent idea, but quite difficult to accomplish. In the first place, manure is almost as scarce as clingstone peaches in Iquitos. The only horses in town are a score of ridgeback broomtails belonging to the water carriers. Cows are hardly more plentiful. Consequently, after months of diligent, piecemeal gleaning, you amass only a minute pile of manure. There are no commercial fertilizers. As an inadequate substitute, people buy rotted mahogany and cedar sawdust from the sawmills.

The Russells of Chanticleer, however, had one of the few productive truck gardens in Iquitos. They were in part indebted for this good fortune to old Kurt Riess, who had located a rare section of rich black soil near Iquitos and hauled it to Chanticleer to fill his bricked-in garden plots. Equally important, Ray owned a half ton of bird guano which he had flown by RDC Catalina from coastal Peru. He kept the stuff under lock and key like a horde of gold doubloons.

Ray was well paid by the RDC, but he had not paid to have the guano flown over the hill at twenty-five cents a pound, the prevailing rate for air express. Ray had lived in Iquitos over a year before he decided to import his family from Lima. He rightfully insisted that, if his wife and children were to live in scarcity-ridden Iquitos, they would have to be equipped with the essentials of healthy living. These were the days before Faucett assumed the operation of the Catalinas on a commercial basis. The two ships were intended exclusively for the use of the RDC. Ray, then, obtained authorization to transport his family and their household necessities to Iquitos at government expense. He loaded Lib, the two kids, their refrigerator, spring beds, crates of tinned food, four bicycles, and the half ton of bird excreta aboard Condor Biggs' Cat and bade farewell to the metropolis.

The Russells' flight over the hill is one of the epics of Andean aviation history. From Chiclayo, it took them three weeks to reach the Pearl of the Amazon! Every dawn for twenty dawns, Condor Biggs corkscrewed into the air above Chiclayo to twenty thousand feet and headed the Cat into the ominous front, sniffing for a hole to go through or a top to climb over. On the twelfth day morning, the Russells looked down to find themselves over the ocean. The headwinds were blowing the Cat backwards faster than its straining engines were pushing it forwards! In two hours of flying eastward, they had travelled fifteen miles towards the west!

Because of their harrowing journey to the land of promise, the Russells had no desire to leave Iquitos until they left for good. They were happy in near self-sufficiency at Chanticleer amid their livestock and poultry. At Chanticleer, the union of Kurt Riess' good earth and Chincha Island's good guano produced fresh vegetables never or rarely seen on the Iquitos market: tomatoes, onions, butter beans, green beans, radishes, cabbages, carrots, and lettuce.

The Russells knew of the tales whispered by the barefooted folk who hurried by the high wall. "Doesn't the Meester know," they muttered, "that Chanticleer is cursed? Doesn't he know that every night the ghost of the leper Riess rings the bell at the front gate and roams the portal rattling each door?" The rapid turnover of Lib's servants, despite high wages, was a tribute to the effectiveness of *el leproso's* haunting.

When Ray rented Chanticleer from Riess' mestiza widow, merchants and officials downtown shook their heads in disapproval. "The place is contaminated," they told him. "The German contracted leprosy and lived there for years before he died. His widow may have it, too, for she shut herself up behind that high wall after Riess' death and never appeared in public."

Ray and Lib set about exorcizing the spirit of el leproso Riess from Chanticleer. Before moving in, they sealed each room and subjected the whole house to a thorough fumigation. After moving in, they entertained frequently. The stream of guests passing through the grilled gate rang the suspended bell so constantly that el leproso Riess had little opportunity to ring on his own account. Neither did he have the liberty of the portal for his nocturnal ramblings. After dinner, "Iron Man" Russell would rouse his male guests for his favorite parlor game, the "Pig Race." At the word "go," the contestants dashed along the portal to the rear of the house, where Ray stood at the gate of the pig corral, flashlight in hand. The corral was a large enclosure, studded with trees. Ray would squirt erratic streams of light from his flashlight impartially about the enclosure to help the peering contestants locate a young pig. There were shouts, squeals, and spills as the guests and piglets hurtled about in the half-light. The first to grab a pig, dash back along the portal, dragging the protesting chanchito behind him, and reach the spot where the ladies were seated was the winner. If the party was large, Ray ran the race in several heats. The din of the pig race, I am sure, rather than the fumigation, drove the ghost of el leproso Riess in despair from the haunts of Chanticleer.

12

$\mathcal{I}$N IQUITOS, two worlds met—the dynamic twentieth century world of the European and Yankee, and the static, timeless world of the jungle aborigine. The white man reached out his hand from Iquitos and wormed acquisitive fingers up the hundreds of waterways of Loreto to rake in the fruits of the jungle. In the hinterland, commerce brought contact but no fusion of the two worlds. In the metropolis, the two cultures poured together to produce a strange blend, not quite a true synthesis, yet not so distinct and unmixed as the layers of a pousse cafe. In Iquitos, the white-skinned merchant, in his starched white suit and complaining shoes, joined the brown-skinned cholo in

Beware the Jabberwock!

his faded, patched trousers and shoeless feet, at the Alhambra theatre to watch the antics of Abbott and Costello. But the merchant returned to a tile-fronted home with hardwood floors, and ate his imported dinner at a mahogany table from fine English china. The cholo returned to the traditional palm leaf and pole hut of the jungle to eat his rice, yuca, and fish, squatting on the floor, from a halved *tutumbo* gourd. The Spanish Augustinian padres expounded the dogmas of the Roman Catholic Church to white and aborigine alike in the moldy interior of the *iglesia matriz* on the Plaza de Armas. While the whites, especially the men, paid a tepid allegiance to the State religion, the cholo, anything but tepid in this respect, surrounded himself with a web of liturgical rites in which the threads of Christianity, paganism, and witchcraft were inextricably woven.

The cholo's awareness of the supernatural was so acute that it pervaded every phase of his day-to-day existence. His life, health, and well-being were conditioned by a host of forces in which the tangible and intangible became inseparable.

The trees, the water, and air about the cholo were filled with goblins, most of whom were intent on causing some ill to man. The *chullachaqui* was a creature with a hideous face, one huge foot, and one shriveled foot, that hobbled about the jungle, frightening unwary travellers from the trail so that they became lost and plunged about in desperate fear until the chullachaqui, tiring of the game, killed them. In the depths of the rivers lived the *yacuruna* (in the Quechua tongue, "Man of the Water") who hacked the smooth surface of the rivers with his machete to make the waves, and stirred up the treacherous whirlpools to trap the Loretano's canoe. The *yayay mamen* took the form of a small swift bird, rarely seen, whose agonizing cry filled the forest stillness. Its mournful call seemed actually to say, "Ay Ay mama," in intense grief. So poignant was the call of this evil spirit that children were enticed into the forest where they became lost and were turned into these small birds, destined to cry forever for their mothers.

Chanticleer had its leprous ghost; Tacu Tacu had its *tunche*. There is no spirit in the jungle that is more dreaded than the tunche. People lower their voices when the tunche is mentioned, as if the very sound of its name will bring on a visitation. If Lib Russell failed to fortify her servants for more than a short time against the nightly prowlings of el leproso Riess, Dot and I made no attempt to keep Antonia or Petronila in the house after 9:00 p. m. Antonia saw to it that she and her children were gathered safely in their own home before the tunche began swooping over the housetops, filling the night air with prolonged and lugubrious whistles which announced that death was about to visit someone in the neighborhood. Dot and I lay in bed many a night, listening to that hair-raising sequence of three whistles followed by a silence. We were never able to catch a glimpse of the tunche. People said it went about in the guise of an owl-like bird. Bird or spirit, the tunche seemed to have set aside our house for special attention.

In Loreto, modern medicine was making its first tentative sorties into the domain of folk cures and sorcery. The program of the American-financed and supervised Health and Sanitation Mission was only the courageous beginning of a tremendous task in mass education. Our majordomo Walter cut his foot, and a bad infection developed. Dot insisted that Antonia take him to the Mission's free clinic for treatment. After a couple of treatments, the infection seemed just as severe. Antonia, having given the Señora's treatment a fair try, marched Walter off to a medicine man, taking along a pair of her best chickens. According to Antonia, some brujo had cast a spell on Walter. The brujo she was consulting was very powerful and would draw out the evil of the first brujo by his incantations and *chupadas* or suckings of the infected wound. When we saw Walter after his treatment, his foot looked as nasty as before; but several days later, the swelling disappeared and the foot healed. Antonia was as laconic and stolid as usual. Though she passed no judgment, it was clear to us that the brujos would give the clinics of the Health and Sanitation Mission abundant competition.

In Iquitos, we found that having a tricky liver was quite the rage. We learned about livers from Antonia. Except for her *hígado,* Antonia was a paragon of health. She never had fevers, headaches, toothaches, or the grippe. She didn't even become *constipada* as the Loretanos refer (most disconcertingly for the Norteamericano) to the common head cold. She did have an hígado, though. When her hígado flared up, she would send Petronila to advise that she would not be at work that day.

One evening, Antonia's hígado picked a very inopportune time to be fractious, and with astounding results. We were having people for dinner. The guests had arrived and their appetites were whetted by vermouth and pisco cocktails when Antonia announced that she had a pain in her hígado and had to go home immediately. Dot pleaded with her to stay at least until the dinner was served, but off she went. The next morning, Petronila appeared to announce sheepishly that she had a new baby brother, born about a half hour after Antonia had left Tacu Tacu. The new baby had arrived, as do the majority of Loretan babies, without the assistance of a medico.

Dot and I were stunned at the instantaneous transformation of an ailing hígado into a baby. We had not once suspected Antonia's pregnancy. Her squat body looked just as square and squat that night as it did the day she first came to work.

A week later, at Antonia's request we named the baby. From a choice of three names she selected "Sidney," after Dot's brother-in-law in a Jap internment camp in Shanghai.

In due time, Antonia brought little Sydney to visit his godparents in Tacu Tacu. Sydney was a healthy baby, with the traditional gray eyes and light hair of the Peréz family. But his beauty was marred by a large, puffy raspberry birthmark on his forehead, the shape of a quarter moon. "Too bad the baby has that ugly mole," Dot remarked to me in English. Antonia got the drift of the remark, for she replied in Spanish, *"Sí, Señora, es una lástima,"* she agreed. And looking Dot squarely in the face, which she seldom did, yet without any bitterness in her eyes or voice, she said, "You are to blame for the birthmark, Señora. Do you remember several months before the baby was born, when the sun became dark at midday? I was afraid, Señora. There were no clouds, yet the sun became dark at midday. You wanted that I look at the dark sun through a smoked glass. I was afraid to look, but you commanded me. I looked quickly and saw that the sun was not round and shiny like a coin but dark and eaten away like an old moon. I did evil to look, and I ran into the kitchen trembling. You see, Señora, the dark sun has cursed my baby, and you are to blame, Señora."

The upper classes of Iquitos, for all their sophistication, were not immune to the intoxicating fumes rising from the caldron of popular folklore. In time, everyone succumbed to some extent to the witchery of the jungle. There were too many fantastic, dangerous creatures and plants, too many perils actually lurking in the foliage, in the mud, and under the murky waters for one to separate fact from fiction. The real perils of the jungle made themselves sufficiently obvious to lend a degree of reality to a host of nebulous fables and old wives' tales.

For instance, one heard of the *champsa negra,* a man-eating black alligator, with hypnotic eyes. Just as you were about to relegate the champsa negra to the rubbish heap of fantasy, *El Oriente* would announce that a ten-year-old boy had been dragged under the waters of Moronacocha by an alligator, only a few feet away from the Iquitos Regatta Club. After reading the account, you were not so sure about discarding the alligator with the evil eyes.

You heard stories of the *yacu mama* (in the Quechua tongue "Mother of the Water"), the giant boa constrictor. The stories sounded too much like the fabrications of Rudyard Kipling to be credible. The half dozen boas that Dot and I saw were really minding their own business, as most wild animals do, but we were so frightened by the mere sight of these dappled black and yellow monsters that we were ready to put them in a class with the tunche and other spirit animals.

Dot met our largest boa on very intimate terms. Dot, Pablo Fernández, and I were biking along a trail running between the Itaya and Nanay rivers, bound for Quistococha, a lake about fifteen kilometers from town. Pablo and I were about one hundred yards ahead of Dot speeding down a slight decline in the winding trail when her shriek brought us to a skidding halt. She was rattling down the slope at full tilt on her Bianchi, which had long before worn out its hand brakes. A few yards ahead of her, a boa had thrust its head out of the undergrowth and was on its way across the trail. "What shall I do!" Dot howled. "Gun 'er!" I yelled. "Pump like hell!" At that moment, the boa accelerated its pace and a collision seemed inevitable. Instinctively, I closed my eyes for an instant. I opened them in time to see the rear wheel of Dot's Bianchi flash by the raised head of the boa, missing it by inches. Her feet were off the pedals tucked up as high as she could get them. The fifteen-foot body of the boa stretched almost from one margin of the trail to the other, forcing Dot to brush the edge of the undergrowth to avoid a collision. By the time she reached the spot where we were waiting, the boa had disappeared into the jungle.

Our last encounter with yacu mama was in the water. It was during flood time, and Dot and I had paddled in a dugout canoe to inundated Iquitos Island, lying directly in front of the city across a kilometer-wide stretch of the Amazon. The jungle in flood time is more easily penetrated by canoe than it is in the dry season by foot. You work your canoe along canopied *sacaritas* or canals into hidden lagoons, landlocked during the dry season. So thick are the aquatic plants floating on the surface that you see no water unless you dig for it. The paddling is hard as you force the prow of your hollowed log among Victoria Regia lily pads, five feet in diameter and clustered about gorgeous rose-white blooms the size of a head of lettuce. The riotous profusion of nature is overwhelming—everything is so huge, so plentiful, so varied. Wading birds of all kinds rise with shrill calls from the reeds along the banks of the *cocha*. There is the slender *avaporoto* with curious orange spurs on its wings, and the snowy egret, so wary that it is difficult to slip up on one no matter how quietly you work your paddle.

The day we encountered the boa we were attempting to work within shooting range of a group of six egrets. Dot squatted in the prow while I paddled stern with a .22 rifle across my knees. As the prow slipped alongside the top branches of a flooded bush, Dot's back stiffened, and she whispered hoarsely, "There's a *snake* in those branches."

I laid my paddle in the bottom of the canoe, threw the safety on the rifle, and let our slight momentum carry the canoe forward. From my position, I could not see the hidden snake and realized that the canoe would have to pass by the bush before I could see to shoot. It seemed an eternity as the canoe inched past the bush, its side on a level with the snake's lair. At last, I saw. It was a boa entwined in the branches of the bush, its body submerged except for the triangular head. The boa probably hoped as fervently as we did that there would be no trouble. But it was too close for comfort. I blasted at the head. There was a churning of waters and the head disappeared. We abandoned our pursuit of the egrets and paddled hard for the open Amazon and home.

Although Iquitos was beset on all sides with water, and every Iquiteño could swim, swimming was never popular. In the summer season, when the Amazon dropped and the large sandy *playas* appeared, timid bathers made brief sorties into the muddy waters. During this season, General Morla took parties of would-be bathers aboard his launch. The General and his aides themselves had no intention of swimming. They brought along no bathing suits and remained securely encased in their high boots and starched uniforms.

If the General and his officers would rather have faced a firing squad than to have dived off the anchored launch, they were insistent that their guests not miss the pleasure. They seemed particularly desirous that the ladies go for a swim. Dot and Peg were always urged with special insistence to plunge into the river. *"Pierdan ustedes cuidado, Señoras,"* the General would assure them. "There is nothing to fear. The waters are perfectly safe." When the Señoras still appeared dubious, the General would say, *"Un momento, Señoras.* I will prove to you that the waters are safe." The General would then order one of the crew to dive in and swim about the launch to reassure the ladies. The soldier obeyed his orders but with no excess of glee. The demonstration over, the General would proudly point out the confirmation of his theory. "You see, Señoras! No alligators, no boas, no electric eels, no sting rays, no *pañas*, no *caneros!* The prevalence of these creatures is greatly exaggerated by the cholo class."

The paña and the canero are, perhaps, the most dreaded fish of tropical American rivers, although both are small fish. The paña or *piraña* (serrasalinus piraya) is a chunky, blunt-nosed fish about a foot long, but its jaws are armed with sharp, triangular, saw-like teeth. The paña is extremely rapacious, and in swarms, its attack is devastating. Aurelio, Tacu Tacu's yardman, had spent several years as a commercial fisherman in the vicinity of Iquitos. He and his companions once had the misfortune of ensnaring a school of paña in their nets. The snapping demons cut the heavy net cords to shreds and allowed the other fish to escape. Aurelio, in his attempt to haul in the net, plunged a hand into the water. He yelled in pain as a paña hit, snapping off his index finger neatly at a second joint. Contrary to fish generally, a disturbance in the water seems to attract the paña and incite him to attack. Once blood has been shed in the water his fury knows no bounds. Hope Morris, on one of her trips to Iquitos over the Pichis trail, watched one of the mules laden with canvas mail pouches be cut to shreds within a few minutes as it splashed across a river ford at the rear of the caravan.

Even more terrible, in a sense, than the paña, and certainly more unusual in his habits, is the diminutive canero (of the family Pygidiidae for the benefit of you ichthyologists). The canero is seldom more than six inches long, and its thin body is coated heavily with mucus. The canero's slender body and slipperiness enable it to enter the orifices of man or beast, particularly the penis, vulva, and rectum. Once inside, it lodges itself firmly by means of spines on the gill plates, and lives on the blood of the host animal as would a tick or other parasite. Unless the canero is removed, death will eventually result. These creatures can often be removed only by surgery. However, an Australian missionary living near Yurimaguas on the Huallaga River claimed that he had succeeded in dislodging the canero from a number of victims by administering internally the juice from the green fruit of the *huito* tree mixed with water.

The fear of the paña and the canero is so implanted in the real Loretano—the man who spends so much of his life in a canoe that his arms and torso have reached unusual development, while his legs are almost vestigial by contrast—that he enters the water only when unavoidable. Yet, the Loretano is extremely cleanly in his personal habits. He bathes at least once a day, but not in the river. In deference to the paña and canero, the Loretano, man and woman, sits cross-legged in the safety of a canoe moored to the river bank or on the edge of a raft, scoops up water from the river with a tutumbo gourd, pours it over his body, and proceeds to lather up. Foolish children and rash outlanders alone provoke the river devils by bathing in el Amazonas.

One of the most vivid manifestations of the extent to which the quasi-superstition or, if you will, the wisdom, of the aborigine pervades all levels of Iquiteño society is the case of the *zúngaro dorado*. A zúngaro is the Loretanism for a catfish, and a zúngaro dorado is a variety of yellow or golden catfish. These huge golden cats are caught most abundantly near the banks, in large nets, during the *creciente,* when fish of all kinds take advantage of the rising waters to seek feed amid the drowned vegetation. Although Iquitos is surrounded by rivers apparently abounding in fish, we found that fish was even more difficult to obtain in the market than meat. Dot, therefore, was delighted to find the market well supplied during the flood season with a fish called zúngaro dorado. We tried some and found it delicious.

We were so thrilled with our discovery that we asked the Prefect and his wife to dinner. The zúngaro steaks baked in canned Brazilian butter were set before the guests. "What fish is this?" asked Betty de Echecopar, in pleased anticipation. "Why, zúngaro dorado, of course," we carolled. "It's the only plentiful fish on the market, very good and not expensive." The Prefect and his Señora looked from one to another, seeking in each other's eyes what to say next. "Don't you care for zúngaro?" Dot asked. "If you don't, Antonia can easily prepare a heart of palm omelette." Don Carlos Echecopar smiled one of his bland smiles. "If convenient, the omelette would be very nice, Señora." "Perhaps," volunteered Betty de Echecopar, "you do not realize why zúngaro dorado is plentiful in the market? You must learn to be suspicious of anything that is plentiful in the Iquitos market. You see," continued Betty, "few people eat zúngaro dorado because it makes your skin break out with *manchas,* discolored blotches that remain permanently. Did no one tell you this? It is true of all zúngaros with a scaleless skin."

In the days that followed, Dot and I found that everyone subscribed to the mancha theory. Looking back, we remembered that Antonia had not been at all enthusiastic about the zúngaro, but she had said no more than that the zúngaro "was not good to eat." We had paid no attention to her because the testing of the zúngaro had been proof enough for us. Dot and I continued to eat zúngaro dorado, popular superstition be hanged. However, each time the zúngaro was served, our relish for it decreased until, shortly, there was no relish left. We stopped buying zúngaro and began examining our skins for suspicious signs.

In a very short time, Madre Selva lays her hand on a man— be he a barefooted Indian, a judge of the Superior Court, a Prefect of the Department, or a Yanqui Vice Consul—and convinces him that he must reckon with her children—reckon with chullachaqui, the yacuruna, the yayay mamen, the tunche, the brujo, the champsa negra, the yacu mama, the paña, the canero, and the zúngaro dorado.

13

*P*ERU IS bordered by five countries—Ecuador and Colombia on the north, Brazil and Bolivia on the east, and Chile on the south. With the exception of Chile, the most extensive portions of the boundaries between these countries and Peru lie in the remote, thinly-populated Upper Amazon Valley.

During Spain's colonial rule, no definite boundaries existed between the various political subdivisions of the Spanish colonies in America and the Portuguese colony of Brazil. In South America, Spanish colonial rule divided the continent into three viceroyalties: New Granada, comprising what is now Venezuela, Colombia, and Ecuador; Peru, comprising what is now Peru,

Thunder Over the Jungle

Chile, and part of Bolivia; and La Plata, comprising what is now Argentina, Uruguay, Paraguay, and part of Bolivia. Each viceroyalty was divided into a number of *audiencias,* which, in turn, were made up of provinces and municipalities. At the time of the independence from Spain, territorial subdivisions of the viceroyalties roughly determined the boundaries of the various infant republics.

The patriot governments agreed to accept in principle the *uti possidetis* of 1810 as a basis in working out the eventual definitive boundaries of their respective territories. The principle of uti possidetis vests in belligerents as absolute property the territory under their actual control at the time of agreement. In the vast, trackless, undeveloped Upper Amazon Valley, the decision of who has actual control over what territory has not proved an easy matter to decide over the conference table.

Throughout the nineteenth century and up to the present, Peru has had her share of boundary controversies with all her Amazonian neighbors. Her disputes with Brazil and Bolivia resulted in nothing more serious than small-scale clashes between jungle pioneers and isolated garrisons before a stable boundary agreement was reached. But Peru's boundary disputes with Colombia and Ecuador led it to military operations on a large scale.

I arrived in Iquitos in time to observe the final stages of settlement of the long-standing boundary dispute between Ecuador and Peru. This assignment was the most absorbing of my various duties. I was fortunate in being able to visit a number of remote Peruvian garrisons buried deep in the jungle along the new boundary line still in the stage of demarcation. From my observations, I believe that the new Peru-Ecuador boundary stands an excellent chance of bringing to a permanent end the last of a list of outstanding disputes that have fostered suspicion, ill-will, and bloodshed between Peru and her several neighbors.

For a clear understanding of the boundary demarcation work, it is necessary to present a brief history of the boundary dispute between Peru and Ecuador. I do not pretend to offer an entirely unbiased picture of the background of the dispute. My sources of information—both personal contacts and printed material—have been largely Peruvian, because of the location of my post. But since the final settlement has favored the Peruvian claim over the Ecuadorean, the implication is that Peru had the sounder case.

Peru based her fundamental claim to the area in dispute between herself and Ecuador on the *Real Cédula* (Royal Decree) of 1802. By this decree, the King of Spain ordered (almost a decade before the first outbreaks of revolutionary activity in his American colonies) the creation of the provinces of Maynas and Quijos, comprising a large portion of what is now northern coastal, Andean, and Amazonian Peru. In addition, the Real Cédula transferred the territory comprising these two provinces from the viceroyalty of New Granada (in which present-day Ecuador was located) to the viceroyalty of Peru. When Peru emerged as an independent nation, in 1821, she laid claim to the territory within the jurisdiction of the defunct viceroyalty of Peru. Peru further insisted that her sovereignty over the northern province of Maynas, together with those of Tumbes and Jaen, was proved beyond a doubt because these three provinces took the oath of independence from Spain in 1821, along with the other provinces of Peru. Ecuador contested the validity of the Peruvian claim, and there commenced a dispute that alternately smoked and flared up for over a century. In 1828, Peruvian troops invaded Ecuador, which, at the time, was federated with Colombia and Venezuela in the short-lived Republic of Gran Colombia. The Peruvian aim of annexing the port of Guayaquil failed when the invaders were defeated by a composite force of Colombians and Ecuadoreans. War over territorial sovereignty again broke out in 1859, when Peru discovered that Ecuador had attempted to liquidate a portion of her foreign debt by transferring to her creditors a section of land in the *Oriente* (all land east of the Andes is known as *El Oriente*), claimed also by Peru. The Peruvian fleet blocked the Ecuadorean coast and forced a humiliating boundary treaty on the leader of the Guayaquil faction of Ecuadorean politics. This treaty was later repudiated by both the Ecuadorean and Peruvian governments.

Relations between Peru and Ecuador smoldered along throughout the rest of the nineteenth century and into the twentieth. Boundary agreements, in 1887 and 1890, proved to be fleeting and unsatisfactory. In 1904, both countries agreed to submit the touchy matter to the King of Spain for arbitration. However, the findings of the Spanish king were withheld for fear that war would break out between the two countries upon the announcement of his decision. Years passed, and the two countries came no closer to a reconciliation of their differences. In 1936, President Roosevelt became arbitrator of the dispute, but the arbitration made little headway and was followed, in July and August, 1941, by a renewal of armed conflict.

During the fourscore years prior to the outbreak of World War II, Peru succeeded in strengthening her claim to the Oriente by a vigorous program of occupation. On the other hand, Ecuador drained away her energies in a prolonged orgy of internal political strife in which the coast dwellers of Guayaquil repeatedly defied the authorities at Quito, the capital in the highlands. Hence, Ecuador was at a disadvantage in the settlement of disputed boundary lines, for she made no serious attempt to colonize the areas she claimed in the Upper Amazon drainage.

Peru's first efforts to incorporate the montaña section with the coastal and Andean sections were given impetus by General Ramón Castilla, for many years President of the Republic. In 1861, General Castilla created the *Departamento Fluvial y Militar de Loreto,* purely an administrative zone of the Peruvian

Navy. Castilla bolstered his decree by positive action. He dispatched a naval mission to England to arrange for the construction of a number of river craft to be used for the exploration and defense of the vast network of Amazonian waterways to which Peru laid claim. The naval mission was successful. In February, 1864, a flotilla of four river steamers, under the command of Capitán Federico Alzamora, dropped anchor in the broad Amazon off the palm-thatched village of Iquitos, inhabited by Indians of the Iquitos tribe and a handful of Peruvian whites from the mountain country around Moyobamba. The steamers were significantly named the *Morona, Pastaza, Napo,* and *Putumayo,* after four of the great affluents of the Upper Río Amazonas.

The arrival of the flotilla of gunboats, followed by the establishment of a naval base, furnished the impetus for the impressive growth of Iquitos. From a handful of palm huts in 1864, Iquitos had grown to a cosmopolitan city of forty thousand by 1906, famed as the most bustling river port of the nation, the Pearl of the Amazon. In 1868, the littoral Province of Loreto was raised to the category of a department, on a par with the other departments of Peru, the equivalent of our states. In 1897, the increasing importance of Iquitos as the gathering and distributing point for the booming wild rubber industry was evidenced by a law transferring the capital of Loreto from the ancient colonial city of Moyobamba, high in the Andes, to Iquitos, the adolescent jungle metropolis in the lowlands.

As a consequence of the foresight and energy of the Peruvian Government and the stimulating effects of the rubber boom, Peru assured herself of the strongest talking point in any international boundary dispute—that of possession. In addition, Peru set about lashing her marooned Amazonian colony to her centers of population in old Peru—to the Andes and to the coast. In 1908, Iquitos and Lima were joined over jungle plain and mountain wall by wireless telegraph. Upon the completion of the Panama Canal, in 1914, Peruvian ships ran scheduled trips between Callao and Iquitos, 7,500 miles apart. In 1928, transportation by airplane between Iquitos and the coast was inaugurated. As a final bond, the Government, in the late thirties, began the construction of a trans-Andean highway to link Lima with Pucallpa, on the Ucayali River.

In contrast, Ecuador was strong only in verbal vehemence. Extreme Ecuadorean claims reached out to embrace even Iquitos and beyond, just as Peruvian maps shoved the green of the *Departamento de Loreto* within sight of the city limits of Quito, the Ecuadorean capital. However boldly Ecuador announced her determination to back her claims with armed might, the fact remained that she was not equipped to fight in her jungle back yard. She had no rock in the Oriente—no Iquitos—to which to tie. She had no ships linking Guayaquil and the Amazon; no air service or roads spanning the mountains and traversing the rain forest. The garrisons that Ecuador planted in the wilderness of the montaña had to be maintained under the most unfavorable conditions. Troops and supplies were forced to descend from the Andean backbone of Ecuador to the Amazonian lowlands over tortuous trails and by canoe and raft on treacherous mountain rivers. What Ecuador's chances for military success were in the coastal sector of the conflict, I cannot say; but in the Oriente, her campaign, by necessity, operated on a shoestring.

The hostilities that broke out between Peru and Ecuador in July, 1941, and lasted into August, took place chiefly along a narrow section of coast line on the southern shore of the Gulf of Guayaquil. Peruvian troops forced a crossing of the frontier formed by the Zarumilla River and invaded the Ecuadorean Province of El Oro. Ecuador, in a desperate attempt to halt the Peruvian drive, rushed munitions from Guayaquil by sea to her southern port of Puerto Bolívar, where they were hurried by rail through the city of Machala to the battlefront. But, by this time, the poorly equipped Ecuadoreans were in full rout. They had no time to stop for supplies as they rushed past the waiting freight cars. The Peruvians moved up and captured the entire supply train intact. Machala and Puerto Bolívar fell to the Peruvians, whose drive northward was then halted by topography—by lack of a land route over the marshy jungle coast separating them from Ecuador's great port of Guayaquil.

The only large-scale engagement along the vast unpeopled Amazon frontier occurred far to the northeast of the Zarumilla frontier, on the Napo River, less than one degree south of the Equator. Here, on August 11, 1941, troops of General Morla's Jungle Division drove three hundred Ecuadoreans from their garrison of Rocafuerte (Strong Rock) into the river, where many drowned in the swift current.

Dot and I, in January, 1944, flew from Iquitos to the Roca-fuerte battleground with the Military Attaché for Air, of the American Embassy in Lima. We were weathered in for three days at this historic spot, which afforded ample time for every Peruvian officer in the garrison to re-fight the battle for our benefit. The Ecuadorean garrison of Rocafuerte was situated on a high bluff dominating the north bank of the Río Napo, at its confluence with the Río Aguarico. About a half mile down river from Rocafuerte, and on the same side of the Napo, Peru had planted her strongest jungle outpost—called Pantoja, gar-risoned by about six hundred soldiers. The two garrisons were separated only by a shallow ravine through which ran a brook no more than a yard wide. Spanning the brook was the *puente internacional*, a roofed foot-bridge. On one side of the interna-tional bridge stood the sentry box of Ecuador; on the other side, within spitting distance, the sentry box of Peru. Set thus, cheek by jowl, in a jungle wilderness, with nothing to do but listen to the patter of the rain, watch the empty Napo slip by, and watch one another, it is amazing that sheer boredom did not precipitate a fight long before August 11, 1941.

Thus, by the end of August, the Peruvians, having won a smashing initial victory on both the coastal and Amazonian fronts, were ready to accept the good offices that streamed along the cableways from a number of the other American republics. A truce was arranged which froze the battlefronts until Peru and Ecuador signed a Protocol of Peace, Friendship, and Fron-tiers on January 29, 1942.

The agreement of peace between the two belligerents came as one of the by-products of the momentous Conference of Foreign Ministers of the American Republics that met at Río de Janeiro in January, 1942, to formulate a policy of Pan-American solidarity in the face of the hulking Axis threat from the west and from the east. The United States, confronted with a long, uphill, two-front war, wanted internal peace and unity in the Americas. Only a united Pan-America could pour its energies and products into the fight for survival. Peru and Ecuador rose to the occasion, and signed a treaty designed to insure peace by establishing between the two countries a definitive frontier line that would eliminate century-old discussions and frictions.

For the work of demarcation, the Protocol divided the boundary into two sections—the shorter western section of the Coastal and Andean area, and the much more extensive eastern or Amazonian section. The western section of the line began on the Gulf of Guayaquil, west of Machala, ran up the Zarumilla River and generally southeastwards through the mountains to the confluence of the Chinchipe River with the San Francisco River, on the eastern slope of the Andes. At this point, the eastern section of the boundary began, running generally northeastwards, cutting across the upper reaches of the northern affluents of the Amazon to where the line ended in the junction of the frontiers of Ecuador, Colombia, and Peru, on the Putumayo River. The Protocol further stipulated that the United States, Argentina, Brazil, and Chile would guarantee the faithful execution of the Protocol.

Finally, the Protocol provided that, in the actual survey of the boundary line, Peru and Ecuador were to grant "such reciprocal concessions as may be considered convenient for the purpose of adjusting the frontier line to geographic realities" and that "such rectifications should be effected with the collaboration" of the four mediating countries.

The Protocol of Río de Janeiro was a clear victory for Peru. It assured Peru of the integrity, under her flag, of her western provinces of Tumbes, Jaen, and Maynas. It also finally established the sovereignty of Peru in Amazonia—over the Amazon River, the Marañón River, and all their northern and southern affluents—in belated fulfillment, proclaimed the Peruvian Government, of the stipulations of the King of Spain's Royal Decree of 1802.

In accordance with the Protocol, Peru and Ecuador appointed a Mixed Boundary Demarcation Commission, consisting of representatives of each country, and divided into two parties, one to work in the western section of the boundary and the other in the eastern section. The demarcation work in the western section progressed rapidly because of its much shorter extent and easier accessibility. The demarcation of the eastern section, however, entailed the survey of approximately five hundred miles of the most remote, inaccessible, unexplored terrain in the world. A mere glance at the map will give one an idea of how vast and arduous was the undertaking.

Iquitos was the headquarters for the eastern section of the Boundary Commission, where results of field work were studied and discussed before being forwarded to the respective ministries of foreign relations in Lima and Quito.

The Peruvian delegation to the Commission was made up exclusively of officers of the Peruvian Navy, all men of high professional calibre. The President of the delegation was Capitán Barandiarán, who had made a distinguished record as an instructor at the *Escuela Naval*, at La Punta, Peru's Annapolis. Capitán Barandiarán did not live to see the completion of the survey, however. A wound on his foot became infected. The infection spread, other complications developed, and the captain died in March of 1944. Don Carlos Echecopar was appointed the new President of the Peruvian delegation upon the death of Capitán Barandiarán.

Ecuador's delegation was headed by Doctor Luis Tufiño, a rotund, mild-mannered civilian. Dr. Tufiño would enter the Vice Consulate, mopping his face and neck with a handkerchief. Sinking into a chair, he would express the hope that the demarcation would hurry to a conclusion. He longed to escape from the enervating heat of the Peruvian lowlands and return to the brisk delight of nine-thousand-foot Quito, where the temperature averages fifty-four degrees Fahrenheit the year round.

One section of the Protocol requires that the boundary line run in a straight line from the confluence of the Río Bobonaza with the Río Pastazo to the confluence of the Río Cunambo with the Río Pintoyacu, which together form the Río Tigre. The distance between these two points, as the crow flies, is about fifty miles. The boundary commission decided to hack a trocha or trail, studded at frequent intervals with stone surveyor's monuments, along this section of the boundary line. The assignment took eight exhausting, hungry, disease-ridden months to complete.

On my way to Lima to keep my big date with Dot, I travelled with Lieutenant (j. g.) Antonio Bustamante, of the Peruvian Boundary Commission. Antonio had sweated out the entire Pastaza-Tigre trocha and was on his way to Lima for a breather. He was gaunt from malnutrition, over-exertion, and malaria; his skin was as yellow as a pigskin glove. Antonio was one patriotic Peruvian who got a good look at what his country and Ecuador had been fighting over for a century, and he came away wondering *why.* "There was nothing but solitude," Antonio told me, his large brown eyes squeezed forward in his drawn face, "nothing but dense vegetation shutting out the sun so that your sweat was always clammy. There were no people there, not even wild Indians, no food, few animals, and many insects." The Boundary Commission decided to hew no more boulevards along the boundary. Instead, the field parties ascended the principal rivers and placed markers at the points where the rivers cut the boundary line.

14

$\mathcal{T}$ HE Río de Janeiro Protocol placed definite obligations upon the United States to assist in bringing the demarcation of the Peru-Ecuador boundary to a successful conclusion. Accordingly, the Department of State appointed the geographer, Dr. George M. McBride, who had won distinction by his studies of the land systems of Mexico and Chile, as United States technical advisor to the Peru-Ecuador Boundary Commission. Dr. McBride was so busy shuttling between Lima and Quito that he had no time to make a personal check on developments beyond the hill. It was, therefore, up to the American Vice Consul in Iquitos to keep his eyes open for thunderheads over the jungle.

Bag-Ears, the Demarcating Duck

Mr. Hull facilitated the mapping of the boundary by offering Peru and Ecuador the assistance of the United States Army Air Corps. Early one afternoon, Joaquín, who kept a careful tab on all aircraft that appeared over the city, called me to the balcony of the Vice Consulate. A plane approached from the direction of the Andes. It was a stranger—a clip-winged, thick-set Grumman Widgeon, like LAN's two, but painted orange and black, with white stripes.

An hour later, the Gran Hotel Malecón Palace was jammed with a detachment of the Second Photo Charting Squadron of the United States Army Air Corps, consisting of seven enlisted men and three officers, under the command of Major Philip C. Doran. Major Doran's orders were to establish twenty points along the eastern section of the Peru-Ecuador border by celestial readings from the ground as the initial step in working up an accurate aerial map of the region. The points were then to be photographed from a plane at a low altitude—around fifteen hundred feet. Finally, these points were to be tied in with high-altitude strip photographs taken at twenty thousand feet. The longitude and latitude readings of Major Doran's ground party, combined with the low-altitude photographs of the points and their immediate surroundings and the broad sweep of the high-altitude photographs would complete the material for the preparation of the final aerial map. Our Government, in return for the liberty afforded our mapping party by Peru and Ecuador, agreed to make the photographs and maps available to these countries to facilitate the demarcation of the boundary line.

The points which Major Doran's party were to establish were located on the upper reaches of six of the great northern tributaries of the Amazon and Marañón rivers. The assignment was no trifling affair. The nearest of the points to be established was approximately 250 airline miles from the base of operations at Iquitos, and the most distant, around 350 miles. The plan was to use the Grumman duck to fly the ground party to the location of the points, or as close as conditions permitted. The Grumman would also take the low-altitude photographs.

Weather was the most formidable obstacle. Clear skies by night and day are required to shoot the stars and to take aerial photographs. Someone in the Pentagon Building must have gotten his weather intelligence scrambled, for the mapping party reached Iquitos in January, at the beginning of the wet season, instead of in July, at the beginning of the dry season. Consequently, the weather became progressively fouler during the entire job. Day after day the duck sat moored to the river bank because of the encompassing mists squatting on the tree tops. Night after night, the key stars were unable to pierce the cloud blanket.

Then Major Doran sent a radiogram to me from a remote Peruvian garrison on the Río Pataza. "Chronometers ruined by weather stop Further work impossible stop Send duck for us," the message read. When the Major reached Iquitos, three days later, he had to wait a week before the RDC Catalina arrived from Lima. Once in Lima, it took him two weeks to locate new chronometers and return to Iquitos. Finally, having travelled seventeen hundred miles and consumed a month to find his new timepieces, Major Doran resumed his work on the Río Pastaza.

A number of the points to be established were not located on the main rivers, but on some narrow, jungle-canopied, serpentine tributaries that afforded no room for the duck to alight. The mapping party entered such tributaries by launch. Two of the main rivers—the Tigre and Morona—looped and twisted so much that the duck could not be used at all.

Major Doran obtained the use of a thirty-six-foot launch belonging to the Forest Service of the Peruvian Department of Agriculture. One morning, I climbed down the embankment in front of the Malecón to the river's edge to see the party off on its trip up the Río Tigre. The launch, painted a forest green, sat low in the muddy water, stuffed with men and provisions. In lieu of a crow's nest, the good ship *Lancha Forestal Número 1* flaunted a chicken coop, made of green slats, lashed to the cabin roof. Legs and feathers of half-stifled pullets poked out between the slats. The gangplank was hauled aboard, and the launch swung out into the swift current. The American Vice Consul waved mournfully from the shore and then reluctantly climbed the embankment to resume his pencil pushing.

In two weeks, the expedition returned, having ascended the Río Tigre for two hundred miles as the crow flies. Everything had gone well for a change. The points were successfully taken. Everyone looked like an intrepid explorer, bearded and bronzed. The green chicken coop was empty, but the cabin roof was piled with stalks of bananas, arranged in a crude corral about a river turtle weighing over a hundred pounds, turned, for safe keeping, on his back. Enviously, I listened to tales of shooting at the ruby eyes of alligators, caught in the probing finger of the launch's searchlight, and of a herd of fifty peccaries surprised in a long chain swimming across the river. These stay-at-home days were the most trying of my consular career. To be planted in the middle of the wild Amazonian jungle, yet not to see it! "An exigency of the Service," Uncle Charlie would say.

Fortunately, these days did not last. I owed my escapes from paper shuffling to Captain Thomas G. Abbey and his spunky duck, Bag-Ears. A marine at eighteen in World War I, and for years a commercial pilot, Tom Abbey, in his early forties, became senior pilot for Major Doran's mapping party. Tom's informality, unfailing courtesy, and kindliness were blended with just the right amount of drive, resourcefulness, and professional skill to win the respect and devotion of every officer and enlisted man in the mapping party.

Although Tom had a complete immunity to Spanish and put across his ideas to Peruvians in pidgin English punctuated with elaborate gestures and winning smiles, he was Uncle Sam's most effective ambassador of good will in the Peruvian Amazon. Tom was no social lion. When in Iquitos, he shyly avoided dances and receptions. He drank only when courtesy required it. It was his amazing skill as a pilot, his demonstrated abundance of corazón, or heart, in ticklish flying conditions, his quiet modesty, his natural, almost Latin courtesy, and his eagerness to help others, that sold Capitán Abbey to the officers of the Peruvian Army in Iquitos.

You have met Tom Abbey. Let me introduce his ship, Bag-Ears. Bag-Ears was the mapping party's only plane, the Grumman Widgeon. It had been acquired from the Gulf Oil Company, for whom I had worked in Venezuela. Gulf's colors had been left unchanged except for the white star on the fuselage. For the first few weeks after the Grumman's arrival, it was referred to simply as "the duck." But one morning, Tom Abbey arrived at the Itaya Base to find "Bag-Ears" painted in large white letters on each side of the plane's snout. Sergeant George Moore, the ship's mechanic, was credited with the inspiration. The two pontoons dangling from the near extremity of either wing resembled a pair of extended ear lobes, especially when the ship was in flight. Bag-Ears, an unlovely name, but just the right one. Tom Abbey and Bag-Ears made flying history in the montaña.

My first expedition with the mapping party in Bag-Ears was a modest one. We flew 250 miles westward from Iquitos, up the Marañón River to the garrison of Barranca, located on a high bluff dominating the river, about midway between the mouths of the Morona and Pastaza rivers. Barranca was used as a field base for the points to be established far up the Río Pastaza. To give Bag-Ears a greater range, I had asked General Morla to ship twenty barrels of aviation gasoline to Barranca on one of the trips of his garrison-provisioning launch, the *Huayna Capac*.

When we emerged from the hatch in Bag-Ears' snout and stepped onto the red clay bank, we were greeted by Lieutenant José Cacho Bernales, who commanded Barranca's fifty soldiers. Teniente Cacho was, beyond all doubt, the most garrulous, lusty extrovert in the Peruvian Army. He shone especially at banquets, where he would not only make a dozen speeches himself, but, when the heavy-tongued United States-er groped for words, Cacho would leap to his feet and make a speech for him. Teniente Cacho hurried down the steps to the landing. His heavy black beard looked all the blacker by contrast to his faded khaki shirt and tattered straw hat. "Hola, Aabbee!" he roared in uninhibited delight, giving Tom Abbey a tremendous bear hug. Releasing Tom from his embrace, he continued, "I insist that you and Señor CONsool accompany me to the *Comandancia*, where I have a bottle of very special aguardiente reserved for the occasion. Ay, what aguardiente!" he exclaimed, kissing his fingertips. "It is *suave*, Señores, smooth like the coo of a dove."

At this point, Abbey had me explain to the disappointed Teniente that he had to leave immediately for Puerto Pardo, on the Río Pastaza, to bring food and equipment to Major Doran. On Abbey's promise that he would be back for the drink as soon as possible, Teniente Cacho furnished several soldiers to help gas up the plane. In a half hour, Abbey was off, accompanied only by Sergeant Moore, so that the ship's load would be as light as possible.

Bag-Ears was gone for twenty-four hours, leaving Co-pilot Lieutenant Art Double and me at the mercy of Teniente Cacho's unbounded hospitality. Ay, what aguardiente! But, Señores, it went down like a blowtorch rather than smoothly like the coo of a dove!

That evening, Art Double and I dined at the Comandancia with Teniente Cacho and his wife. Señora de Cacho was a plump little Limeña and, like all Limeñas, she talked with the rapidity of a machine gun. She kept up such a steady bombardment of chatter that even the Teniente found it difficult to propose more than a dozen toasts during the meal. She told us that life in the garrison was very *triste* after Lima. In all the eight months that she had been in Barranca, she had hardly put a foot outside the Comandancia. "Why go out in the sun?" she said. "There is nothing to do in the sun but perspire."

Each moment his wife stopped for breath, Cacho would quickly raise his wineglass, nod his head to each of us, and explode with "SALOOD, Señor CONsool; SaLOOD, Teniente DOObleh!" Art and I returned fire, saluding with becoming alacrity for the first few courses. Towards the end of the meal, however, I am afraid that our toasting and acknowledgments of toasting lacked some of the spark demanded by protocol. Between goblet liftings of aguardiente, pisco, sauterne, and hot Lima beer we bolted a bewildering number of variations on the starch theme. A barefooted private first served rice gruel, followed by boiled chicken and boiled rice, fried rice patties, beans, and fried yuca. The pièce de résistance was a tin of paté de foie gras, the last of a stock of delicacies that Señora de Cacho had brought with her from Lima.

Fortunately for Art and me, Teniente Cacho's liquor supply gave out at the yuca course. Our host then turned his abounding energy to his pets. Although we ate in the half light of a single candle and a sooty kerosene lamp, Teniente Cacho would reach unerringly about the room and return to the table with a new pet on every trip. He first produced a monkey and a land tortoise. Then came a procession of parrots, from vest pocket parakeets to macaws. He held the smaller parrots up to his mouth and let them extract bits of rice from between his lips. One by one, he placed them on his shoulders and head, from where they hopped to the table, striding cross-footed from plate to plate, sampling food and tracking paté and rice grains all about.

After the parrots, we were introduced to a motley gang of domestic cats. Teniente Cacho felt each cat carefully as would an army doctor examining an inductee for sound limbs. "They are still too thin," he announced professionally. "It will be another month before they are ready." "Ready for what?" I queried. "To eat, of course," announced Teniente Cacho. "Why, Señor CONsool, have you never tasted *gato al horno?* Roasted just so, with a flavoring of red wine and ringed with baked bananas? *Bien sabroso,* Señor CONsool, most tasty!" he exclaimed, kissing his fingertips.

"It is so Señores," Señora de Cacho hastened to assure us.
"My husband is an excellent cook and a recognized gourmet.
Beef and pork are so scarce here that we must look for substitutes. But far better than gato al horno is a roast *majás* stuffed
with rice." *"Eso, sí!"* agreed Teniente Cacho. "It was stupid of
me to forget the majás. With your permission," he said, rising
from the table, "I will get him." Teniente Cacho dived under a
bench in the far corner of the room. Out of the shadows came
complaints from the majás, the scratching of claws on the board
floor, followed by a curse from Teniente Cacho. He approached
the table sucking his injured finger and carrying the squirming
majás by the scruff of the neck. "It is time we ate the majás.
He has become surly." The majás, one of Amazonia's many
rodents, was about the size and shape of a dachshund, except
that its ears were small and its coat reddish and spotted with
gray, like a fawn's. "Tomorrow evening, Señores, we will eat
the majás," announced Teniente Cacho. "You cannot imagine
how savoury is the flesh of the majás."

Having wined and dined and met all the birds and beasts,
Art and I groped our way by candlelight up the narrow stairs of
the Comandancia to our sleeping quarters. We slipped under
our mosquito bars and fell into a troubled sleep. Our nightmares were almost identical. I dreamed that I was lying on a
huge pile of steaming rice, my flesh roasted to a crackling brown,
a banana in my mouth, while all about sat solemn cats licking
their whiskers and periodically raising their glasses on high and
crying "Salud, Señor CONsool!"

I was awakened while it was still dark by a squadron of
mosquitoes peeling off above my head and making power dives
onto my face. In my thrashings, I had pulled the netting up,
leaving a large aperture. I then became aware that mosquitoes
weren't my only trouble. My bladder ached with Teniente
Cacho's wine cellar. What to do? The nearest "chicago" was
an outhouse, fifty yards from the Comandancia. Getting there
would entail stumbling down the creaky stairs to the living room,
awakening the Comandante and his wife, not to mention the

monkey, the parrots, the cats, and the majás. "Chicago" was out of the question. I stepped out on the porch. The bright moon revealed the tempting convenience of the open railing and the sloping tin roof covering the downstairs porch.

In the morning, on my way downstairs, I was confronted with a sign nailed to the porch railing. The sign read: *Favor de no orinar en el techo,* and was signed by José Cacho Bernales, Comandante. Evidently, the Veesay CONsool Norteamericano was not the first guest to inundate the Comandante's roof. The object of the sign, I discovered, was to preserve the purity of the Comandancia's water supply, which drained off the roof into a series of gasoline drums.

Art Double and I were denied the experience of eating majás al horno stuffed with rice, for, about noon, Bag-Ears suddenly roared over Barranca, buzzing the Comandancia so intimately that Teniente Cacho dashed from the building, thinking the roof had been swept away. All was well with Major Doran up the Pastaza; another week would complete the work there. We were to return to Iquitos as soon as the ship was gassed.

Teniente Cacho had not been idle that morning. He had radioed Iquitos for permission to proceed to the metropolis with Abbey. He and his wife had not been away from the garrison for eight months. The presence of Bag-Ears was an opportunity not to be missed. The trip by Casa Kahn's river steamer *Huallaga,* that stopped at Barranca once a month to trade, consumed a week. Bag-Ears could whisk them to the wonders of Iquitos in two hours. The Cachos were dressed for the occasion. The Teniente was clean-shaven and smartly attired in a clean uniform and well-polished, knee-high lace boots. His Señora, who, we were surprised to learn, was the sister-in-law of author-cosmopolite Carleton Beals, climbed aboard in a flowered silk dress, white platform shoes, and bag to match.

Two hours later, as our taxi rattled down Jirón Lima, from the Itaya Base towards the Plaza de Armas, I realized for the first time what Iquitos was. It takes a visit to Barranca or to any primitive hamlet along the rivers of Loreto to bring home the magic of Iquitos. To the Loretano of the jungle, Iquitos, in spite of its open sewers and roving livestock, is, in fact, the Pearl of the Amazon, the Paris, New York, and Río de Janeiro of his world. An adaptation of my father's traditional dictum, pronounced every time we New Mexicans visited New York, applies with more vivid significance to Iquitos: "Until you hit Iquitos, you are camping out."

A month later, I again flew with Abbey in Bag-Ears. This trip was more extensive and gave me an understanding of one of the knottiest problems confronting the Peru-Ecuador Mixed Boundary Demarcation Commission. The trip was an exploratory one, with the purpose of locating the sites of two points on the Santiago River, preparatory to Major Doran moving his ground party into that inaccessible region.

The Río Santiago flows parallel to the Río Morona in a north-south direction entering the Marañón some eighty beeline miles west of Barranca. It is difficult of access from the east because its confluence with the Marañón is about ten miles above the limit of steam navigation on the Marañón. Forming the watershed between the Morona and Santiago rivers, and extending south of the Río Marañón, is the Sierra Campánquiz, a heavily-timbered mountain range rising about three thousand feet above the flat rain forest to the east. The mighty Marañón at this point cuts through the Sierra Campánquiz in a seven-mile gorge called the Pongo de Manseriche. Once through the *pongo*, the Marañón, like the fabled River Xanadu, abandons for good its "caverns measureless to man" for the unrestraining immensity of the near-sea-level jungle plain.

At the down-river terminus of the pongo is located the important garrison of Borja, upon which a number of subsidiary garrisons in the mountainous country west of the pongo depend for re-enforcements and supplies. Commercial river steamers and the supply steamers of the Jungle Division go no farther upstream than Borja. The pongo is passable only by canoe, balsa raft, and small open boats. At all times, the passage is dangerous. The low water of summer exposes treacherous rocks. Winter's redoubled volume of water increases the speed of the current and the treachery of waves and whirlpools. To insure communication with up-river garrisons when the pongo is too dangerous to navigate, a foot trail was built from Borja along the northern slope of the gorge to the subsidiary garrison of Pinglo, located at the mouth of the Río Santiago. Arriving in Borja, Abbey set Bag-Ears expertly down in the swift current and nosed her with an easy jolt into the embankment. We walked to the Comandancia over a path paved with rounded river stones. We, of stoneless Iquitos, were impressed by the abundance of stones—loose stones lying about the ground and limestone outcroppings in the ridge behind the garrison.

We stayed in Borja just long enough to borrow three soldiers. We planned to leave them at one of the point sights on the Río Santiago to make a clearing for Major Doran and his party. The soldiers—a corporal with shoes, and two barefooted privates —came aboard with their Mausers, machetes, and enough fariña flour for five days. It was their first flight. I watched them as Abbey gunned the ship over the choppy waters and rose into the air. Their stolid aborigine faces betrayed no emotion. Nonchalantly, they were by-passing centuries of painful evolution in human transportation. In a flash they had been whisked from earthbound pre-Egyptian times to twentieth century travel by air. They skipped the horse, wheel, sail, steamship, steam locomotive, and automobile.

Our first point, about fifteen miles up the Río Santiago from its confluence with the Marañón, was a mere hedge-hop from Borja. We breezed through the pongo at fifteen hundred feet, about midway between the water and ridge tops on either side. We were not too high to make out the etched confusion of the waters—the swirls, the eddies, the whirlpools, the cross currents. Now and then, we picked out the trunk of a giant tree plunging along through the current-patterns, its branches and roots projecting grotesquely from the muddy waters. All this we saw in a few brief minutes, and then we passed from the gorge into a broad inter-mountain valley, where the waters of the Río Santiago, pouring into those of the Marañón, produced such a flood behind the bottleneck of the pongo that the waters backed up and spread out, forming a huge lake as placid as a millpond.

I never had the opportunity of shooting the Pongo de Manseriche, although I would have given a great deal to have done so. I have a first-hand account, however, from Captain Robert E. Hervey, formerly Military Attaché for Air of the American Embassy at Lima, who travelled from Pinglo to Borja on a balsa-log raft. Bob had flown over from Lima to make an inspection of the garrisons under General Morla's command. He visited Borja and decided to hike by trocha from Borja to Pinglo. The eleven-kilometer tramp took Bob and his crew five sweating hours to complete. The prospect of repeating this ordeal on the return to Borja was so grim that the party voted to risk the pongo. The soldiers at Pinglo lashed together twenty-five balsa logs with lianas, equipped the raft with a rudder-oar, and a platform raised a couple of feet off the logs for the eight passengers and duffle.

The following morning the balsa was towed by a dugout canoe through the millpond until the clumsy raft was sucked with increasing speed into the bottleneck. The precipitous, matted walls of the canyon seemed to rush to a juncture as the raft churned deeper into the gorge. The stocky rudder man, stripped down to his shorts, tensed as the raft rushed towards a spot where the waters boiled with particular fury. Working his ungainly boom oar feverishly, he attempted to skirt the rough spot. The raft did not respond. It struck the three-foot breakers, drenching everyone to the waist, and passed through them into a huge swirling *remolino* or whirlpool. The balsa pivoted sharply around and creaked with the strain. Several of the lianas parted, but the raft held together and passed to safety beyond the whirlpool. The trip that had taken five tedious hours by trail, they completed in one hour by raft! Less fortunate voyagers have spent many hours trapped in some gigantic vortex of the Marañón, spinning around and around.

Once through the pongo, Abbey headed Bag-Ears northwards

up the Río Santiago. Spotting a clearing and a house near our point site, Abbey set the ship down in the center of the swift mountain river. He did not attempt to edge into the bank. Sergeant Moore threw out the anchor. The cable stretched taut. Bag-Ears pivoted and hauled like a bronc snubbed to a post. Repeatedly, the anchor lost its grip on the bottom and sent Bag-Ears slipping downstream tail first in spasmodic jerks. Then, the anchor caught firmly.

Finally, the help we needed appeared from the farmhouse. A canoe came alongside and took the three soldiers aboard from the starboard hatch. Our hands were bleeding before we broke the anchor's grip on the bottom.

Abbey put the spurs to Bag-Ears, and we crow-hopped over the chop to a laborious take-off. We ascended the river for approximately seventy-five miles until the Santiago bent westward in a right-angled turn. Here, we spotted Cahuide, one of the most remote of Peru's garrisons, built on a bluff where the Santiago bends and where the Río Yaupi comes in from the north. Abbey circled and dropped for an acuatizaje. The choppy water looked ominous. Instinctively, we braced ourselves for the shock. There were a series of rough jolts as the ship's bottom slapped the water, bounced into the air, and slapped again and again like a flat stone skipping across a pond. Cameras, knapsacks, and empty gasoline tins hurtled around inside the fuselage like ice in a cocktail shaker. I had a feeling that we were going to nose over and would be trapped inside, but the fuselage settled into the water, and we dragged to a safe stop.

Cahuide, probably the Jungle Division's newest garrison, was established in 1941, at the time of the conflict with Ecuador. As we climbed the path to the garrison, we were struck by the stimulating upland feel of the air, so welcome after the oppressiveness of the tierra caliente. Here, at about one thousand feet above sea level, there were no mosquitoes. Cahuide was pushed into the borderland as far as the terms of the Río Protocol would allow; in fact, the garrison was planted right on the intended boundary. On the Ecuadorean side, there was only jungle.

There is something thrilling about an international boundary line; about looking across into the territory of another nation. At Cahuide, isolation intensifies the thrill. You are on a frontier rather than a boundary line. There is nothing to indicate that two sovereign countries at this point come together. The matted hills and the unharnessed river seem to be a law unto themselves.

The most serious disagreement that arose between the Peruvian and Ecuadorean delegations of the Boundary Commission was over the demarcation of the boundary line between the Chinchipe-San Francisco point and the confluence of the Río Santiago with the Río Yaupi. This disagreement was the result of insufficient knowledge of the territory on the part of the statesmen who drafted the Río Protocol, and was finally settled by aerial photographs of the region taken by the A-29 photo reconnaissance planes based at Talara. These were the same planes that took the high-elevation strip photographs of the entire boundary area to complement the work of Major Doran's ground party.

The A-29s were also sent into the field during the rainy season. The Iquitos field was still just as much of a cow pasture as it had been in 1922 when Faucett's *Oriole* struck a chuck hole and shattered its propeller. The RDC was still awaiting the arrival of equipment and had not begun the rebuilding of the field into an all-weather landing strip. After several near crashes on the slithery, mushy death trap, Iquitos was abandoned as a base for the high-elevation photography, and all flights were made from Talara. Even though the non-aquatic A-29s arrived no more in Iquitos to wrack my nerves, their prop-wash blew into my office from three hundred miles away. One morning, General Morla, who occupied the apartment adjoining the Vice Consulate, entered the office. His usually enigmatic face showed a trace of irritation as he seated himself. "Kehlee, the military planes of your country based at Talara have been causing me some embarrassment," the General began with un-Latin directness. "As you realize, my command extends westward into the

Andes. Recently, I have received radio reports from several of my garrisons along the border with Ecuador of the appearance of unidentified airplanes. My commanders naturally request instructions as to what attitude they should adopt toward these planes. You can appreciate, Kehlee," continued the General, "that the situation is awkward. I am forced to assume that the planes are those of your photographic squadron from Talara, and on the basis of this assumption, I inform my garrisons that the planes are friendly and that an attitude of passivity should be adopted. But what if those friendly photographic planes should turn out to be Japanese bombers? What then, amigo Kehlee—when my garrisons are caught off-guard in an attitude of passivity?"

I assured the General that his point was well made—very well made. I had never seen anything more powerful in those remote garrisons than Mauser rifles and .30 calibre machine guns. But speculation as to whether a handful of foot soldiers in a jungle clearing wouldn't be better off by adopting an attitude of passivity rather than one of militant aggressiveness, when confronted by high-flying bombers, was beside the point. General Morla had a valid complaint, and there was no reason why the American commander of the Talara base shouldn't make use of an idle American corporal who had been installed in the Malecón Palace with a radio set for the purpose of assisting planes landing at Iquitos. It would be a simple matter for Talara to radio Corporal Klunk of the departure of every photo-charting mission likely to poke its nose over the hill into General Morla's bailiwick. I forwarded the General's request to the American Military Attaché at the Embassy in Lima and directly to the Commander at Talara.

Evidently, the solution to the problem was not so simple as we had thought, for the unheralded planes continued to violate the command of the Jungle Division. A couple of months passed. The situation became as embarrassing for me as for General Morla. One morning, after I had given up hope of any co-operation from coastal Peru, Corporal Klunk appeared at the office wearing a triumphant smile. "The message from Talara," he said, handing me a slip of paper. I read it with as much awe as if it were a top secret advice of the D-Day invasion. Gleefully, I rushed Joaquín, at a high lope, off to the Comandancia with a letter advising General Morla that three A-29s had departed from Talara at eight o'clock that morning to photograph the Santiago-Zamora watershed. The letter so placated General Morla that he suggested I forego transmitting the information by official consular communication. "It will be sufficient," he pleasantly conceded, "that the Corporal place an informal pencilled note under the door of my apartment."

15

$\mathcal{E}$ ARLY ONE morning towards the end of May, Bag-Ears rose off the river, circled to the west, and headed for the invisible Andes. For several minutes, the rising sun spotlighted the ship's orange hide and made it shine until distance extinguished the light. Aboard were Tom Abbey, Major Doran, and the last of the mapping party. It was not pleasant to see them go. That speck on the horizon spelled for me an end to five months of cherished companionship and rare adventure. All that was left in Iquitos of the Second Photo Charting Squadron were memories, and Corporal Klunk sitting disconsolately by his silent radio on the third floor of the Gran Hotel Malecón Palace.

The Voice from the Clay

A month later, the vigilance of Corporal Klunk was rewarded. A long-awaited B-34 was coming in from Talara, en route to Manaos, Brazil, piloted by Major Payne, Second Mapping's top kick from squadron headquarters in Laredo, Texas.

The B-34 offered even more. To my surprise and delight, Tom Abbey climbed out of the ship on the heels of Major Payne. He brought news of the old crowd. Tom himself had graduated to B-34's and was to direct the operation of the squadron's photographic planes in Brazil. Bag-Ears had been turned over to Art Double and was scheduled for work in the Brazilian jungle.

The last time I saw Tom Abbey alive was about two months later, early in September and shortly after Dot and I had reached Iquitos. Tom sat his B-34 nonchalantly down on the now dry Bergieri field. A few minutes later, Art Double skimmed Bag-Ears over the surface of the Amazon and taxied up the Itaya. Both Tom and Art had been to the States. Art had taken Bag-Ears to receive a new brace of engines for the Brazilian venture. He left the plane in the shops and dashed for home, arriving just in time to rush his wife to the hospital for the birth of their first baby. Tom's furlough miscarried. Instead of two weeks with his wife he had barely twenty-four hours when a telegram ordered him back to the jungle.

In celebration, Tom, Art, Dot, and I had dinner at Don Martín's. The dinner was nice. Don Martín went to special pains to make it so. He brought out from hiding some of his fine cut crystal in which to serve the wine. The roast chicken was excellent, and for dessert we passed up the usual bananas and guava preserves for a can of freestone peaches that Don Martín must have saved for months. And—the rarest of all tributes from

189

Don Martín—there was not a cat to be seen during the whole meal, not even his favorite brindle with the ulcerated belly.

As we lingered over the peaches, Tom dropped the chit chat. "I'm worried about Major Payne," he confided. "Klunk received word that he left Manaos early this morning in his B-34 on a non-stop flight to Cali, Colombia. An hour ago, Cali still had no report from him. It must be about thirteen hundred miles, with no place to sit down; and Payne has to cross both the eastern and central cordilleras before he reaches the Cauca Valley, where he can land. Even if the weather is good the whole way, he won't have more than thirty minutes of gas left when he hits Cali. If he's delayed by a front over the mountains, there's no telling." Tom reached for a toothpick. "Well," he said, "we'll see what news we get tomorrow."

Dot and I went to the movies after the dinner. Tom and Art set off for the Malecón Palace and an early bed. We lent them our bicycles and watched the two aviators pedal uncertainly down the dimly lighted street. As they wobbled under the street lamp at the corner Tom looked back at us and yelled, "Hey, this crate of yours is too temperamental. Give me back my B-34." The cyclists disappeared around the corner.

The following morning, Dot and I were still in bed when we heard the roar of Abbey's plane. At the office, Corporal Klunk told me that no word had been heard from Major Payne and that Abbey had taken off for Manaos to see what he could learn.

It was midday, September 6, 1943, the day after Abbey's departure for Manaos. Dot and I were eating lunch at Tacu Tacu when the telephone rang. It was Thomas Parsons, the Booth Steamship agent. Mr. Parsons' voice was strained. "I say, I just heard that an American bomber crashed a few minutes ago on the Bergieri field! My foreman just came with the news. I had sent him to the field with gasoline . . ."

I pedaled like mad down Punchana Road, through the Plaza de Armas, past the Central Market. As I approached the field, I saw with relief that it was empty. But beyond the far end of the runway, out from the scrub forest, rose a thick pillar of smoke. The pillar stood straight, black, and ominous in the still, blue air. I tried to reason away that dread plume. Parsons must be wrong, I thought. What American bomber could it be? Abbey's was the last one here, and I would have heard his drone had he returned from Manaos. Someone must be burning brush. I looked again at the black pillar, and I knew that it was not burning brush.

The road I followed paralleled the airfield and ended at the Regatta Club, on Moronacocha. I abandoned my bike and hurried through several hundred yards of scrub jungle towards the base of the smoke column. I emerged from the scrub into a nightmare clearing. It was not a natural clearing. It was one blasted out of the jungle by a terrible impact and explosion. At one moment, there had been trees, shrubs, and grass; at the next, there was a charred arena fifty yards across, ringed with a low broken wall of flames eating outwards. On the periphery of the clearing and inside, poking about in charred, smoking, twisted piles of debris, were perhaps fifty people, mostly Peruvian soldiers. Among the crowd, I picked out Art Double, Art's co-pilot, and Corporal Klunk. Art's eyes were dull with shock. "Abbey?" I asked him. Art nodded his head.

I didn't want to ask any more questions. One look at Art's face made the questions stick in my throat. Questions, the mere sound of one's voice, were not in order in that place. The horrible visual testimony was strewn all about. Yet, I had to ask questions. The Embassy would require the ship's number, the names of the dead, the names of the survivors, if any. After the telegraphic advice, the Embassy would want a full report. I had to ask questions.

Art told his story in a flat emotionless voice. "Abbey slipped into the field about 11:00 this morning from Manaos. He came in so low and quietly that, if he hadn't radioed Klunk, we might never have heard him arrive. He arranged for gasoline to be hauled to the field. Major Payne was still missing, Tom said, and he was going to look for him. He had a hunch that the Major had run into trouble in the mountains southeast of Cali. Abbey gassed the ship up full—every drop she could take. There were seven aboard. The ship was very heavy. The runway was rough and short, but Abbey figured he could make it. After all, he had done it before."

"When Abbey started down the runway," Art continued in the same expressionless voice, "I remember I looked at my watch. It was 12:30. The plane seemed to drag to the left. Its wheels were still on the ground far down the runway. Then the plane hit a bad bump and left the ground. Abbey didn't have enough forward speed. In another hundred yards, his left wheel struck the ground. The jungle was ahead. There was no more room. Abbey lifted the nose to avoid the trees. The ship climbed several hundred feet into the air and then stalled off on the port wing. We saw it dive into the trees beyond the runway. There was an explosion, flames, and smoke. We started to run towards the spot. There was another explosion before we got there. I think they're all dead except a corporal who was thrown clear when the ship crashed. They took him to Santa Rosa Hospital. Don't know how bad off he is."

The next three hours were a grisly nightmare. One by one, the six broken, carbonized bodies were exhumed from the wreckage. Identification was difficult. The bodies had not only been burnt to a cinder by the flaming gasoline, but most of the victims suffered skull fractures so severe that only part of the head remained. We found a few blackened dog tags loose in the debris, but none in direct association with the bodies. Identification was positive only in the case of the flight surgeon, whose watch, bearing his name, still encircled his wrist. With Abbey and the co-pilot, we were reasonably sure. The balance, we identified as best we could by elimination.

Iquitos offered no embalming facilities. The climate dictated a twenty-four-hour burial law. General Morla instructed Lieutenant-Colonel Gómez, his Chief of Staff, to render the dead soldiers full military honors. The bodies were to lie in state in the Casino Militar until the funeral the following day. The General had reached the scene of the crash a few minutes after I did.

When I told him that it was Abbey, his usually inscrutable face betrayed emotion. "Abbey!" he said. "What a terrible thing!"

It was my job, however, to arrange for the caskets, the black-rimmed death and funeral announcement cards, the flowers, the transportation to the cemetery, the burial plot, and a thousand and one details. I accomplished the job only because all of Iquitos rallied to my assistance.

Charapa Bardales, so called because his wrinkled, leathery neck resembled that of the river turtle, ran an undertaker's establishment in the rear of his secondhand furniture store. The shingle over the entrance advertising the store was not too reassuring. It read: *modus vivendi*. Once inside, however, Señor Bardales assured me that he would do everything possible to furnish six caskets plus six metal casket linings by evening. "The casket linings will be the most difficult to obtain," he said. "Sheet metal is very scarce, Señor CONsool." The Charapa was as good as his word. By dusk, the six caskets draped with one large American flag were resting in state under a military guard of honor in the main ballroom of the Casino Militar.

There were no commercial florists in the city. Garden flowers grew reluctantly in the hardpan clay. The cost of importing flowers from Lima, the nearest flower market, was prohibitive. The Drewry's, living out at the Loretana sawmill, were the only people in town with a garden worthy of the name. Even the climbing mauve-red bougainvilla, an almost universal appurtenance of whitewashed walls in a thousand Spanish-American cities, was rarely seen in Iquitos. Small pink roses, bound in tight bouquets or woven into wreaths were the only flowers available in sufficient quantity for commercial purposes. Paper flowers were used often in lieu of real ones. In spite of the difficulty in obtaining flowers, an impressive number of floral offerings were sent by the officials and private citizens of the city. Hundreds of personal cards poured into the Vice Consulate—cards bearing the single word, *Pésame*, [condolence].

The funeral was held in the afternoon of the day following the crash. I was told afterwards by many old-time residents that

Iquitos had never before honored its dead with such a solemn, impressive farewell. It is true that the crash was Loreto's biggest and most sensational aerial disaster. It is true that many of the spectators jamming the sidewalks of the Plaza de Armas were drawn primarily by curiosity. That would be true in any community. But overshadowing this was a feeling of genuine community sorrow. The Peruvians of Iquitos and the Norteamericanos of Iquitos were drawn close together in the tragedy.

The caskets of the three American officers—Tom Abbey, his co-pilot, and the flight surgeon—were carried on the shoulders of their Peruvian peers from the Casino to a small truck draped in black. They were arranged side by side and covered with an American flag and a number of wreaths. On the second truck were placed the caskets of the three sergeants, borne on the shoulders of three sergeants of the Jungle Division. Drawn up at attention in front of the Casino were three companies of the Twenty-Fifth Infantry Battalion of the Jungle Division, the drum and bugle corps, a detachment from the Itaya aviation squadron, in gleaming white uniforms, carrying bayoneted rifles, and a detachment of naval personnel from the gunboat flotilla.

At the cemetery, a simple funeral service in English was conducted by two American Protestant missionaries residing in Iquitos. A Requiem Mass for the Catholic crash victims had been said that morning in the main church on the Plaza de Armas. Taps sounded. A plane from the Itaya Base flew low over the crowd and dropped a bouquet—the final tribute from the men of the Peruvian Air Corps to their brothers of the American Air Corps who had died in the line of duty. The niches were sealed. The crowd moved away. Captain Thomas Abbey and his crew—Captain Robert C. Badertscher, Lieutenant Willard F. Starns, Sergeant Earl E. Duff, Sergeant Donald M. Joyce, and Sergeant Eugene H. Walters—rested among real friends.

The group funeral was followed four days later by that of Corporal Lucien H. Rettstatt, the sole survivor of the crash. Everything possible, within the limited facilities of the Santa

Rosa Hospital, was done to save Rettstatt, who suffered from general burns and a severe concussion of the head. Doctor Fischer, of the Health and Sanitation Mission, and a Peruvian Army doctor did their best. Blood plasma was flown in from Manaos. There was talk of flying the injured lad to Lima by Catalina, but the plan was abandoned when the doctors agreed that it would be more dangerous to subject him to that arduous flight than to keep him in Iquitos.

Had it not been for the heroism of two Peruvian lieutenants, Rettstatt would have burned to death with the others. A small artillery barracks was located towards the upper end of the Bergieri field. The two officers and a number of enlisted men of the barracks watched the abortive take-off. As soon as the crash occurred, they started at a run towards the spot. The two officers were the first to arrive on the scene, several minutes before the arrival of Art Double and the other American soldiers. One gas tank had exploded with the impact of the ship, and the flames in the center of the blasted area were still mountainous. Low flames of burning grass ringed the circle. Strewn between the ring of flame and the roaring inferno in the center, they noticed several bodies that had been thrown clear of the wreckage when the bomber broke up. One of the bodies moved and groaned. It was Corporal Rettstatt. The officers rushed through the flaming ring into the charred area, seized the corporal, and dragged him to safety. Hardly had they reached the edge of the clearing when the second gas tank exploded, filling the whole arena with liquid fire. Had the Peruvians reached the corporal a few seconds later, they would have been carbonized along with him.

In those early September days, there was no rest. Between the two funerals, Manuel Prado, President of Peru, arrived in Iquitos. The visit was of tremendous significance, for it dramatically spotlighted the beginning of the end of the isolation of Peruvian Amazonia from the rest of the nation. From the birth of the Peruvian Republic in 1821 until that day in 1943, no President of Peru had crossed the Andes to set foot in the montaña. Manuel Prado's arrival at Peru's great backdoor port, by gunboat, after inaugurating the Pucallpa Road, was the most exciting event in the history of Loreto.

Just imagine if all the presidents of the United States from Washington down to the present time had never ventured west of the Appalachian Mountains! Then, one fine day, the innovator, Franklin Roosevelt, crossed the mountains and trekked through the great *Wild West* to the backdoor port of San Francisco. What a fuss there'd be!

Innovator Manuel Prado was in and out of Iquitos for four days. He was a man of iron. Every minute of his stay was crammed with activity. He made speeches, watched school children parade, reviewed the flower of the Jungle Division, flew to various frontier garrisons, went to church, attended banquets, danced the waltz criollo and the samba, was crushed by delirious mobs, and hugged and was hugged by hundreds of Loretanos, exalted and humble alike, including yours truly, the American Vice Consul, and Antonia, the American Vice Consul's cook. Antonia was thereafter known in Punchana as *La Abrazada,* the embraced one.

In this dizzy welter of rushings about, President Prado found the time to send his aide-de-camp, Major Mario Saona, to represent him at the funeral of Corporal Lucien Rettstatt, and, later, the President personally laid a wreath on the graves of the American aviators.

One of the final acts of President Prado's visit was the inauguration of the work on the Rubber Development Corporation's all-weather, 6,000-foot airfield. The infamous, death-dealing Bergieri field was to be worked over, surfaced and extended into an airfield that would offer a safe landing to all types of planes in all kinds of weather. RDC's airfield construction personnel had been stewing in idleness in Iquitos for eight months for lack of bulldozers and other earth-moving equipment. At last, the equipment had arrived.

The ceremony of inauguration was simple. Francis Truslow, RDC chief in Peru, made a speech, and Señor Prado made one in reply. Then the obliging President climbed aboard a huge bulldozer, and, assisted by Brooky Brookshire, had a whale of a good time shoving about tons of red earth and mowing down the scrub forest.

As I watched the President of Peru scrape the soil of Loreto, the tragedy underlying the ceremony rose out of the red clay and with charred lips cried, "Too late! Too late for the men of the B-34!"

At the same moment, Colombian horsemen, far to the northwest, were leading a string of pack horses down a mountain trail. To the back of each pack horse was lashed a long canvas-wrapped bundle. Help came too late in Colombia, too—too late for the men of Major Payne's B-34.

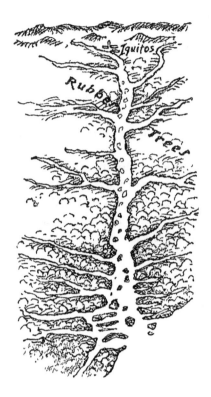

16

𝒯HE CONTRIBUTION of Peru's Amazonia to the supply of strategic commodities flowing to the United States from Latin American countries was an important one. The montaña's strategic trio was composed of rubber, barbasco, and mahogany lumber. By seniority, the dean of the trio was rubber. In fact, the modern history of the entire Amazon Valley may be summed up in the one fabulous word. Prior to the discovery of the new world by Columbus, the aborigines of Mexico and Central and South America knew the use of rubber. They slashed the smooth, wood-ash-colored bark of the Hevea brasiliensis and collected the milky sap, or latex, in cups fastened to the trunk of the

The Putumayo Scandals

wounded tree. The latex was then coagulated into a solid object whose shape was determined by molds. The Mayas of Yucatan and the Aztecs of Mexico used large solid rubber balls in an exciting game, the precursor of basketball-soccer, in which the players were not allowed the use of their hands to propel the ball through a small stone hoop set vertically, high in the ball court wall. Making a goal was apparently such a difficult feat that the lucky player was, as a reward, entitled to the clothing of all the spectators. When the rubber ball passed through the ring, there was a roar of approval from the crowd, followed immediately by a mad stampede for the gate to elude the tunic-grasping agents of the champion.

The use of rubber by the American aborigines was recorded by many Europeans, from the sixteenth century conquistadores to the French and British explorer-scientists of the eighteenth and nineteenth centuries. In 1736, the French scientist, Charles Marie de la Condamine, was intrigued by the skill with which the Indians of the Esmeraldas Coast of Ecuador tapped the rubber trees and fashioned elastic sheets from the coagulated latex. La Condamine put his observations to use and was probably the first European to manufacture a rubber article—a pouch to protect his quadrant against the weather. La Condamine saw many more rubber trees in his descent of the Amazon (1743-44) and is credited with being the first person to attract the attention of Europe to rubber, by the samples he brought back.

A century after La Condamine, the English explorer-scientist, Richard Spruce, witnessed the first flush of the rubber boom, the years in which rubber emerged from the category of a jungle curiosity to that of a mighty economic force. Spruce left Manaos, a sleepy Brazilian town at the confluence of the Río Negro and the Amazon, in 1850, on a plant-collecting expedition that carried him up the Río Negro, through the Casiquiare waterway, and into the headwaters of the Orinoco River. Four years later, he returned to Manaos by the same route. The sleepy village had changed to a throbbing metropolis to whose new jetty, steamboats were moored; whose streets were jammed with speculators and adventurers from all over the world, their pockets stuffed with money and their heads burning with the fever of black gold.

After Charles Goodyear discovered how to vulcanize rubber, in 1839, each new invention of mechanical and electrical devices in which rubber was an essential element inflated the black ball of Amazonian rubber to a greater size. In twenty-five years, Manaos shot up from a village of 3,000 to a seething metropolis of 100,000 inhabitants. Ocean liners steamed up the Amazon for a thousand miles, laden with the delicacies of Europe, and returned stuffed with smoke-blackened rubber balls smelling like rancid hams.

Higher and higher up the Amazon and its tributaries pushed the rubber-gathering *seringuero* in his canoe. Loreto became infected with the fever. As Manaos was the entrepôt for the wild rubber production of the Brazilian Amazon, so Iquitos became the entrepôt for the black balls rolling out of the Peruvian Amazon. Exports of Peruvian rubber began about 1882. By 1897, rubber exports from Iquitos amounted to 9 per cent of the value of all Peruvian exports, and by 1907, to 21 per cent.

Iquitos repeated the experience of Manaos on a modest scale, growing from a few palm leaf shacks in 1864 to a city of forty thousand inhabitants by 1906. The Gran Hotel Malecón Palace and scores of similarly ornate buildings, faced from street level to roof with glazed, multicolored English and Portuguese tiles, sprang up along the low ridge between the Amazon and the Nanay rivers. Don Martín's restaurant clientele paid fabulous prices for their meals, but they dined on paté de fois gras, Huntley and Palmer's biscuits, Crosse and Blackwell jams, Irish butter, and Portuguese hams, washed down with French champagne and British ginger beer in brown earthenware bottles. All the while, a grand piano and string quartette played soothing dinner music.

There seemed to be no ceiling to the crazy spiral of prosperity. The invention of the automobile and the demand for rubber tires brought the Amazonian rubber market to a peak of speculation and spending in 1909 and 1910. The price of rubber skyrocketed out of sight, to three dollars a pound! Then, suddenly, the distended black ball burst, blowing the elaborate credit structure of the Amazonian rubber market to bits. Down below the tree tops fell the price of rubber. The hubbub of Manaos and Iquitos faded away. The silence, mildew, and lethargy of the jungle settled upon the two cities. Rubber production tottered to a standstill. In 1917, the last big year of Peruvian production, approximately five and a half million pounds of rubber were produced. The following year, that production was cut by half. In 1919, practically no rubber came to the Iquitos warehouses.

The roots of the dramatic collapse went back to 1850, when scientist Richard Spruce watched Brazilian seringueros bleed rubber trees near Santarem. Spruce studied the rubber-yielding trees carefully and gathered a great deal of valuable information concerning them. The British Government, through its alert botanical institute, Kew Gardens, requested Spruce to obtain rubber plants. But Spruce had no opportunity to transport rubber seeds or seedlings to England. The Brazilian Government was understandably jealous of her unique position in the world rubber market and was determined to safeguard her monopoly. This, Brazil managed to do until the fateful year of 1872, when Henry Wickham, also commissioned for the job by the British Government, succeeded in snatching seventy thousand Hevea seeds from the Río Tapajoz area, smuggled them aboard a special ship at Santarem, and dashed for the broad Atlantic. Once in London, the seeds were rushed to specially prepared hot-houses in Kew Gardens. Seedlings of the

Tapajoz seeds were transported to the Botanical Gardens in Colombo, Ceylon, and, in 1896, the first rubber plantations were started in Malaya and Sumatra. The beginning of the end of Amazonian wild rubber production was at hand. Henry Wickham snatched much more than a handful of seeds from the Brazilian jungle; he made off bodily with an industry, a way of life, and the prosperity of the world's largest valley.

The wild Amazonian rubber tree and its kidnapped plantation cousin of the East Indies are essentially the same tree, but a number of factors made the production costs of plantation rubber only a fraction of those of wild rubber. The Malayan rubber tree, through grafting and the development of selected strains, yielded from ten to seventeen pounds annually per tree, while the yield per tree in the Amazon forest was only about one-half to one-third that much. In the plantation, where the rubber trees were arranged closely together in orderly rows, one worker could tap several hundred trees; in the Amazon forest, the rubber trees were widely scattered, making it necessary to cut an *estrada* or path through the vegetation to each tree so that a seringuero did well if he attended to one hundred trees. Scientific tapping methods (neat spiraled cuts made with a special tapping knife near the base of the tree), supervised by experts, were the practice in plantations, with the double purpose of protecting the health of the tree and obtaining a maximum yield of latex. In the tangled vastness of the Amazon jungle, such supervision was impossible. Indians, outfitted with a *machadiño*, or hatchet, by greedy, irresponsible patrones, hacked ugly, chevron-shaped wounds in the tender bark of the Hevea, thus wasting the tapping surface and endangering the life of the tree.

Most important, the rubber plantations of Malaya and Sumatra were surrounded by densely populated regions supplying a large number of low-wage workers. By contrast, the Amazon Valley was, and still is, an empty wilderness, settled in infrequent clusters along the river banks. Lack of hands to do the work was the major problem facing the rubber operator. In Brazil, thousands of rubber workers were recruited from the drought-stricken state of Ceará, on the *nose* of Brazil. The rubber gatherers of the headwaters of the Amazon—of Bolivia, Peru, Ecuador, and Colombia—were jungle and Andean Indians pressed into service by varying degrees of force.

Given two such contrasting sets of conditions, it was only a matter of time before plantation rubber of Malaya and Sumatra brought disaster to the Amazonian wild rubber industry. In 1905, the plantations produced only an insignificant part of the world's rubber supply, but by 1910, Malaya and Sumatra produced 9 per cent; by 1914, 60 per cent; and by 1925, 93 per cent. Wild rubber of the Amazon could not compete in price with plantation rubber of the East Indies.

The story of the recruiting of labor for rubber gathering in the Peruvian Oriente is typical of what occurred in all sections of the Upper Amazon Valley. The story is not pleasant, for the protection of law could hardly reach across the Andes into so remote an area.

I remember that my hair stood on end as I sat in the sheltered quiet of the Hispanic Foundation in Washington, prior to my departure for Lima, and read Document 1366 of the 62nd Congress, dated February 7, 1913. The title of the publication was, *Slavery in Peru—Message from the President of the United States (W. H. Taft) transmitting report of the Secretary of State with accompanying papers concerning the alleged existence of slavery in Peru.* The President's message to Congress was based on the report of an American Consul sent to Iquitos in 1912 to investigate the treatment of the Indian rubber workers on the Putamayo River, and on material in the British *Blue Book,* containing the findings of British diplomatic investigators.

An editorial in the *London Times* of July 15, 1912, commented on the *Blue Book* report in these stirring words: "The *Blue Book* shows that in an immense territory which Peru professes to govern the worst evils of plantation slavery which our forefathers labored to suppress are at this moment equalled or surpassed. They are so horrible that they might seem incredible were their existence supported by less trustworthy evidence."

The atrocity charges contained in these reports were aimed specifically at The Peruvian Amazon Company, Ltd., a rubber-gathering organization largely financed—ironically enough—by British capital. The immense concession granted to the company by the Peruvian Government sprawled over approximately nineteen thousand square miles (an area greater than that of Massachusetts, Connecticut, Rhode Island, and Delaware combined) of low-lying jungle country north and south of the Putumayo River. The series of sensational exposés was touched off by an article entitled "The Devil's Paradise," appearing in the London magazine *Truth* in September, 1909. The article charged the Peruvian Amazon Company with brutal and shameless exploitation of thousands of primitive Indians in the Putumayo area, whom the Company forced to work rubber. The article was based on the declarations of W. E. Hardenburg, an American civil engineer, who had just arrived in London, after a trip down the Putumayo River.

"The Devil's Paradise" raised such a stir that the British Foreign Office took the matter up with the London office of the Peruvian Amazon Company. The British directors professed themselves as surprised and horrified at the report as the man on the street. Blame for the atrocities was shifted to the shoulders of Julio C. Arana & Brothers, a Peruvian company conducting the actual operations on the Putumayo for the parent British company.

Interest in the Putumayo atrocities remained so keen that, in 1910, the Foreign Office sent Roger Casement, British Consul General at Río de Janeiro, Brazil, to investigate conditions in the Putumayo area. The ostensible purpose of Casement's assignment was to determine the condition and treatment of British subjects working in the Putumayo. Most of these British subjects were West Indian negroes, many from Barbados, a considerable number of whom were employed as gang foremen in outlying rubber gathering camps. In addition, Casement was under secret instructions to investigate the methods used by the company to collect rubber, and the treatment afforded the aborigine rubber gatherers by the supervisory employees of the company. Casement spent several months on the Igaraparaná and the Caraparaná rivers (northern affluents of the Putumayo), where the Peruvian Amazon Company concentrated the major part of its activities.

The publication of the ensuing Casement report created an explosion that rocked the Upper Amazon and brought knighthood to its author. Casement charged that the Witoto tribe of Indians (embracing the related Boras, Andoques, and Ocainas), which numbered about fifty thousand at the time that the Peruvian Amazon Company began its operations along the Putumayo, had been reduced by the time of his visit to the pitiful remnant of about eight thousand. This near extermination, Casement claimed, was the result of every conceivable kind of atrocity and abuse visited upon the backward Indians by the production-mad minions of Julio Arana. Section camp bosses, who received a commission on all the rubber gathered in their area, had personal gain as an incentive to drive the Indian workers harder and harder.

The Witotos were, and still are, a Stone Age people, accustomed to a free, nomadic life of hunting, fishing, and sporadic agriculture. They were ill-suited to the regimentation and production schedule of the Peruvian Amazon Company. It is true that the Witotos coveted the trade goods—the machetes, colored prints, beads, mirrors, food—given to them in payment for the rubber they delivered. But the Witotos also liked to work at their own tempo, taking liberal leaves of absence from rubber gathering to hunt, fish, farm a little, dance, drink masato, and make raids on neighboring tribes in search of women.

Besides the two main headquarters of the Company—La Chorrera on the Río Igaraparaná and El Encanto on the Río Caraparaná—there were numerous section camps where rubber was gathered for shipment by launch to the main camps and from there to Iquitos. The foremen in these remote sections ruled as despotically as their isolation and Winchesters permitted.

The sworn testimony that Casement took from a number of

West Indian negroes is filled with tales of lawlessness that equal anything in the bloody history of the march of the Yankee pioneers across the Western plains and mountains of the United States. Strange to say, a number of the negro witnesses confessed their guilt in some of the most outrageous of the atrocities. Recalcitrant Witotos were flogged, burned, mutilated, beheaded with machetes, and just plain shot. Casement reported that he saw many Indians whose backs bore the scars of severe lashings. The Indians were required to carry the heavy rubber balls on their backs, over long, muddy trochas.

The Indian women were a constant bone of contention. When section bosses appropriated the wives of Indian leaders, bloody retaliation frequently resulted. In revenge for the attacks by the Indians, Company employees, armed with the almighty Winchester .44, set forth to shoot up the jungle.

As a result of Casement's report, the Peruvian Government, in 1911, sent a judicial commission to the Putumayo to investigate the atrocity charges and bring the culprits to justice. The commission issued 215 warrants for arrest, but only a small number of those indicted were caught. Escape was easy. There was no police force in the area, and the adjoining boundaries of Colombia and Brazil offered a ready sanctuary.

The atrocity accusations of the British press continued even after the Peruvian judicial investigation. In August, 1912, a triple international commission, composed of Carlos Rey de Castro, Consul General of Peru at Manaos; George B. Michell, British Consul at Iquitos; and James S. Fuller, American Consul at Iquitos, chugged up the Putumayo aboard the 100-ton *Liberal,* the flagship of the Peruvian Amazon Company, to investigate the condition of the Indians. About the same time, a special police force, appointed by the Peruvian Government, reached the Putumayo concession to keep law and order, and track down the criminals still at large.

The consular commission remained on the Putumayo for three months. The reports of the British and American consuls stress, time and again, their impatience at being unable to make an independent investigation among the Indians. Messrs. Michell and Fuller had hoped to charter their own launch in Iquitos in order to insure their freedom of movement. As it turned out, they were unable to move a hand in that vast, empty region, except as the guests of the Peruvian Amazon Company. They felt that they were victims of a carefully rehearsed tourist excursion, designed to show them only what their hosts wanted them to see and hear. Señor Arana programmed their every hour. The two consuls attended spectacular Indian dances given in their honor; were photographed with naked Witoto babies in their arms; and inspected naked Witoto men and women to see with their own eyes that they were healthy, contented specimens, not famished, overworked, mutilated slaves.

However, the Company managers at La Chorrera and El Encanto, in written statements to the commission, admitted that their predecessors had sanctioned the existence of terrible abuses, but insisted that these conditions no longer existed under the new regime. The Indians were paid in merchandise on a fair basis (money was of no value to them) for every kilogram of rubber delivered to the Company. The managers pointed out that, since January, 1911, all commissions paid to supervisory employees on the amount of rubber produced in the section camps had been eliminated, and replaced by straight salaries. They also stated that the trails had been widened and improved to make the journeys of the burden carriers easier and that a Company regulation was then in effect limiting the maximum load of an adult male Indian to sixty-six pounds, which he was obliged to carry for no longer than four hours at a stretch. The manager at La Chorrera mentioned Señor Arana's plan to inaugurate a school for the Indian children, but that the project was at a standstill until a schoolteacher could be found in Iquitos.

It is significant that these reforms and projected reforms—which appear to be meagre enough—came at the end of the Amazonian rubber boom, at the moment of triumph for East Indian plantation rubber. In fact, the Company was already in liquidation at the time that the three consuls reached the Putumayo.

When I reached Iquitos, the crack of the overseer's whip and the screams of Witotos echoing through the cloistered reading rooms of the Library of Congress still rang loudly in my ears. It was true that black gold had been buried and all but forgotten in the swamps of depression for a quarter of a century. But, now, the United States was set on reviving the dead. Not long after my arrival, I met the ghost of the Putumayo. I met him on the baseball field near the Bergieri airport. Every Sunday morning, "frightfully-keen-on-sports-you-know" Baron Drewry would stomp down the hall of the Malecón Palace arousing sleepy mapping-party boys, RDC-ites and the American Vice Consul. He would herd us, together with any Peruvian recruits he could collar, out to the field for a game of softball in the broiling sun. One Sunday, a short, sinewy Peruvian appeared on the field, dressed in blue trunks and track shoes. He played right field on the opposing team and amazed us by snagging fly after fly out of the air. On top of this, he knocked two home runs, one with bases loaded. This Amazonian Babe Ruth was Luis Arana, the ghost of the Putumayo, the son of celebrated Julio C. Arana of the Peruvian Amazon Company.

I became acquainted with Luis Arana. Although about forty years old, Luis' trim physical condition made him appear ten years younger. Luis' fondness for baseball and his fluent command of English were acquired in the twenties at the Massachusetts Institute of Technology, where he took a degree in civil engineering. In Iquitos, he was engaged in the exportation of jungle products, in partnership with Frenchman Pierre Schuler, the Belgian Consul. In addition to his business activities, Luis taught mathematics in the local Colegio Nacional.

In Luis' office one day, the conversation turned to the old rubber boom, to the Putumayo, to what I had read in Washington. Luis' gray eyes became cold and hard when Sir Roger Casement was mentioned. "The report of that illustrious gentleman," said Luis, "is a pack of lies. Believe me that 95 per cent of the atrocity charges are false. Casement was nothing more than an exalted blackmailer in the hire of East Indian rubber plantation interests, whose purpose was to destroy the demand for Peruvian rubber, even if they had to smear it with Witoto blood to accomplish their ends.

"Do you know what the British finally did with their trusted agent?" Luis asked me in his high-pitched voice. "Well, they hanged *Sir* Roger Casement by the neck for treason during the other war with Germany."

Carlos Rey de Castro, Peruvian member of the International Commission denied the truth of the sensational charges contained in the Hardenburg article and in the Casement and Michell reports. He furnished proof that Hardenburg was an indigent rascal, who lived by forgery and blackmail. Rey de Castro countered with some even more sensational charges against the United States and Great Britain. He accused these two countries of entering into a conspiracy against Peru, in general, and against Julio Arana & Brothers, in particular, in order to ingratiate themselves with Colombia, who held out the promise of certain concessions (among them oil leases) in return for British and Yankee assistance in her boundary dispute with Peru.

Such are the lurid outlines of the era of black gold in the Peruvian montaña. More than a search for rubber, it was a search for a supply of labor. Rubber was worked all over the montaña, but activity was especially intensive in the Putumayo region, because of its relatively dense population of potential workers. At all times and in all places it has been true that, in the meeting of two civilizations, the backward has necessarily suffered. The tragic fate of the North American Indian is our own case history.

17

$\mathcal{L}$ONG, THEN, before the outbreak of World War II, Peruvian
rubber production, like Scrooge's partner, Marley, was dead as
a doornail. The United States, in dire need of natural rubber,
faced the discouraging necessity of reviving a dead industry.
The initial step taken was an international agreement whereby
the United States, through the Rubber Development Corporation, undertook to finance and supervise the revival of the
rubber industry in eastern Peru. Similar agreements were made
in other rubber-producing countries of Latin America. Iquitos
was chosen as the logical field headquarters for the program.
Credits were to be extended to responsible patrones or entrepe-

Tío Sam
Gathers Rubber

neurs to enable them to hire rubber workers and to supply them with food and equipment. As Peru was not in a position to furnish food and tools for the rubber workers, the RDC had to import these essentials from the United States.

All rubber produced was to be purchased by the Rubber Development Corporation on a grade basis, at fixed, guaranteed prices for shipment to the United States. Out of the total production of rubber, Peru was entitled to retain an annual quota of around 470 tons to take care of her minimum basic needs.

The men in Washington who formulated our Government's rubber procurement policy had read about the atrocities of the rubber boom, and they were determined that the United States should in no way be responsible for a return of such conditions. As if getting rubber and getting it quickly were not enough of a problem, the RDC was saddled with the responsibility of carrying out a program of economic justice and welfare on behalf of the laboring man of Loreto.

The RDC intended to prevent a recurrence of the form of debt-slavery in vogue under the old patrón system by importing rubber workers' food and supplies direct from the States by the Amazon route and selling the supplies at cost to the patrones. The patrones would be obligated to pass these supplies on to their seringueros at only a slight mark-up. The patrón was also obligated to pay fixed prices per kilo for all rubber produced by his men. Folders were distributed that informed the seringuero of what prices he should expect. The RDC policy was to be enforced by its field technicians, who were to travel the rivers by crew and launch, and check up on the patrones.

The plan was an excellent one on paper, but in practice, it

was only partially successful. In the first place, it would have taken an army of field inspectors to enforce an adequate compliance with the price regulations. Ray Russell and his half dozen field technicians, operating out of Iquitos, had more than they could do to encourage the production of rubber without worrying whether Maximino Gómez, far up the Río Ucayali, was charging his peones too much for tinned milk and machetes. Much RDC equipment was sold by patrones for black-market prices, and to individuals who never intended to wield a tapping knife. Some of the equipment that reached the seringuero passed quickly through his hands to others. The ordinary Loretano was more content to eat his rice and beans out of the traditional halved tutumbo gourd than from an RDC tin plate, especially if he could sell the tin plate to some river trader for three times what he had paid for it.

To the big-time merchants lining the malecón of Iquitos, the RDC policy was nonsense. It grieved them to see barge-loads of scarce food and equipment discharged at Iquitos, none of which went to their shelves. "If the United States," they would comment, "wants plenty of rubber in a hurry, why doesn't it chuck all this bureaucracy and red tape, pay a dollar a pound, and let us handle the rest. For a dollar a pound, the trees would bleed themselves. As it is, a man would rather plant barbasco than work rubber, and the little rubber that is coming in costs your Government more than a dollar a pound, if you add on the tremendous overhead of the RDC organization." The observations of the malecón merchants, if tinged by self-interest, certainly made good horse-sense.

For the first two years, it seemed that the old king of the jungle would never awake from his coma, despite repeated RDC hypodermics. A great lethargy and indifference pervaded the whole montaña. "Iron Man" Russell paddled the rivers and tramped the jungle until he was limp with despondency, but no one was working rubber. I can remember the flurry of excitement in Otto Losa's tile-fronted office when, in May, 1943, the first token shipments of rubber, totaling about ten tons, were flown from Iquitos to Belem do Pará, at the mouth of the Amazon.

The turning point came in 1944. The jungle monarch did not leap to his feet, but at least he began to stir. The pungent, smoke-stained balls gradually piled up in the RDC warehouse, a block from the Vice Consulate. In February, a record shipment of seventy-five gross tons of rubber slipped downstream aboard the RDC barge *Manhattan*. In July, just before Dot and I left for Chile, the *Manhattan* departed with 160 gross tons of rubber, the largest individual shipment from Peru since "Iron Man" Russell began prowling the montaña. When we read about the amount of natural rubber it took to manufacture one tire for a B-29, we hoped that RDC Brazil was having more luck reviving the industry than was RDC Peru.

Reviving a dead industry in the obstacle-infested montaña was a gigantic task, one that took time. Ray Russell, as chief field technician of a wilderness area roughly the size of Texas, yet thinly settled with a roving population about equal to that of Wyoming, had a man-sized job on his hands. Ray was publicity agent in a world without mail service, radio, newspapers, and sound trucks. Rubber had to be called back to life by direct word of mouth, by thousands of personal calls at tiny villages and single dwellings. In the maze of trees, waterways, and trails, Ray had to search out rubber trees, locate patrones who would undertake to find labor, decide whether the patrón was a reasonably safe risk for an RDC loan, and then figure out a way to get food and supplies to the spot from the warehouse in Iquitos, often hundreds of miles away.

Time in the montaña is as plentiful as the waters of the Amazon. In time, Ray learned that he could not tie up his launch at some fifty-shack village and expect to get his business accomplished in a few hours. Social amenities came before asperities of business, and the social amenities often ran for several days and nights.

In May, 1943, Ray made a survey trip in the mountainous country of the Upper Marañón River above the Pongo de Manseriche. He chartered a Faucett plane and flew from Chiclayo over the westernmost ranges of the Andes and landed at an hacienda near Bellavista, on the Marañón. Here, the Marañón runs in a south-north direction, through profound gorges, until it bends eastwards and bursts through the Pongo de Manseriche onto the Amazonian jungle plain. The purpose of the trip was to survey the region as far downstream as Borja for rubber trees and labor supply. This mountainous area beyond the limits of steam navigation offered to the rubber program the advantage of its elevation of around three thousand feet. This meant that rubber could be worked the year round, for there was no danger of inundation by the rising rivers.

But freedom from inundation offered small comfort in view of the inaccessibility of the country, the hazards of transportation, and the casual ways of the Indians. The distance from Bellavista to Borja by trail and canoe along the Marañón is about 150 miles. The journey took Ray three arduous weeks to complete. His guides, porters, canoemen and raftsmen were Aguaruna Indians, a sub-tribe of the large, head-hunting Jívaro tribe that inhabits the eastern slopes of the Andes along the Peru-Ecuador border. The fathers of Ray's escorts had settled their score with the caucheros by massacring all the whites in the Upper Marañón, toward the end of the rubber boom. The present generation earned a precarious but untrammeled living by panning gold, hunting, fishing, informal planting, and swapping their women for coveted cloth, shirts, trousers, shotguns, ammunition, tobacco, and salt. When they ran out of women, they replenished their stock by raiding the neighboring tribe.

On the fourth day of the journey, the party came to a stopping place called Miraná. Miraná proved to be more of a stopping place than its half dozen houses would seem to warrant. The porters refused to go on. There were things to be done in Miraná. For the next two days, Ray witnessed the formation and indoctrination of a war party. Indian men and a few women arrived at Miraná all day long in small groups. The men were dressed for an occasion. Their faces were painted red, blue, and green; on their heads, they wore crowns of toucan feathers, around their necks many necklaces. Finally, the warriors numbered about twenty. All were armed—some with shotguns, others with spears, blowguns, and machetes. Ray learned through his guide, who spoke both Aguaruna and Spanish, that one of the young men of the tribe had been killed a few days before by a rival tribe about twenty miles away, on the Chiriaco River. Ray and his party would be welcome to accompany the raiding party after the ceremonial prelude.

The core of the morale-bolstering festival was the drinking of masato. Masato is an alcoholic food-drink made from yuca root (the source of tapioca) and consumed by all Indians of the montaña. Its preparation is interesting. The yuca root is peeled, and boiled until soft in earthenware pots over an open fire. The boiled root is then pounded with a club into a semi-pulp. The women-folk gather around the pile of boiled, mashed yuca and chew the roots in their mouths, spitting the masticated remains back into a common pot. The enzyme ptyalin of the women's saliva converts the starch of the yuca into sugar. The boiled, beaten, chewed mass is allowed to ferment for several days, after which the brew is strained through a gourd colander and is ready to serve—a thick, yellowish liquid. If you are bent on preparing superior masato, make certain that your chewers are toothless crones. The resulting beverage will be *más dulce*— smoother—for the crone will have to gum the yuca longer than a maiden with teeth, thus affording the enzyme ptyalin more time to act on the starch of the yuca.

As the masato drinking got under way, a dance and chant began, to the accompaniment of a drum. Later, as night fell, the thin, plaintive piping of a reed flute joined the drum. The masato went the rounds in a single tutumbo gourd cup, passed from drinker to drinker by a young girl. Apparently, it was proper etiquette to recognize the presence of the cupbearer only after she had been standing in front of the drinker for a half minute. The drinker then cleared his throat in a prolonged hack, spat on the floor, accepted the gourd, drank several gulps, spat again, and returned the gourd to the server. The cupbearer, before serving the next person, would clean the rim of the gourd with her thumb. "Iron Man" Russell, the complete diplomat, accepted one round of masato before he slipped outside the hut where he had set up his cot under the stars.

Ray didn't learn whether any heads were taken by the raiding party that got under way two days later. He and his party accompanied the warriors for one day on foot, and then their paths split when Ray resumed travel by raft. The obtaining of a shrunken head is the greatest ambition of collectors of jungle curiosities. I saw one on display in a store window in Bogotá, Colombia, and another in Iquitos, the property of the naturalist, Don Guillermo Klug, but I came no closer to owning one. Every member of Major Doran's mapping party hoped to locate one, but none succeeded. The mapping party visited a Jívaro village on the Río Huasaga, a tributary to the Río Pastaza. There Major Doran umpired a blowgun target contest: the target—a banana at thirty paces. The party returned to Iquitos, laden with blowguns, poisoned darts, and pottery, but no one had seen a sign of a shrunken head.

The Jívaro method of reducing heads is, reportedly, as follows: The head, taken from an enemy to revenge a wrong, is impaled on a pole for several days out-of-doors, until partially decomposed. A vertical slit is made from the back of the neck to the crown of the head, and the skull is carefully removed, leaving scalp and skin of the face intact. The inside of the skin is then filled with hot sand and thoroughly charred. Afterwards the skin is smoked over a special fire made of the roots of the *chonta* and *hucunga* palm, the smoke containing enough alum to contract the skin to the desired size. The head is then washed in a strong solution made of the bark of the *renaquilla* tree, which has great astringent properties. Until the head becomes dry, the shape of the jaws is retained by slivers of chonta wood. In the ceremony that follows the shrinking of the head, in which much masato is drunk, the victor addresses insulting tirades to the head, which he carries suspended by a cord around his neck. He makes sure, however, that the spirit of the dead enemy is unable to talk back, by sewing up the lips of the head. Although all the Jívaro tribes reduce the heads of their enemies, there is no indication that they practice cannibalism.

If the head-hunting Jívaros were too busy with their own affairs to assume more than in indifferent attitude towards the RDC program, the Mayo Indians went out of their way to hinder the program. The warlike Mayos range between the Río Yavarí, that forms the border between Brazil and Peru, and the Río Tapiche, a tributary of the Río Ucayali. Estimates place the number of Mayos at one hundred families only, but this tribe made up in ferocity what it lacked in numbers. A number of rubber-workers were killed, their women and children abducted, and their camps rifled. The attacks continued so that no patrón could prevail on his men to work in that area. The Mayos grew so bold that they dared raid Requena, a good-sized town on the Río Ucayali, where they succeeded in carrying off a teen-aged girl. Ray investigated the situation and saw to it that all rubber-workers were armed with shotguns. However, the seringueros complained that shotguns were inadequate against the Mayos who, they insisted, were armed with Winchester rifles smuggled in from Brazil. It was out of the question to obtain rifles for the rubber-workers, for Peruvian law banned the possession of rifles by anyone except the military and police. Then it was whispered that the Mayos were instigated, armed, and led by white men from the other side of the Yavarí River. In Iquitos, people went about sniffing the air and making sage remarks about a Brazilian plot. The excitement finally died down when nobody could agree whether the trouble-makers were the Mayos, the Brasilieros, or the unruly rubber-workers themselves.

One of the most interesting, and certainly the most picturesque, of the Peruvian jungle Indians are the Yaguas. The Yaguas, who number about 5,000, live along small tributaries on the north bank of the Amazon, about midway between Iquitos and the Brazilian border. Although the Yaguas are in constant contact with the whites and are an inoffensive, lazy people, they have clung tenaciously to their native garb. The men dress in a grass skirt made of the fibers of aguaje palm. The skirt resembles a Hawaiian hula skirt. About their necks, the men wear an aguaje fiber bib, and their arm and leg bands are of the same material. The bare parts of their bodies are smeared with bright red dye made from the seeds of the *achiote* tree. The achiote coloring is not only a decoration, but affords the Indians some protection against the bites of insects. The Yagua women are considerably less modest than their men and go about naked except for a narrow strip of cloth around their hips.

As if in justification for wearing the skirts of the family, the Yagua man indulges in a peculiar ritual at the birth of his child— a kind of painless turnabout. When the wife's moment of labor approaches, she retires alone into the jungle near a stream, where, unattended, she gives birth to her child. As soon as the baby is born, she bathes in the stream and returns to the house, where, instead of going to bed, she nurses her prostrate husband who goes through a make-believe labor, complete with grunts, cries, and contortions. The Yaguas are among the few people in the world who grant the father the proper degree of considera-tion at the time of childbirth.

Though "Iron Man" Russell passed unharmed among the head-hunting Jívaros and the Winchester-packing Mayos, he was nearly done in by the peaceful Yaguas. "I was spending the night," Ray said, "in the house of Domingo Vásquez, a patrón in the Yagua country. We had arranged the terms of a rubber loan, and Señor Vásquez had agreed to have fifty men at work as soon as he got supplies. With that, we went to bed. Everyone was fast asleep in his hammock in the big communal room when my hammock rope parted. Vásquez' house was set ten feet off the ground on pilings like most of the country houses. I hit the split cane floor, crashed through, and fell spread-eagled in the mud amid a collection of pigs and chickens. The pigs squealed and rushed over me in mad flight; the chickens beat their wings and cackled frantically. Hardly had I struck the mud when there was another crash, and I was driven deeper in the mire by a great weight falling directly on me with the force of a pile driver. When I recovered, Señor Vásquez was standing over me with a lantern. Beside him stood María, his two-hundred-pound Yagua concubine, attired informally in a pair of mud-stained red bloomers. It was María, the Yagua Princess, whose fall I had broken! 'A thousand pardons, amigo!' expostulated Señor Vásquez. 'For some time, I have been thinking of replacing the flooring with fresh *pona,* but,' he sighed, 'there have been so many distractions . . . !' "

18

$\mathcal{D}$URING one of my stopovers at the garrison-village of Barranca, on the Río Marañón, I was included in the strangest and most effective fishing venture that one may ever expect to witness. I was invited on the expedition by Sargento Elmeri Risco, second in command of the Barranca garrison. The sergeant and I walked for about a mile downstream along the bench overlooking the Marañón, until we came to the junction of a sluggish stream, or *quebrada*, with the main river. Several hundred yards up the quebrada from its mouth were three dugout canoes moored to the mud bank. "We will wait here," announced Sargento Risco.

We squatted on the bank by the empty canoes for half an

The Brazilian Army Prefers Buttons

hour. Finally, a dozen men—civilians from the village—approached in single file along the trail. Three of them carried large bundles of yellow-white roots, long and tapering like a rutabaga, bound together with lianas. Had I not been told that they were going fishing, I would have found no clue to what was planned in the equipment of the fishermen—no line, no hooks, no bait, no nets. Several of the men walked to the mouth of the quebrada, stripped down to their shorts, and began the construction of a woven brushwood weir. They worked quickly in the muddy, chest-deep water, and soon the mouth of the quebrada was snugly muzzled.

While the weir was being constructed, the balance of the party was busy with the whitish root. The three bundles, weighing, in all, perhaps 150 pounds, were dumped into the largest of the canoes, untied and spread about on the bottom. Two of these unorthodox fishermen set to work with heavy clubs, pounding the roots to a pulp. With every blow, milky juice oozed from the mashed roots. River water was then poured into the canoe and mixed thoroughly with the pulp and juice.

Apparently, all was in readiness. Some of the fishermen spread out along both banks of the quebrada, while others, in pairs, entered the extra canoes. Two of the men waded into the water, pushing the laden dugout to the center of the quebrada. There they capsized it. The muddy water of the quebrada turned pale as the milky brew was diffused and moved slowly downstream.

The fishermen watched the placid, impenetrable waters with silent expectancy. Soon the troweled surface of the quebrada erupted. Its calm was whipped and broken from beneath. The

221

watchers voiced shrill, triumphant cries as one, then another, then many fish appeared on the surface, pale bellies up, struggling in a doped, listless fashion. The dazed fish were gathered in as easily as one would gather fallen apples. The fishermen scooped them up with their hands and impaled them with short, forked gigs. The fish were not large—they ranged from several ounces to several pounds—but the numbers and variety that rose to the surface were amazing. The harvest continued right up to the weir, where the fish jammed like driftwood. Within a half hour after the first fish broke the surface, the fishermen were on their way back to the village, laden with several hundred pounds of fish to be split, salted, and dried.

That evening for dinner, Teniente Cacho served fresh, pan-fried *boca chicas* and *palometas*. He noticed that I hesitated over my plate. "Have no fear, Señor CONsool," he assured me. "The root has no effect on the flesh of the fish." Teniente Cacho was right. Whether the magical root poisoned, paralyzed, or asphyxiated the fish, the flesh was as delicious as if the fish had been caught on a Royal Coachman.

Such, then, was my introduction to the potency of the barbasco root, the peer of rubber and mahogany in Loreto's trio of wartime strategics so much needed by the United States. Barbasco had been used by the aborigines of tropical America as a fish poison long before the advent of the Spaniards. European missionaries, explorers, and scientists through the centuries have recorded the use of this plant by the Indians as a quick and effective means of obtaining fish. Although used by the Indians, and known to Europeans for as long as rubber, barbasco remained an obscure jungle plant until very recent years.

A number of people claim the distinction of being the discoverer and publicizer of the insecticidal properties of the barbasco root. If anyone deserves more credit than another in this respect, that person seems to be W. J. Dennis, formerly an American schoolteacher in the Peruvian mountain city of Huancayo. Dennis' interest in barbasco was first aroused on a school picnic back in 1917, when his pupils demonstrated the effectiveness of the root as a fish poison, in the Mantaro River, near Huancayo. Over the years, Dennis made a number of experiments with the powdered barbasco roots, which convinced him that his pupils' fish-stunning root had tremendous possibilities as a commercial insecticide to kill plant parasites, de-bug farm animals, and to free the home of insect pests. Dennis later gained the assistance of visiting American plant specialists and experts in the United States Department of Agriculture in making tests that proved beyond a doubt the bug-killing value of barbasco. An especially desirable feature of the plant was its harmlessness to human beings who consumed the food product sprayed or dusted with the prepared insecticide.

In 1929, Dennis joined an expedition of the Smithsonian Institution, and, for eight months, searched the montaña for barbasco seeds. His unrewarded hunt convinced him that the barbasco plant—a shrub about the size of a lilac bush—produced neither bloom nor seed. The plant could be reproduced only by cuttings.

Though Dennis failed to locate barbasco seeds during his expedition, he did discover a serious man-made obstacle that had to be removed before the commercial cultivation of barbasco would be feasible. The Peruvian Government had passed a law strictly forbidding the use and cultivation of barbasco, in order to eliminate the use of the root for fishing, and thus prevent the possible extermination of fish life in the Amazonian rivers. In the unpoliced montaña, most people ignored the law, but they were careful to conceal their little plot of fish poison from the stranger's view. Dennis appealed to the Prefect of Loreto, at Iquitos, for assistance in obtaining the repeal of the law. The Prefect was impressed by Dennis' conviction that barbasco—a wild jungle plant—could be grown successfully as a cultivated cash crop. The plant required only an abundance of heat and rain. Heat and rain abounded in the montaña. Type of soil seemed secondary. The law forbidding the cultivation of barbasco was repealed, and, in 1931, Dennis exported to the United States the first ton and a half of barbasco root from Peru.

In the decade that preceded Pearl Harbor, shipments of plantation-grown barbasco root from Iquitos (at first to the United States, and then also to Europe) mounted steadily: 16 metric tons in 1933 (a metric ton is a ton of 1,000 kilograms or 2,204 pounds) ; 439, in 1935; 1,302, in 1940; and approximately 2,500, in 1942.

The discovery, by a New Jersey chemist, that barbasco contained an alkaloid known as rotenone, to which its insecticidal powers were attributed, was a spur to greater production. Dynamic John W. Massey, Booth Steamship agent, British Consul, and spark of the Iquitos Chamber of Commerce, directed a vigorous campaign of propaganda to awaken the Loretan farmer to the merits of planting barbasco. Here was a crop ideally suited to Loretan economy. The production of barbasco, as contrasted to that of rubber, could be carried on by the individual small farmer, by his own efforts, on his own land. He did not need a great outlay of capital and effort, or the assistance of a patrón to obtain supplies. Nor was it necessary to subject himself to the uprooted, nomadic life of the seringuero.

The Iquitos Chamber of Commerce erected billboards about town, distributed handbills, and prepared show cases plugging barbasco. John W. Massey was sent up and down the rivers in a hydroplane to make speeches urging the farmer to plant *Huasca Barbasco* (known scientifically as *Lonchocarpus Nicou*) , the variety which contained the highest percentage of rotenone. For the initial planting, the farmer would have to search for wild plants to obtain his *estacas*—a foot-long cutting from the main stem of the bush. After his first harvest, he would be able to replant with cuttings from his own fields. He was advised to plant from four to five thousand cuttings per hectare, a unit of land equivalent to 2.471 acres. Except for weeding while the plant was small, the barbasco required no attention after the initial effort of clearing the land and planting. Jungle heat, jungle rain, and time did the rest.

The farmer was cautioned not to pull his roots before the plant had grown for twenty-four months. If the harvest could be delayed until the plant reached the full maturity of thirty-six months, the farmer would be rewarded with root that would yield the maximum percentage of rotenone. Estimates of yield ranged from 10,000 to 25,000 pounds of root per hectare. The farmer was encouraged to plant a food crop among his barbasco plants, such as yuca, that would yield him a cash crop in eight months and help carry him along until the barbasco matured.

In May, 1942, as had been done with rubber, an international agreement was signed, making the United States the exclusive purchaser of Peruvian barbasco. Producers were guaranteed a price of fifteen and a half cents a pound for whole barbasco root and eighteen cents a pound for ground barbasco root, f. o. b. river steamer in Iquitos. The Commodity Credit Corporation purchased all barbasco for the United States Government by means of irrevocable letters of credit, issued by New York banks to banks in Iquitos. The terms of the letters of credit permitted the shipper to collect up to 80 per cent of the value of the shipment from the Iquitos bank, upon presentation of consular invoice and shipping documents, and the balance after analysis of the barbasco shipment by Government assayers in the States. The basic price per pound was contingent upon the written guarantee of the shipper that the barbasco shipped contained at least 5 per cent of rotenone and no more than 12 per cent moisture. For barbasco that showed, upon analysis, a percentage of rotenone greater than 5 per cent and a moisture content less than 12 per cent, a premium was paid. Conversely, the agreement provided for a proportionate downward revision in price for barbasco shipments not measuring up to minimum specifications.

Compared to the rubber agreement, the barbasco agreement was realistically simple. No United States Government procurement agency was dispatched to the jungle to finance, supply, and supervise the production of barbasco. A stimulating price was guaranteed, and the rest was left to established commercial channels in the locality. However, the United States Government did create an agency, referred to as the Foreign Economic Administration (FEA), that was to supervise and co-ordinate all the commodity procurement programs outside the United States and to assist in providing shipping space for these strategic products. As the nearest FEA office was in Lima, I was instructed by the Embassy to represent the Government's barbasco interests in Iquitos.

At first, my job with the FEA seemed simple enough. Twice a month, I had to transmit a telegraphic report to the FEA representative at Lima, to be cabled by him to Washington, listing the port stock tonnages of the strategic trio—rubber, barbasco, and mahogany lumber—actually on hand in Iquitos, awaiting shipment to the United States, and the tonnages expected to be ready for shipment within the next thirty and sixty days. This report was designed to enable FEA authorities to arrange for adequate shipping facilities to prevent the bottle-necking of strategic cargoes.

I had sent only a few reports when it became apparent that barbasco was hot stuff to FEA in Washington, and that important people were not at all content with the state of affairs on the Upper Amazon. Each fortnightly cable reporting mounting piles of barbasco drew a lengthy coded message from Washington, expressing concern over the alarming increase in barbasco stocks.

The big boys seemed to lay the whole blame for the Amazonian shipping shortage at my feet. Washington seemed to pay no attention to my reports on the sad condition of Amazon River shipping, nor offer any suggestions as to what to do about it. The difficulty lay in transporting the commodities the 2,300 miles downstream to Belem do Pará, at the mouth of the Amazon, for transhipment there aboard ocean-going vessels to the States. Only two steamers offered a scheduled freight service between Iquitos and Belem do Pará. Confronted with a port stock of five hundred metric tons of barbasco, these two venerable, nineteenth-century wood-burners might just as well have been dugout canoes for all the impression they could make in that ever-growing mountain of root.

Even if the steamers had been willing to accept no cargo but barbasco, which was definitely not the case, they could, at best, have hauled away only about 150 metric tons every six to eight weeks. In the meantime, twice that amount of barbasco entered Iquitos from the Río Huallaga plantations alone. Two months was not a bad average for a round trip between Iquitos and Belem do Pará, under ideal conditions. But conditions on the Amazon River were seldom ideal. Any number of misfortunes could overtake the river steamer to slow its trip to three months, six months, or even a year. The ship's Captain might lose a whole week searching for the once plentiful stacks of firewood, wood-gatherers having abandoned their trade for more lucrative enterprises. When found, it was apt to be so green that it sizzled and smouldered ineffectually in the ship's boilers. At Belem do Pará, the Captain was in luck if he did not have to wait in line for days to get a berth in order to discharge his cargo and take aboard the Iquitos-bound freight.

The Amazon River is largely uncharted and unmarked. In the 2,300 miles from Iquitos to Belem do Pará, it is entirely between two banks only twice. For the rest, the Amazon is split up by a confusing series of islands that divert part of the water many miles before it rejoins the main channel. The ship's safety rested in the hands of experienced pilots or *practicantes,* who depended solely on their memory and their keen eyes. But even the most skillful practicante could mistake a shoal for the channel on a starless, rain-swept night. If the ship stuck fast on a sandbar, when the river was on the rise, a few days' wait would give it clearance. But if the river was falling, the ship might have to squat on the sandbar until the river rose again the following year.

Before the war, most of Iquitos' export cargo moved down river in the Brazilian ships of the Government-controlled *Snapp* line. Once a month, a Snapp steamer pulled alongside the pontoon dock. Frequently, the ship was a large one, like the 700-ton *Fortaleza.* As the war progressed, however, fewer and fewer Snapp ships came to Iquitos, and those that arrived were all small-tonnage boats.

The shipping situation in the Upper Amazon could not have been worse, when bottoms were needed with greater urgency than at any time since the rubber boom. Iquitos was marooned at the headwaters of the world's largest river, with only the most tenuous of contacts with the outside world. Topography and the river demanded that Iquitos face eastwards towards the Atlantic, that her products move eastwards, and that her imported food and clothing come from the east. The Amazon River was her life line, yet movement along the line was near a standstill. Information from down river was vague and meagre, the head and the foot of the Amazon being out of touch with one another except by the expensive, roundabout, air and cable routes circling the top side of South America.

Washington's anxiety over the mounting stockpile of barbasco stranded in Iquitos was well-founded. Body lice spread typhus, and typhus could kill more of our soldiers in a short time than months of combat. Barbasco killed the louse and thus prevented typhus. I was on as strategic a front as any G.I., because the barbasco of the Peruvian montaña was the United States' principal source of rotenone.

There was a wild scramble among Iquitos merchants for tonnage allotments aboard the infrequent Pará-bound steamers. They fought and jockeyed for space with a ruthless determination proportionate to the distended sides of their warehouses.

The export merchant of Iquitos dealt in many jungle products, because his supplier and customer—the man in the jungle —was forced by conditions to earn his living in a variety of ways. The Loretano might cut down mahogany trees or gather rubber until he was forced out of the lowlands by rising river water. Then he might plant barbasco and yuca on high ground. But while his crop was maturing, he would have to support himself by hunting peccary and river otter for their skins, or by gathering leche caspi (related to chicle and used in the manufacture of chewing gum) and tagua nuts, from which buttons are made. The FEA and the American Vice Consulate had eyes only for barbasco, but the merchant saw all his products in the light of their seasonal importance and their economic interdependence. He fought to give each its bit of space aboard the tiny steamers.

Good-Neighborly and Let's-Win-the-War appeals from the representative of the United States met with more favorable response than I expected, but such appeals can interest a business man only as long as business conditions permit.

Tagua nuts, or vegetable ivory, was one of barbasco's most formidable rivals for shipping space. Tagua, the fruit of a palm known by the same name, grew in wild abundance, especially along the Napo River. Almost all the tagua shipped from Iquitos was sold in Brazil for the manufacture of buttons. Tagua was not considered a strategic commodity by the United States Government, nor were any shipments made to the United States.

Snapp line steamers suddenly grew hostile to barbasco. My badminton-playing colleague, Theodore Magellan (Teodoro Magalhaes), the Brazilian Consul, was local agent of the line. Teodoro assured me again and again that he desired to do all in his power to help Brazil's ally fight the war, but he protested his inability to over-ride the adamant ship captains. The captains insisted that they had orders from Belem do Pará, not to load barbasco, because it was an unprofitable, disagreeable cargo to handle.

The undesirable characteristics of barbasco—bulk without weight, fumes, sweat, and dust—combined with a freight rate reduction made at the request of the United States, put Snapp in an unreceptive mood toward the product. When barbasco was mentioned to the Captain of the *Jansem de Melo*, the first Brazilian steamer to put in at Iquitos in six months, he roared, "Barbasco! By all the bitches of Belem, I swear I will return empty to Brazil before I take aboard one kilo of that cursed root!"

The Captain did not speak in jest, for the following morning, along the malecón, coursed the report that the *Jansem de Melo* was going to load nothing but tagua nuts. Buttons for Brazil! What had buttons to do with winning the war! I steamed down the malecón to the office of the principal tagua merchant of Iquitos. Coronel Salamón Azerrad, a little man in his seventies, wearing a very high, starched collar, had come from Syria to the Amazon Valley where he, like many of his amazing compatriots, managed to make a fortune amid the débris of the rubber boom. In Brazil, he became a citizen, a tagua king, and a Brazilian *coronel,* which title, I understand, is closely akin to that of a Kentucky colonel. In time, Coronel Azerrad extended his operations to Iquitos.

As I entered his office, the Coronel greeted me with formal coolness. His manner told me that he surmised the purpose of my visit. I attempted to prepare the way with innocuous chitchat. We discussed the latest cocktail-danzant at the Club Iquitos, and the progress of the pipe laying for the municipal water supply. The Coronel's watery eyes remained as inscrutable as ever, his manner as aloofly courteous.

As a way-paver, I was a flop. There was no remedy but a frontal assault. "Estimado Coronel Azerrad," I began, "it is rumored that you intend to make a considerable shipment of tagua nuts aboard the *Jansem de Melo.*" The Coronel smiled innocently. "Only an insignificant quantity, Señor CONsool," he replied. "A trifling three hundred tons."

"But Coronel," I exclaimed, "three hundred tons of tagua will fill the entire ship! There will be space for nothing more!"

"As to that, I cannot say, Señor CONsool," remarked the Coronel. "All I know is that three hundred tons is less than half the tagua I have stored in Iquitos, awaiting shipment these many months."

In desperation, I appealed to the Coronel's patriotism, to his strong advocacy of the Allied cause. I reminded him that barbasco was a strategic war cargo; that tagua was not. Specifically, I requested the Coronel to reduce his shipment of tagua by one hundred tons so that fifty tons of barbasco might go aboard. In a flash of inspiration, I pushed my appeal to a climax. "Mi Coronel," I said, "your glorious country, Brazil, our beloved ally, is training an army that will soon take its place alongside ours on the battlefield of Europe. Would you send your valiant compatriots to war without barbasco powder to destroy the vermin that will inevitably infest their clothing?"

The Coronel fixed me with his watery eyes. Clearly, he was unimpressed. He owned no barbasco, but he did own a mountain of tagua nuts. "Mi estimado Señor Cónsul," countered the Coronel, "what you say about the body lice has certain merit, but I am sure that the valiant Brazilian soldier would prefer to charge into battle with an itching body than without buttons to sustain his trousers."

The interview was at an end. Two days later, the *Jansem de Melo* departed, loaded to gunwales with buttons-to-be for the Brazilian Army.

19

*M*AHOGANY from the Peruvian Amazon made its debut on the world mahogany market in 1928, when Don Pepe O'Neill, representing the Otis Astoria Corporation, of New York, joined hands with Don Carlos Bonilla, a Colombian engineer with a degree from Cambridge, England, to begin sawing operations at the mouth of the Nanay. Lumber dealers in the States, accustomed to handling mahogany from Central America, were reluctant to accept the new Amazonian product. Bonilla was unsuccessful in breaking down this prejudice, until he interested Astoria in starting operations in Loreto. The swampy country and the expense and difficulty of introducing logging machinery

The Voyage of the Dock

limited logging operations to the margins of rivers. A mahogany tree six feet in diameter felled far from water could not be moved by manpower alone. As Astoria exhausted timber in the vicinity of Iquitos, it had to reach farther and farther away from the mill. When I arrived in Iquitos, the bulk of Astoria's logs were floated to the mill from hundreds of miles away, far up the Río Ucayali. Mahogany seedlings planted in the vicinity of the Nanay mill would not be ready for cutting for many years.

Although Astoria and Loretana had more lumber on hand than they had stacking space, the rising waters of the Amazon announced the beginning of another sawing season. Tremendous oval islands, made up of hundreds of gigantic mahogany and cedar logs, began to float into view. Aboard these great rafts rode long-haired Chama Indians from far up the Río Ucayali, where the trees had been felled. These picturesque caretakers had been riding the logs for months. At last, their voyage was over, and tugs towed the booms to the mill for sawing.

The swollen Amazon was not content with bringing logs to Iquitos. She also brought devastation and hunger. She brought them every year in April and May, but this year the visitation promised to be especially severe. For years, Don Pepe O'Neill had marked the crest of the flooding river on the cement base of the log crane at the Astoria mill. The high point fell with amazing precision, year after year, on, or within a few days of, the twentieth of May. In 1944, the crest came unusually early, and, by April 29, the water level stood three inches higher than the all-time recorded high.

The river rose no higher, but Dot and I could see how grim a harvest the chocolate waters were reaping as we chugged upstream toward Iquitos from the Astoria mill. Water washed two feet deep among the boles of the banana plants, whose broad leaves had turned a deathly yellow. Farmers worked desperately in knee-deep water trying to salvage a few kilos of yuca root. Chickens and turkeys, perched disconsolately along the porch railings and on the roofs of the high-stilted houses, surveyed the liquid world beneath them. Cows gathered on tiny patches of elevated land, that still afforded them a dry footing in their drowned pastures. Some farmers had removed their cattle and pigs to the temporary safety of a raft snubbed to the pilings of their elevated huts. People whose homes were not located on high ground or atop high stilts were flooded out. They joined their livestock on the balsas or sat sorrowfully in their canoes.

For a few days, the market of Iquitos was flooded with an unaccustomed plenty. Cattle, hogs, and poultry were sold at sacrificial prices rather than have them drown or starve to death on the rafts. Yuca, beans, corn, and bananas, hastily gathered in the face of the rising flood, were cheap and plentiful. But in a little while, when these were gone, there would be a great scarcity, and inflation and hunger for months to come. The pattern, year after year, was always the same. When the waters dropped, the man of Loreto rushed down to the silted beaches and planted his corn and beans. When the waters rose, the man of Loreto grabbed up a hasty harvest and retreated to his stilt house on the little nob. There, he waited patiently until the beaches appeared once more. Predestined to this futile chasing back and forth, could the man of Loreto aspire to better things?

The steamers that failed to come from Pará increased the hunger. Iquitos, even in low water, could not feed herself. The city lived on what came up the river, from coastal Peru, and from the United States. In 1943, Iquitos was without wheat flour for six months and we ate no bread. When wheat flour finally came, it was Gold Medal flour from New York!

At last, on May 5, our long vigil ended. "The *Ucayali* has arrived!" was the elated cry. The three-thousand-ton ocean-going monster dwarfed our floating dock. It was the biggest ship that had come to Iquitos for years. To us Iquiteños, accustomed to canoes and putt-putt launches, the *Ucayali* was the *Queen Elizabeth* and more. The ship belonged to the Peruvian Government and had come 7,500 miles from Callao, laden with food and merchandise. It had originally been planned to time the arrival of the relief ship with the visit of President Prado, in September of the previous year. The plan was a masterpiece of political strategy, but something had gone wrong. The President had beaten his dinner pail to Loreto by eight months!

The *Ucayali* brought news of other ships on their way to Iquitos. Within a few days, the river bank would be lined with steamers waiting their turn at the dock to discharge and load up. It would be like the old rubber days, when ocean-going steamers from Europe formed queues to receive the rubber balls. The *Ucayali* herself would haul no strategics, for she was taking a straight load of cedar lumber back to Callao, where it would go into the construction of housing and furniture. However, the eighteen-hundred-ton *Perené*, also bringing general merchandise from Callao, had been chartered by the FEA to make a special trip from Iquitos to Belem do Pará with an exclusive cargo of barbasco, rubber, and mahogany lumber. Behind the *Perené* was the tug, *Curaray*, towing not only the *Manhattan* but also another large barge. Bringing up the rear was the little *Morey*.

Times were good indeed. An abundance of food was at hand, and the prospect was good of cleaning out the log-jam of strategic commodities that had oppressed us so long. If there was ever an excuse for a fiesta, we had one. Dot decided to throw a big party in Punchana—appropriately enough, a ship party. The Captain and First Mate of the Good Ship *Tacu Tacu* sent out too many invitations. Obviously, our little ship would founder with so many aboard. Our neighbors at Chalet Crandall obligingly tied up alongside and more than doubled our tonnage.

The deep veranda circling Chalet Crandall made an excellent "A" deck on which were arranged cushion-laden dugout canoes for lifeboats, a ping-pong table, a shuffleboard court, and card tables. Tied to one of the corner pilings of the veranda, with a red ribbon, was a mahogany board anchor, resting in an RDC latex tub filled with water.

Everybody joined in the outfitting of the SS *Tacu Tacu*. The skipper of the Amazon River flotilla flagship, the 250-ton diesel-powered *Amazonas*, practically dismantled his battleship so that the *Tacu Tacu* might be properly rigged out. The Comandante sent sailors from the Punchana Naval Base with the gunboat's gangway, life preservers, and strings of multi-colored signal flags. Dot and I were overcome by the simpático-ness of this gesture. The Connecticut-built *Amazonas* had a gallant record in the conflict with Colombia and Ecuador. She had navigated the Pongo de Manseriche and returned to Iquitos laden with Ecuadorean prisoners. More recently, she had brought President Prado down the Río Ucayali to Iquitos.

The provisioning of the SS *Tacu Tacu*, with its fifty-odd passengers, was a more difficult assignment than its rigging out. Somehow, Dot accomplished the job. For three days, she and Antonia stoked the tiny stove with charcoal, and baked loaf after loaf of golden bread, dozens of rolls, and four pound-cakes. Antonia made a gallon of *taperibá* jam. Walter perched for hours atop Lib Russell's ice cream freezer, while Antonia, Petronila, and the American Vice Consul cranked and cranked. Dot found the only two turkeys in Iquitos that had survived the flood. They went into turkey salad with home-made mayonnaise, chopped hearts of palm, and ripe olives.

Dot also found a fresh pork leg. The leg, too large to go into the oven, was dressed and spiced just before dark the eve of the party. Flashlight in hand, pork leg in basket, Dot was about to set out on her bike to have it roasted in the baker's oven when she was accosted by a nervous, sweaty man from the slaughter-house carrying a pork leg over his shoulder. He asked that the original leg be returned to him. Dot blew up, but surrendered her precious leg when she learned that a belated examination of the carcass of the first pig had disclosed that the animal was severely afflicted with trichinosis. The superintendent of the slaughterhouse sent his apologies and hoped that the replacement leg had not arrived too late. "After all, Señora," said the slaughterhouse man, "The Señor Prefecto, the Señor General, the Señor Alcalde, and other dignitaries will be present. One cannot afford to take chances."

Sunday dawned, with promise of a fine day for the fiesta. The guests were expected at noon, and the fiesta was to continue the rest of the day. Everything was fine. The preparations were nearly complete when Walter burst into the house. "Señor Kehlee!" he shrieked. *"Arrancó el muelle—se ha ido río abajo!"*

I leaped on the Raleigh and dashed down Punchana Road. I got as far as the slaughterhouse, and there it was. There, in the middle of the Amazon, a good two hundred yards from shore and a quarter of a mile below its accustomed location, was the floating dock of Iquitos—the whole 585 feet of it, complete with customs tally house, railroad tracks, freight cars, and lamp posts! The only thing restraining the long, ungainly raft from continuing its voyage to the Atlantic Ocean was a slender cable from a mooring brace to the stern of the anchored *Ucayali*.

Bit by bit, I pieced together the story from individuals in the crowd lining the embankment. About two o'clock that morning, the moorings of the *Ucayali* to the deadheads on the embankment and to the dock suddenly parted. The ship swung out into the river where the crew succeeded in anchoring it a short distance below the dock and well away from shore. Several of the principal land-based cables holding the floating dock in position were apparently loosened or severed at the time that the *Ucayali* broke loose. As a result, the pressure of the flooding Amazon on the dock's remaining cables was too great, and they also broke, along with the heavy anchor chains at the up-river end of the dock. The anchor chains at the down-river end remained intact, however, so that the dock slipped in jerks downstream until it was brought to a stop by a cable that somehow still connected it to the stern of the *Ucayali*.

Opinion as to whether or not the *Ucayali* had been properly moored varied widely. Some defended the Captain. Others maintained that the whole drag of the ship had been supported by the dock alone; that there were no land-based cables, nor were the ship's anchors lowered.

Despite the excitement caused by the unheralded departure of the dock, all the guests were aboard the SS *Tacu Tacu*—all except the Navy. Absent was the Commander-in-Chief of the gunboat flotilla, the captains of all the gunboats, the Port Captain, and the Administrator of Customs. Nevertheless, the pisco sours were served, and the four guitars and the maraca launched a criollo waltz.

Three of the gunboats of the Amazon flotilla—the *Amazonas* and the venerable, wood-burning *América* and *Napo*—were tied up along the embankment below the Punchana Naval Base, not two hundred yards from the fiesta. I carried over a tray of turkey salad and uncontaminated pork for the three skippers standing by, aboard their ships. Raul, the skipper of the *Amazonas*, who had just returned from a tour of duty with the United States Navy, was on the bridge, binoculars in hand. The dock was clearly visible only a half a mile upstream. I didn't need glasses to see that it was no longer tied to the *Ucayali* and that it had slipped another quarter of a mile from its location earlier in the day. "You should have been here a few minutes ago," said Raul. "There was plenty of excitement up there. It was all very clear through the glasses. A big balsa raft, manned by three men and loaded heavily with bananas and yuca, collided full-tilt with the up-river extremity of the dock. I guess the raft was too unwieldy to maneuver. Just before the collision, the three men clung to the *Ucayali's* cable in an attempt to save themselves. The strain of the impact of the balsa and the weight of the men must have been just what was needed. The cable parted. One of the men on the raft was drowned. The dock executed a 180-degree pivot and moved along in jerks, dragging its remaining anchors."

We watched the bustle of activity about the dock. A dozen diminutive river steamers, launches, and tugs nuzzled along each side, bent on restraining the nomadic dock by their collective grunts and wheezes. We spotted Commodore Wilke's two rugged little tugs, the *Dorothy* and the *Jean*, among the pushers. "If they don't succeed in passing a cable or two from the dock to the shore," Raul observed, "I'm afraid the damn thing will move down and crush the gunboats. We wouldn't stand a chance. Those heavy steel pontoons would flatten us like match boxes." "Why don't you get the hell out of the way?" I ventured. "An excellent idea, chum," Raul replied, "but there are a couple of drawbacks. The *Amazonas* could get away in a hurry. She burns oil and we have oil. But the other two," Raul gestured toward the *América* and the *Napo,* "they can't budge. They're wood-burners and they've got no steam up. What's more, they haven't a stick of wood aboard to make steam with. If the dock moves any closer, I'll have to try to tow them away. I wonder if the *Amazonas* could do it—after all, she's no tug boat."

The voyage of the municipal dock to the Atlantic Ocean was checked short of the Punchana Naval Base, and the gunboats of the Amazon River flotilla were delivered from what might have been a crushing defeat. The promised *Perené,* the tug *Curaray* and her two barges, and the *Morey* arrived shortly after the dock broke loose.

The situation was ludicrous, but it was also packed with irony. Iquitos was hungry for the food still aboard the *Ucayali* and *Perené.* Iquitos was surfeited with the raw jungle products glutting her warehouses. Out in the river was the greatest assemblage of ships that Iquitos had seen in many years. Yet, between Iquitos and the ships there was no bond. Their bond, the dock, was in the middle of the river.

It took the ships two months to turn around. Each had to be unloaded at a snail's pace, bundle by bundle, onto tenders and launches. The loading was hardly faster. The barbasco and rubber were loaded by chutes from the embankment. But, by now, the river was dropping rapidly; each day, the distance between the top of the embankment and the deck of the ship was greater; each day, the chutes had to be made longer.

By mid-July, all the ships had left, and the errant dock had been towed in sections back to its original location. Down to Belem do Pará had gone 1,150,000 board feet of mahogany, 710 tons of barbasco, and 160 tons of rubber. The boys up in Washington could relax for a few days.

20

*P*ERU BROKE relations with the Axis at the time of the January, 1942, Conference of Foreign Ministers. This action entailed more than a mere severance of diplomatic relations. Peru agreed to take positive steps to paralyze Axis economic interests within her boundaries, and the United States undertook to supply Peru with a sufficient quantity of manufactured commodities to meet the minimum basic needs of her domestic economy. The officers of the Foreign Service were, logically, the representatives of the United States in this co-operative endeavor with the Peruvian Government. In Iquitos, economic warfare, the settlement of the Peru-Ecuador boundary, and the shipment of strategic jungle

We Make Propaganda

products were the Big Three of my Consular duties. For these three reasons, the Consulate in Iquitos was maintained. My work in economic warfare was never personally satisfying. By nature, it is purely negative, destructive effort. On the other hand, the tracing of a boundary line that underscores the firm resolution of two countries to live in peace with one another, and the shipment of an agricultural product as beneficial to mankind as barbasco were positive, constructive activities.

The two nationals appearing on the *Lista Negra* for Iquitos were the Germans and the Japanese. The German firms considered a menace to the Allied war effort were liquidated, and the nationals themselves deported to camps in the United States.

The Japanese had only begun the infiltration of the montaña at the war's outbreak. Their colony in Iquitos earned a modest living as retail shopkeepers and was far outmatched in number and wealth by the Chinese. Japanese influence in coastal Peru, however, was well entrenched. Thousands of Japanese laborers had entered Peru to work on the large sugar, cotton, and rice plantations of the coastal valleys. At the time of Pearl Harbor, an estimated 25,000 Japanese lived in tight cultural clusters, principally along the coast north and south of Lima. Their hold on Peruvian agriculture and retail commerce was comparable to that of the Japanese in California.

None of the half dozen Japanese shops on the Iquitos Black List were important enough to warrant the appointment of a Peruvian intervener to hasten their liquidation. The withering consequences of inclusion on the List were enough to ruin most of them. Alfredo Ochi, the leader of the colony, set the example to his compatriots by selling his grocery store, *El Patito* (The

241

Little Duck), to a Spanish Republican refugee. Jorge Taka-gishi's dry-goods store, *El Abanico* (The Fan), folded up shortly afterwards. Francisco Hakiwara, who operated a small pastry and candy shop, tried to perpetuate the family business by selling out to his Peruvian-born son. The sign advertising Hakiwara senior's establishment read *El Sol Naciente* (The Rising Sun). Young Hakiwara indicated his complete severance with the old school by amending the shingle to read *El Reflejo del Sol Naci-ente.* Who could get burned in the mere reflection of the rising sun?

There was one Japanese, however, who succeeded, as long as he lived, in defying the attempts of the American Embassy in Lima and the Vice Consulate in Iquitos to have him dis-lodged. This Japanese was a fish expert named Nakashima, employed by the Peruvian Bureau of Fisheries to direct a fish nursery on the Pacaya River, about 125 miles southwest of Iquitos. The nursery, the only one of its kind in the montaña, was dedicated to the protection and propagation of the *paiche,* the Amazon's most useful and interesting fish.

The paiche (*arapaima gigas*) is a hideous fish, encased in scales as thick as armor plate. Its ugliness is exceeded only by its size, for the paiche, reportedly the largest fresh water fish in the world, grows as long as twelve feet and weighs as much as three hundred pounds. It resembles some of the pictorial repro-ductions of armored fish that terrorized the rivers in the early geological eras of Earth history. In fact, scientists claim that the paiche is a hold-over from ancient times, that its anatomy is so obsolete its floating bladder serves also as a lung. For all that, the paiche has been in such demand in Loreto that it is nearing extinction. Because of its size, the paiche is harpooned from a dugout canoe much as the old-time whalers harpooned a whale.

Fresh paiche steaks are as delicious as New England sword-fish; salted paiche is better than dried Boston cod. The bony tongue of a paiche, covered with hundreds of small teeth, makes an excellent rasp; its large rough scales make fine nail files.

The great usefulness of the paiche and its urgent need for protection, made the Pacaya project important to the prosperity of Loreto. The Prefect defended Nakashima against all attempts to dislodge him, on the grounds that the Japanese was not only an expert at his work, but irreplaceable. The Prefect did not find it strange that among seven million Peruvians there could not be found a single capable replacement for one Japanese fish expert.

Reports came to the Vice Consulate that Nakashima was trying to sabotage the rubber program in the Pacaya area by ordering his employees to drive off rubber workers, whom he accused of poaching from his paiche lagoons. Nakashima was also accused of operating a powerful clandestine radio transmitter. What momentous information Nakashima could transmit to the warlords of Tokyo from the unpeopled solitude of the Río Pacaya, my informants could not guess.

I had abandoned all hope of extricating the fish expert from his jungle haunts, when fate stepped in and solved the problem. Nakashima, the immovable, was removed by cancer, and a Peruvian replacement was installed.

Our State Department complemented its campaign to destroy Axis economic influence in Latin America by a program of cultural alignment between the United States and the other American republics. The program was designed to publicize our country to our Latin neighbors, to impress upon them what sort of people we were, how we lived, what we thought about, to what we aspired, and the mighty effort we, with their help, were putting behind our war with the Axis. This program was carried out by scholarships to bring leaders in Latin American cultural and scientific endeavor to study in the United States; by tours of inspection of our military establishments by Latin American soldiers; and by the propagandizing activities of the Co-ordinator of Inter-American Affairs. The CIAA offices in all the Latin American capitals distributed gratis great quantities of educational matter in the form of Spanish language magazines, cartoons, posters, movie film, and radio programs.

The Vice Consulate at Iquitos was the exclusive agent for the distribution of the Co-ordinator's products in the Peruvian Amazon. There might have been a shortage of flour and tapping knives in town, but every RDC Catalina from Lima brought tons of propaganda. Otto Losa would phone the Vice Consulate from the RDC office, a trace of irritation in his voice. "Say, Hank, how about sending over a truck for this damn stuff from the Co-ordinator. There's so much of it, we have no room for our own supplies."

Joaquín would haul the heavy bundles of posters and magazines up the steps of the Malecón Palace and spend the rest of the day making individual rolls of the various posters and pamphlets, securing each with a bit of string. He then set out to leave the posters and magazines at each bar, barber shop, restaurant, and store. Some of the small posters—of President Roosevelt, General Marshall, General Eisenhower, battleships, aircraft carriers, and B-17's—were the self-standing variety. The larger "Illustrated War Series" posters had to be fastened to the wall. Joaquín carried a hammer and a box of tacks in order to accommodate those customers who wanted to have their posters put up.

How much, if any, all this printed material increased the prestige of the United States in the eyes of Iquiteños is a moot question. I do know, though, that the stuff went like hot cakes. It was free, and there was a great dearth of reading matter in Iquitos.

The Co-ordinator's choice product was a slick paper monthly called *En Guardia* (On Guard), filled with excellent colored illustrations and interesting articles. We received only three hundred copies of *En Guardia,* and these were carefully allotted to the intelligentsia. The distribution was a ticklish matter, for everyone was making a collection. One slip-up in Joaquín's delivery schedule would bring a prompt complaint from the neglected collector.

On Saturday afternoons—the time set aside for distribution to the man in the street—the office was stormed by mobs of barefooted cholos, long-haired Chama Indians, enlisted men of the Jungle Division, and Indian women and children, all asking for *proh-pah-GAHN-dah*. Joaquín maintained some semblance of order by barricading the entrance to the office with a heavy mahogany table over which he would dispense the propaganda to the crowd that choked the stairs and bulged out into the street below.

At first, the universal reference to the Co-ordinator's excellent products as "propaganda" seemed to me to contain a bit of sarcasm. "Why can't they be more subtle?" I would complain. Then it dawned on me that we in the United States have twisted the dictionary meaning of the word. When an American exclaims, "Oh, that's just a lot of propaganda!" he indicates that propaganda to him has come to mean a set of ideas or statements that are probably colored or falsified in order to sell a particular program. The Latin American, on the other hand, had retained the classical definition of the word. Propaganda to him is simply legitimate advertising. The Latin American openly makes propaganda to push a scheme of social reform in the same matter-of-fact way that he makes propaganda on behalf of a hair tonic. The Latin American sees no reason why Uncle Sam shouldn't make a little propaganda too.

21

$\mathcal{T}$HE MONTHS slipped by our chalet on Punchana Road as imperceptibly as the abandoned balsa rafts that swept past on the broad shoulders of the Amazon. Our lives had settled into the amiably monotonous pattern of the hot country. Dot and I had become acostumbradoed to the Pearl of the Amazon. We had grown to love the kindly, hospitable, waltzing Iquiteños. They had accepted us without reservation and had made us one of them. Iquitos was our home.

But there were times when we knew that we weren't so well acostumbradoed to the Pearl after all. We knew that we could never succeed in mastering the art of living to the degree

From Parrots to Penguins

that the real Iquiteño had mastered it. The Iquiteño knew how to "set loose" amid a host of environmental annoyances. He seemed amiably impervious to rain, sun, mud, dust, heat, open sewers, empty water tanks, yuca, fried pork, turkey buzzards, mosquitoes, chiggers, errant hogs, belly worms, and isolation. Dot and I found that every few months these *cositas de la vida*, these trifles of living, settled so thickly about us that we could no longer "set loose."

During these visits of the miseries, we did not want to await the day—two, three, four years hence—when Iquitos would have all those projected amenities that would transform it into the most agreeable place to live in Peru: a water supply and sewage disposal system, more than one paved street, a modern hospital, an adequate power plant, a real hotel, and an all-weather airport.

As 1944 grew older, reports from the outside world of movement filled us with restlessness. Ambassador Norweb was now in Portugal; George Widney was transferred to British Guiana; Bob Hervey to Paraguay. Everybody was on the move but us. To be on the move was the important thing. Where didn't matter.

One day the Lima pouch brought an announcement that threw the Vice Consulate into a turmoil of speculation. It was a copy of an airgram from the State Department to the Embassy at Lima, announcing the appointment of Anthony Edward Starcevic as Vice Consul in the Foreign Service Auxiliary and assigned for duty at Iquitos.

The airgram said nothing of the fate of the Vice Consul at Iquitos. One thing was certain. The Department wasn't sending an assistant at this late date. It could only mean that a transfer was in the wind. But where?

In due time, Edward Anthony reached Iquitos in Condor Biggs' Catalina. In five minutes, I learned that my successor was not called Edward Anthony but Tony; that, far from a babe in the woods, he was seasoned for Iquitos. Tony grew up in smoggy Pittsburgh, where he acquired an A.B., a fluency in Yugoslav and Polish, and a knowledge of the meat-packing business. With these qualifications, he departed for Mexico to study archaeology in the University of Mexico and then capitalize on his book-learning by mining mica in Oaxaca.

I breezed Tony through his indoctrination at Iquitos. We worked as if each day might bring my travel orders. A month passed without a word from the Department. The office was shipshape, ready for momentary transfer. Finally, we faced something that I had been postponing for a long time—the regulation requiring an annual change of combination of the safe. While I was alone, I had no intention of disengaging the safe's tumblers and then being unable to set up a new combination. Together, Tony and I could afford to flirt with danger. We flirted for three days. Our series of mishaps began when we contrived to get the safe's lock jammed in the "locked" position with the door open. We flipped a coin to determine which of us would sleep with the safe the first night. The second day, we got the open door un-locked, but the tumblers refused to be reconciled to any com-bination, even the old one. By noon of the third day, we decided to give it one more try before sending Uncle Charlie a coded SOS. The recalcitrant safe, as if in consideration for the pres-tige of the Vice Consulate, capitulated with surprising meekness.

The summer sandbar at the upriver point of Iquitos Island had crept halfway across the shrunken Amazon when the news finally came. I decoded as far as "You will proceed as soon as practicable to . . ." and stopped for breath. Dot and I had speculated and aspired for weeks. We longed for the fleshpots. We hoped in terms of Río de Janeiro, Montevideo, Santiago. The next couple of code groups were garbled, but, when un-scrambled, they left no doubt that we were headed for Punta Arenas, Chile, We combed the lodge-pole length of Chile from the arid nitrate deserts of the north as far south as the smiling lake region of Puerto Montt. Could Punta Arenas be another hermit like Iquitos?

Another hermit was right! We found Punta Arenas perched on the southernmost tip of South America. Iquitos and Punta Arenas were brothers in isolation; the one, the world's most interior city, the other, the world's most southerly. That was all. The rest was screaming contrast. We were swapping the Amazon River for the Straits of Magellan! The view of lush Iquitos Island for bleak, treeless Tierra del Fuego! The heart of a continent for its extremity, where Atlantic and Pacific mingled! A home three degrees south of the Equator for one thirteen degrees north of the Antarctic Circle! The torrid blast of an electric fan for the congealing blast of Cape Horn! A winter of inundating brown water for one of blanketing snow! Pork and yuca for mutton and potatoes! Parrots for penguins! Seersuckers for tweeds!

"Tweeds! Oh my gosh!" Dot cried. She dashed from the office to Tacu Tacu to see what remained of our woolen clothes. A year's onslaught by moths and cockroaches had done them no good. There were no dry-cleaning facilities in town. For lack of commercial gasoline, Dot and Antonia scrubbed the clothes in a tub filled with ninety octane aviation gasoline from the Itaya Air Base. They worked in the backyard so that an explosion would not damage Tacu Tacu. The extent of the moths' infiltration was astounding. A myriad died in the searing bath. The clothes hung on the line for three days, yet the odor of gasoline would not fade. "Perhaps I shouldn't have cleaned them," Dot said, surveying the riddled rags. "There are more holes now than when the moths were inside."

We had to travel to the Straits of Magellan via Lima and the Embassy at Santiago, Chile, from where Punta Arenas' Vice Consulate was supervised. Afraid to deplete the Department's travel appropriation at one blow, we pared down our possessions to the minimum, for the costly plane ride over the Andes. We disposed of our household goods and our pets. Our White Jersey rooster, Moche, was in great demand. I was stopped a dozen times a day on the street by important people who wanted to buy him. The disposal of the rooster became a ticklish matter. In a protective move, I sold him to the Prefect for fifty soles. Invasion-Barge Gertrude of the Alice-Blue eggs went to Antonia. At last, we were ready for our four-thousand-mile expedition from the equatorial jungle into the Antarctic. Our equipment consisted of threadbare seersuckers, a couple of riddled woolen suits, a guitar, two hammocks, two jaguar skins, a blow-gun, two folding beach chairs, the Raleigh, the Bianchi, and Pepe, the parrot.

Pepe would probably be allergic to penguins and icebergs, but we couldn't leave him behind. Pepe was no ordinary parrot; Pepe was a *chirricles*. The chirricles is the aristocrat of the Amazonian parrot world, and Pepe had no peer among chirricleses. He was handsome, spunky, brilliantly roguish, and packed with joie de vivre. Pepe wore a black skull-cap, a coral collar, white vest, yellow knickers, black gaiters, and shamrock-green cutaway. He had a voice as pleasing as his snappy attire. Instead of the raucous voice of ordinary parrots, Pepe spoke in a cheery, melodic whistle. When perfectly camouflaged in his favorite hibiscus bush, Dot would locate him by calling "Pep-eee." His clear, musical reply would echo from the green and yellow depths of the bush where he dined on yellow hibiscus bells.

Personable Pepe, though no larger than a robin, was the complete companion. He went on shopping expeditions, perched on Dot's bicycle basket, whistling impudently at all the girls. We took him on canoe trips to the lagoons of Iquitos Island, where he tramped around on the huge lily pads until we hauled him back into the dugout by his leg leash. At home, during shower time Pepe would sit on the drainage valve of the water tank and try to drown out the sound of spraying water by a mad aria of whistles and screeches.

Pepe, an omnivorous gourmet, poked his black beak into one gastronomic adventure after another. He would gain access to the table top by climbing a pant leg or skirt. Once up, he made straight for the flower bowl for his first course of hibiscus blooms. He then made forays about the table, eating everything he could grab. Chocolate cake and corn on the cob were his favorite foods. For liquid refreshment, Pepe drank everything from limeades to pisco-vermouth cocktails. When agreeably looped, Pepe delighted in switching about with Dot's green velvet hair bow (mounted on a comb) set in his tail. As Pepe had no cage, we found it almost impossible to keep him away from the table. No matter where we confined him, he managed to get loose and come billing his way up your leg. At night, we scratched Pepe's head before he retired through a hole in the lid of Dot's pink hat box, to sleep quietly until daylight.

So Pepe, the chirricles, completely spoiled but completely lovable, set out with us to Chile. In Pepe, we took a bit of the gayety and courage of Loreto. Señor Ortíz, the cabinet maker, built a compact mahogany cage for Pepe, with sliding doors. Covered with a green and white striped hood, it looked just like a vanity case.

Our series of despedidas culminated in a grand despedida-final held in the Club Iquitos. The Gran Oquesta Jazz Band Bolognesi played as never before, and two hundred good friends made the floor vibrate as it had never before vibrated. At midnight, the waltz criollo and the samba ceased for a moment to give way to the *Star Spangled Banner* and the *Wedding March*. It was our first wedding anniversary. Champagne was poured to the two hundred. There was a collective toast; then, a marathon of embraces—two hundred abrazos! Each embracing friend carried a filled champagne glass—so did Dot and I. The technique was so smooth not a drop was spilled.

We could hardly believe that we were the *agasajados*, the regaled ones; that this was *our* despedida. We had taken part in so many despedidas for others; we had crossed the Andes so many times, only to return to Iquitos. It seemed inconceivable that we would board the Cat this time not to return. Our despedida, like all Iquitos despedidas, was an excuse for a danzant. But it was more than that. People seemed really saddened by our departure. They would miss us as we would miss them. We would go away leaving good friends of ours, and through us, of Tío Sam.

On the morning of our departure, even Chenivesse's light plant gave us a parting abrazo by knocking off work. The alarm clock went off at 4:30. We groped about in the dark, took our red worm pills, got dressed, and waited in the dark on the porch for the taxi. At five o'clock, the taxi's single eye pierced the murk of Punchana Road. As we bounced past Antonia's shack, Dot burst into tears. In the half light, standing at the edge of the road, was Antonia, Petronila, and Walter, all weeping and waving. *"Adiós Señora! Que le vaya bien!"* they cried.

Condor Biggs taxied out of the Itaya into the Amazon just as the sun peeped over the jungle. Inside the striped vanity case, surrounded with cotton, was Pepe the chirricles. Condor Biggs climbed to his usual twenty thousand feet that day, but Pepe made the crossing with perfect nonchalance without oxygen.

In clammy, fog-shrouded Lima, Pepe perched cozily on a radiator in the Hotel Bolívar and gave vent to his fiery Loretan patriotism. Pepe had spent his early youth in an atmosphere conducive to militant patriotism. The man who captured fuzzy Pepe, by felling the palm tree in which Pepe's ma had hollowed a nest, was Señor Guerrero (warrior), owner of an hacienda on the Río Napo, called *Tempestad* (tempest), a short distance downstream from the Pantoja-Rocafuerte battleground. The outburst of patriotism came when Dot innocently offered him a slice of banana. Pepe accepted it with his usual alacrity. He took a ravenous bite, and then his face registered surprise, disgust, and rage. He spat out the banana and filled the room with imprecations.

Pepe's conduct baffled us. Granted, the bananas weren't as tasty as a Loretan plátano, but, after all, a banana was a banana. But where did Lima get its bananas? "They come from Guayaquil, Señor," said the head waiter of the Bolívar. We were proud of our patriotic Loretano who preferred to starve rather than eat an Ecuadorean banana.

We sent a telegram to the editor of *El Oriente,* asking him to inform Iquitos of the little Loretan's courageous passage of the Andes *sin oxigeno,* his patriotism in the affair of the Ecuadorean banana, and to predict his triumphant entry into Santiago.

Gallant Pepe came near fulfilling our predictions. He made his way from Callao to Valparaiso in the gun turret of the Chilean freighter *Tubul,* formerly an American ship on the Murmansk run. In Santiago, he confused the personnel of the hotel by emitting a series of defiant whistles from the depths of the striped vanity case. The doorman, the desk clerk, the elevator boy, the bellhop were all at a loss to locate the source of the elusive raspberries.

The Santiago winter did not down Pepe—the grime of soft coal, the sleet, the damp, penetrating cold. We left Pepe on the tepid radiator in the hotel bathroom and walked the streets to keep warm. The rain came down harder, and we sought shelter in a museum filled with trophies of the conquest of Peru in the War of the Pacific: fragments of the Peruvian monitor *Huáscar;* personal effects of Peruvian generals who died in combat; tattered Peruvian flags captured on the outskirts of Lima. It was very depressing.

We dragged back to the drab hotel, filled with nostalgia for Loreto, for the smiling skies, the luxuriant heat of the jungle, the gay Iquiteños, the vals criollo, Chalet Tacu Tacu, for yuca, beans, and fried pork. We unlocked our room. It was still clammy cold. Dot opened the bathroom door and let out a shriek. I rushed in after her. Water was spattered all over. The tragedy was overwhelming. "I forgot to put the lid down!" Dot wailed. Tempestuous Pepe of Pantoja, our indomitable Loretano, had met his end, drowned in a Chilean "chicago"!

Dot and I unashamedly cried over the loss of Pepe. But now we realized what was wrong. We were still strangers in this new country. Pepe had been a symbol of the wonderful interdependence and resulting comradeship we had known with our friends left behind in Iquitos. The fleshpots of the big city that we had yearned for at Tacu Tacu were only pleasant trimmings.

Dancing of an evening in the gold brocaded ballroom of Santiago's beautiful Hotel Carillon wasn't half as satisfying as a *baile* at General Morla's Casino Militar. We would have to turn the page to this new chapter in the lives of the Dancing Diplomats, as our fellow VEEsay CONsools at the Embassy in Lima jokingly called us.

Dot perked up, dried her eyes, and opened the letter we had just received confirming our reservations at the Hotel Cosmos, in Punta Arenas, down on Magellan's strait. "Lookee," she said between sniffs, "they have a penguin crest on their stationery. I have a feeling we are going to like Punta Arenas, too, Hanque!"

CPSIA information can be obtained at www.ICGtesting.com
Printed in the USA
LVOW01s1245101013

356317LV00004B/563/P